Baseball and Philosophy

Popular Culture and Philosophy™
Series Editor: William Irwin

Baseball and Philosophy

Thinking Outside the Batter's Box

Edited by
ERIC BRONSON

OPEN COURT
Chicago and La Salle, Illinois

Volume 6 in the series, Popular Culture and Philosophy™

To order books from Open Court, call toll free 1-800-815-2280, or visit our website at www.opencourtbooks.com.

The photographs on pages 3, 33, 69, 105, 139, 229, 257, and 285 appear courtesy of The National Baseball Hall of Fame and Museum Library. The Homestead Grays picture on page 169 was supplied by Rob Ruck. The Champions of the Baseball Club, 1905, photograph on page 201 is used by permission of the Picture Collection, The Branch Libraries, The New York Public Library, Asor, Lenox, and Tilden Foundations.

Open Court Publishing Company is a division of Carus Publishing Company.

Library of Congress Cataloging-in-Publication Data

Baseball and philosophy : thinking outside the batter's box / edited by Eric Bronson.
    p. cm. -- (Popular culture and philosophy ; 6)
      Includes bibliographical references and index.
      ISBN 0-8126-9556-9 (trade paperback : alk. paper)
      1. Baseball--Social aspects--United States. 2. Sports--Philosophy.
    I. Bronson, Eric, 1971- II. Series.
    GV867.64 .B365 2004
    796.357'01—dc22

                                  2003023346

To Rabstick Park, wiffle ball field of dreams

Contents

Foreword

Philosophy takes time. So does baseball.

Philosophy is sometimes strictly logical, sometimes mystical. Likewise baseball. Ted Williams made such a thorough study of the act of hitting a baseball that most witnesses regard his achievement as science. He argued (loudly and without doubt) that he had come to understand (if not invent) the only proper angle for a bat to describe as it crossed the plate. He maintained that by "getting my pitch," that is, by never giving in to the pitcher who works just off the corners or beyond the upper and lower edges of the strike zone, he could essentially beat the logic of the game, which, of course, has it that good pitching will beat good hitting. On the other hand, Nomar Garciaparra, whom Ted Williams admired immoderately, is apparently convinced that he cannot hit at all if he doesn't adjust his batting gloves with precisely the same sequence of irritating, spastic, tugs before every pitch, which is as logical as not changing your socks when you're on a hitting streak.

These observations would seem to suggest that a book entitled *Baseball and Philosophy* describes a better coupling than, say, *Pole Vaulting and Philosophy*. Moreover, baseball has spawned remarkable philosophers over the decades. Consider Satchel Paige ("Don't look back; something may be gaining on you"); Yogi Berra ("It ain't over 'til it's over"), and Casey Stengel ("The Mets is a very good thing. They give everybody a job. Just like the WPA"). But the best argument for this book is that up and down the lineup, the philosophers involved herein are having such a good time. The achievement of this volume is like the accomplishment of a game in the perfect ballyard on City Island Park in the middle of the Susquehanna River in Harrisburg, Pennsylvania on a night with no mosquitoes. The essays in this book remind the reader that philosophy is fun, and that creatively building unlikely connections between such concerns as faith in the Cubs and faith in God can help us learn how to think. Similarly, the AA game in Harrisburg of a mild summer night reminds us that baseball is a happy invention. The game before us there is, like a simple proposition, the thing itself. Nobody in City Island Park is angry about what the players are making or how much the beer costs, let alone whether the next Major League work stoppage should be called a strike or a lock-out.

This book appears at an especially appropriate time in baseball's long history. Fans can witness these days an entertaining conflict between two schools of baseball thought. In one camp sit the managers who play hunches and the old scouts, who swear they can spot the sole prospect on a high school team just by watching the players get off the team bus. In the opposing dugout are Bill James and his disciples, who have come to understand the game in terms of statistical measures far more complicated than batting average. These mathematicians rate the value of a hitter strictly in terms of the likelihood that he will somehow do something other than make an out. Unlike traditional baseball men, they do not say things like, "He looks like a ball player."

Of course the lovely thing about baseball is that it resists mastery, no matter the tools employed by the player, the manager, the general manager, the owner, the mathematician . . . or the thinker. In that respect, too, the game is the right bailiwick for philosophers, who can argue forever about the definition of "the real fan" or "the wonder of the rules," secure in the knowledge that the pastime will endure their needling and thrive. It is deep and easy at once, this old game. Or as the great baseball philosopher Johnny Pesky has been known to say from the end of the bench, "It's such a simple game, and so hard to play."

BILL LITTLEFIELD

Bill Littlefield hosts National Public Radio's "Only A Game." He is co-editor of *Fall Classics: The Best Writing about the World Series' First 100 Years* and author of the baseball novel *Prospect.*

Acknowledgments

Writing a book, like playing baseball, is only enjoyable if one's teammates are good, or at least likeable.

I am very thankful to the baseball gods that the authors in this book are true professionals who love what they do. For all their hard work and cheery dispositions, especially in the off season, I can do no more than tip my cap.

A special thank you goes out to Bill Irwin who gave us the green light and waved us home. Like all good coaches, he makes us play our best, and like a true friend, his faith and trust never waver. And thanks to Greg Bassham for his vast generosity, his consistent, kind words, and his genuine cigars. With Bill and Greg on the field, it's always an honor to wear their uniform.

Two first ballot Hall of Famers who deserve special credit are Tim Wiles and W.C. Burdick. For their great work in Cooperstown, they should be enshrined.

To David Ramsay Steele in the front office, whose sharp vision helped us hit the curve balls, before we ever saw them coming, and to Carolyn Madia Gray, whose wit and wisdom see us through, I give a hearty high-five.

Of course, baseball is a family game, and no one can capture its spirit without a loving and supporting cast. To my parents who always stood at the dugout steps for every strikeout and every hit, the game ball is always yours. Thanks also to Team Prescott who withstood all the broken bats and errant throws with grace and love.

Standing ovations also go to Evelyn Bronson, Michael J. McGrath, William N. Irwin, John Loyd, Robert Guldner, Steve Libenson, Ray Doswell, Abigail Myers, Jimmy Murphy, Jason Klein, and of course, Betty Morris.

At Berkeley College, where I play my home games, Arthur Blumenthal and Phil Krebs help make the game fun. And finally, thanks to William Moya and my students who never lose faith, through the long practices, and all the rainy days.

Pre-Game Warm-up:
Who's on First?

Baseball has always been a thinking person's game. Just ask the wise philosophers, Abbot and Costello.

Their baseball dream team featured "Who" at first base, "What" at second base, and "Why" out in left field. That's a formidable lineup when you stop and think about it. If any of us could keep track of the Whos, Whats, and Whys in our lives, our daily grind would be a whole lot easier to bear. Poor Costello, though, never could seem to get it right, and most of the time, we can't either. "Who" are we? "What" should we do? "Why" are we here? Throw in "I Don't Know" at third base and you have the foundation for some of the most perplexing philosophical discussions throughout the ages, all on the field at the same time. Can you blame Costello for not getting it straight?

Played without time limits, baseball encourages its participants to pause and think. There is time enough for infield shifts, meetings at the mound, phone calls to the bullpen, and time in between for armchair managing. It's not unusual for St. Louis Cardinals manager Tony LaRussa to don his reading glasses during the game, as he pours over the latest statistics. Or, think of cerebral Atlanta Braves pitcher Greg Maddux (a.k.a. "the Professor"), shaking off sign after sign, as he paints the corners with off-speed pitches.

There is also something about baseball that appeals to men and women of letters. Off the field, intellectuals like Bart Giamatti (Yale University President and later Baseball Commissioner), scientist Stephen Jay Gould, and political commentator George Will spent years seeking to understand baseball's place in American popular culture. When Giamatti wrote his now famous article for *Harper's Magazine*, he noted how baseball happily takes you through the summer and early fall, but "just when the days are all twilight, when you need it most, it stops."

Every year, scores of new baseball books are published to help us make it through the twilight. Such stories cover unforgettable childhood memories, heartbreaking World Series losses, and improbable last inning victories. But up until now, no one has asked the philosophical questions that lie at the heart of the baseball diamond—the "Whos," "Whats," and "Whys."

Why do we root for teams against all odds? Who are we as Americans, and why is baseball our national pastime? What do batting averages have to do with a hitter's ability? Who makes the rules? Why is the hidden ball trick legal, while hidden profits on your tax returns is not?

To help us through such philosophical puzzles, we've asked All-Star philosophers and academics in North America (with assists from Europe and the Middle East) to join the team. For many of our contributors, this book is the culmination of many years of extensive writing and teaching in the philosophy of sport. Others have coached or played the game before being called to the Big Leagues of academia. Filling out the roster are wide-eyed rookies who lead seemingly intellectual lives, assiduously checking box scores and eating ballpark franks on the sly. Give any one of them a dusty old book or a broken-in glove and "they won't care if they ever get back . . ."

The Ancient Greeks believed that true philosophers should have sound minds *and* sound bodies. They understood that loving wisdom means sharpening your analytic tools along with your hand-eye coordination. Baseball, like philosophy, is a complicated process of ideas and achievements, set-backs and stars. These chapters, then, promise a rational investigation into the sometimes serious, sometimes hilarious inner workings of baseball.

After reading this book, we hope you'll have a deeper appreciation for philosophical reasoning and a more informed respect for the greatest game on earth. Who's on first? What's on second? Everybody seems to have an opinion. Agree with us faithfully or disagree angrily. Or, just scratch your head like Costello, and say, "I don't give a darn." We know what you mean.

"That's our shortstop."

First Inning:
Hometown Heroes

We all have fond memories of root, root, rooting for the home team, and we've all dreamed about hitting that game-winning home run in front of our home crowd. Joe Kraus argues that baseball's strong attachment to home is good turf for many rich philosophical issues. Paul Horan and Jason Solomon explain how legal precedent takes a back seat to ethics when the home team is on trial. If Major League Baseball still hopes to contract the Minnesota Twins, it had better prepare for a long, expensive fight with Minnesota's family and friends.

1 | "There's No Place Like Home!"

JOE KRAUS

When my three-year-old son hits a wiffle ball, we shout together, "run," and he takes off. Never mind that he usually heads toward what would be third base if we'd bother to lay out bases; he runs in a straight line until I call out "first base." Then, he veers to the right, runs until I shout, "second base," and then turns and goes again until I yell, "third base." When he makes his final turn and heads back in the general direction where he started, he's on his own. At some random point toward what would be the plate, he slows almost completely, goes to his knees, and performs a slow-motion headfirst slide. When he stops, it's my job to wave my hands and declare, umpire-style, "sa-a-afe."

Put more simply, under his rules, he gets to invent home. The sequence is always the same—a hit, a run with three turns, and a slide—but the particular spot where he stops is always different. If he's fresh and the ball made a particularly satisfying thump when he hit it, he might make it almost all of the way back to where he's discarded his bat. If it's getting late and the field we've chosen isn't all that open, he might stop just past the invisible third base. Either way, home is where he says it is. He stops and rests when he decides he's ready.

The more I watch him, the more I get the sense that real baseball isn't all that different. Home is always wherever the plate is—it's always the same spot where you hit—but there is something arbitrary about even that. We take a spot and decide

7

that it is different from all of the other places on the field. Other sports require you to get a ball or puck into some goal or end zone, but only baseball assigns a special value to one particular spot. You score when you reach that spot yourself, without the ball, without ramming through the opposition. You score when you return to where you started, when you manage to get home safely.

If you've played or watched baseball for a long time, you probably take the rules for granted. They make sense once you've lived with them for a while, and I know that I have a hard time imagining how they could be fundamentally different. (That's one reason that so many of us Americans look at cricket and shake our heads; how can something so baseball-like seem so weird?) When you come to it fresh, though, when you experience it again through the eyes of a three-year-old, it starts to raise some intriguing questions. Why is it that home "counts" only after you leave it and return? Why do we call it "home" at all? And how is baseball in the broader sense a "home" for the team that has home field advantage and for the fans that embrace it? We shout "home, home!" when someone on our team rounds third base trying to beat the throw from right field, and we "root, root, root for the home team," but what exactly do we mean when we say those things? French philosopher Gaston Bachelard may have some answers for us.

Bachelard's Philosophy of Home

"Home," whether we're talking about baseball, the house where you grew up, or your town or city of residence, is surprisingly difficult to define on its own terms. In order to say what it is, you almost always have to explain what it is not. That is, you have to refer to the threat from which your home shields you, the threat that your home is supposed to render invisible. In baseball, that means that home is the place where you are not "out," and it's distinct from the other three bases because once you're safe at home, you're safe permanently; you no longer have to run farther or risk anything else. With your own house, it's the place where other people cannot bother you, the place where you get to apply your own rules or, at least, know the rules that your parents, landlord, or mortgage-lender have made for you. Nobody can interfere with you or even criticize you if you want to walk around naked, let the dog kiss you on the lips, or pour orange juice instead of milk on your cereal.

The power of the home is real. In prehistoric times it was the place in which you could rest and sleep, the place where you were most free from the prowling beasts that might otherwise catch you. Today too, in loving homes, children frequently associate their security with their quiet rooms. (In abusive or shattered homes, kids often find their "home" somewhere outside the house.) In the American legal system, you have rights within your house that you do not have outside it. Even if the police suspect you of certain crimes, they cannot enter your home without specific approval from a judge; that is, they cannot question you as fully, cannot arrest you as easily, and cannot impose all of the laws of the land on you. If you are nineteen years old and drinking beer on a park bench, you're subject to arrest. Do it in your own home without making noise that disturbs the neighbors, and nobody (except your parents) can touch you. Even in the twenty-first century, your own front door really does protect you from much of what goes on outside of it.

Defining the home, then, calls for the difficult trick of explaining simultaneously what it is and what it protects you from. Bachelard describes that seeming contradiction as "the most interminable of dialectics."[1] In his view, we need a sense of home in order to understand who we are because our home is "our first universe."[2] It is the secure, comfortable place from which we experience the world, either by looking out the window or through our reflections and daydreams on our outside experiences. At the same time, Bachelard argues, we need to feel a sense of potential threat in order to recognize how our house makes us feel at home. We need to maintain a kernel of fear, even if we repress it, in order to appreciate what the home does for us. As he puts it, "Without it, man would be a dispersed being. . . Before he is 'cast into the world', as claimed by certain hasty metaphysics, man is laid in the cradle of his house."[3] We experience home as a place of ease and shelter, but we can do so only by retaining some sense of its opposite.

---

[1] All references to Gaston Bachelard are from *The Poetics of Space*, translated by Maria Jolas (Boston: Beacon Press, 1994), p. 5.

[2] *Ibid.*, p. 4.

[3] *Ibid.*, p. 7.

When it comes to baseball, this idea plays out from the very start. The goal is to get "home," and yet, every batter starts off at home. As soon as you walk up to face the pitcher, you're already standing at the place you're eventually trying to reach. It's not hard to imagine Jerry Seinfeld asking the question, "So, why leave? Why not just stay at home in the first place and forget about first, second, and third bases?" The answer, of course, is that "home" in baseball doesn't count until you've left it, until you've gone for a "run" and returned. That's in the same vein as Joseph Campbell's famous discussion of the journey that literary and mythological heroes often take. Known as the "monomyth," it says that the hero must leave his comfortable known world, strike out on his own to find adventure, and then return home a changed man.[4] Think of Ulysses wearing a Giants cap as he ventures to Hades and back and you'll have the idea.

Put differently, home doesn't become meaningful until you have experienced the risk that lies in front of it. You can't score until after you have confronted the pitcher and those fielders who are trying to stop you. It's Bachelard's dialectic: you need to know both the idea of home and the real threat of getting out in order to experience the satisfaction of truly making it home. The original Homer told us that when he wrote *The Odyssey* 3,000 years ago: home is all the sweeter when you've braved adventures to get back to it.

'Canny' Get a Hit at Last?

Stepping up to the plate, though, is about more than just remembering the fear that you might get struck out, thrown out, tagged out, caught stealing, or forced out. In fact, good hitters usually talk about having so much confidence that they forget about the chance of failing even though the very best manage to score only slightly more than 100 runs a season in roughly 650 plate appearances. Hitting is supposed to be thrilling. It's supposed to give you the sense that you can accomplish something significant, that you can take the bat in your hands and make its power your own. As fans, we share in that same excitement, actually amplifying it. Before Mighty Casey stepped up to

---

[4] Joseph Campbell, *The Hero with a Thousand Faces* (Princeton: Princeton University Press, 1972).

the plate, all Mudville rose and cheered. Whenever Sammy Sosa steps into the on-deck circle, spreads his legs, puts his hands at opposite ends of the bat, and stretches upward, we Cubs fans get the sense that a century of futility might really end in our lifetime.

Many hitters have characteristic rituals for batting, rituals that seem designed to show just how at home they feel at the plate. Joe Morgan used to stare intently at the pitcher, his body completely still but his back elbow flapping up and down like a chicken wing. Kirby Puckett would rock from one hip to another, shaking his backside at anyone sitting along the third base line. One of my old favorites, Ruppert Jones, used to stretch his mouth so wide that I was certain he could fit a baseball all the way in. And, according to my mother—my mother!— Mark Grace adjusts his jock strap between every pitch and then takes two quick tugs on his jersey above his heart as if he is puffing out his chest. Think about it, where else but home can a grown man act like a chicken, shake his butt, contort his face into all manner of bizarre expressions, or adjust his crotch? In that respect, such batters treat home plate as their real home, as a private place where they can apply their own rules even if they happen to be standing in front of 30,000 fans and who knows how many more watching on television.

The comfort that hitters demonstrate is a direct response to the anxious excitement that they feel. The two competing emotions are in tension with each other; the plate is both a familiar place and one that promises them some new challenge. The best hitters can be comfortable, or at least assert that they are comfortable, only after they know and then deny that they know how difficult their job is. Anyone who has ever held a bat knows that it is almost impossible to hit a Pedro Martinez fastball, and that would be true even without the difficulty of accounting for the possibility that he might throw a knee-buckling curveball instead. Most major leaguers who have successfully hit such a fastball, however, will also tell you that they did so because they were able to block out just how difficult it is. You can do what you know to be almost impossible only by forgetting that it is impossible.

Bachelard's dialectic relates to that necessary tension because it, too, relies on a sense of repression. We know the security of home only because we know and manage to forget what it is that home protects us from. In that light, such an attitude toward home, whether of the house or plate variety, reflects Sigmund Freud's sense of the uncanny, the sensation that a thing is both foreign and familiar at the same time. As Freud defines it, the uncanny is "that class of the terrifying which leads back to something long known to us, once very familiar."[5] That is, the uncanny is something that frightens us because it almost, but not quite, brings to mind some fact that we have repressed. For most instances of the uncanny, that means some aspect of sexuality or death with which we have not come to grips. In baseball, uncanny describes the thrill you feel stepping up to the plate, the hope that you can hit a home run despite what statistics and personal history tell you: that you are far more likely to get out.

For Freud, the haunted house—the haunted home—is one of the most common species of the uncanny. The German word for "uncanny" is *unheimlich*, literally un-home-like. As Freud argues, we are drawn to such a place because it brings unusual clarity to the dynamic that Bachelard later explores. We see what looks like a regular home, the kind of place within which we have known comfort and security. Yet, within it, we also know fear and discomfort. According to Freud, we feel a kind of terrifying relief in seeing our repressed fears made manifest: there really were monsters in the closet all along; those knocks and pings were ghosts after all. Freudian psycho-therapy works on that principle. The more you talk with a psychologist, the clearer your fears become; once you name and confront them, you can move on.

All of that is not to say that home plate is haunted in quite the same way. It isn't, unless you happen to be a Brooklyn Dodgers fan. Instead, the baseball home is uncanny because, while it invites hitters to make themselves at home on it, it also promises to get them out. "Step up to me," it says. "Make yourself at home; then, give me a moment, and I'll send you back to your dugout." It is simultaneously solid and insubstantial, simultaneously encouraging and demoralizing. And that tension is another reason that it is so satisfying to score a run. Once you've rounded third and slid back into home, it's no longer the same place. You've exorcised it. You've confronted the ghost that whispers, "out, out—you're going to make an out," and you've beaten it.

---

[5] See "The Uncanny," in *Collected Papers of Sigmund Freud*, Volume 4, translated by Joan Riviere (London: Hogarth Press, 1934), pp. 369–370.

You're home, and there is no more tension. You're home, and you're safe . . . at least until your team bats around again.

A Little Elbow Room, or Making Yourself at Home with 30,000+ Pals

What's true for the people who play baseball is true in different ways for those of us who mostly just watch it. On the one hand, a baseball stadium becomes a kind of home for many of us who go often. Whether it's a big league stadium where you can leave your peanut shells scattered beneath your seat or a high school field where you know the person who chalks the base paths every Thursday, it's a personal space. You can keep score with your private notation system, sound off authoritatively on what Bud Selig is doing wrong, or tell an ump that he's missed a call even when you are 140 feet and a bad angle away from the plate. The first few minutes in your seat are all about settling in, finding a place to hang your jacket or purse, balancing your scorecard and any food or drinks you have, and re-familiarizing yourself with the field, scoreboard, and likeliest vendor routes. After that, it's your space, you belong there, and, if it's a sunny day, it really can make you sing, "I don't care if I ever get back." That's also why it's annoying to have someone next to you get up every inning; it's as if someone keeps walking through your living room.

On the other hand, we often talk about our stadiums in ways that reflect Bachelard's sense of the danger from which such a home protects us. For every seeming positive feature of a field, there's a negative-sounding one. Some territory is "fair" and some is "foul." There is an "in-" field, and then there is the much larger expanse of the "out-" field. Wrigley Field is simultaneously "the friendly confines" and, according to singer and life-long Cubs fan Steve Goodman, an "ivy-covered burial ground."[6] And,

---

[6] The line is from "A Dying Cubs Fan's Last Request," recorded as a single in 1981 and available, among other places, on *No Big Surprise: Anthology*, Red Pajamas Records. In the song, a dying Cubs fan requests that his friends spread his ashes around Wrigley Field as he recounts the many ways in which the Cubs have disappointed him during his life. Goodman was himself suffering from leukemia when he wrote the song, and he died three years later. His wife reportedly did spread his ashes in the outfield, but there is no official record proving that Wrigley is, in fact, a burial ground.

Fenway Park, a beloved landmark in Boston, has as its most famous architectural feature "the Green Monster." There are elements that seem comforting, such as the three bases lined up around the infield, and there are elements that sound threatening, such as the warning track, the bullpen, or the mound. Be comfortable, the ballpark seems to say, but stay alert for trouble. The front of your ticket promises a section, a row, and a seat reserved for you; the back of it reminds you in fine print that you run the risk of getting clocked by a foul ball at any time.

In many cases, that sense of a stadium as home comes to define an area outside it as well. In Baltimore, Camden Yards has transformed from an old industrial area into a neighborhood that has a national identity. In Chicago, the area known as Lakeview for over a century has evolved in the last fifteen to twenty years into Wrigleyville, a place as famous for the bars and restaurants around it as it is for the baseball itself. Anaheim, a city that once blurred into the greater Los Angeles area even though it was home to Disneyland, has become a more concrete place courtesy of the Disney Corporation's renaming the Angels to reflect their home. And the *Field of Dreams* movie site in Dyersville, Iowa is a national tourist site, proving that, once they built it, people really did come.

Those places, at least those places in the sense that they are "homes" to many people, exist because baseball is there. Without it they are not just nondescript neighborhoods, but, in some important ways, they cease to exist. Gertrude Stein once famously said of her home town, Oakland, "there's no there there,"[7] meaning that, once her childhood home was torn down, there was nothing to identify it as a place, nothing to characterize it. That was before the West-Coast expansion of major league baseball, of course, and now Oakland has a "there" again, a franchise anchored in 2003 by the best starting rotation in baseball.

The most famous example of a baseball team giving a sense of home to a community was Brooklyn, where the Dodgers, "dem bums," were the heart of the community from the turn of the century until 1958. When owner Walter O'Malley moved the

---

[7] The quotation appears in Gertrude Stein, *Everybody's Autobiography* (Cambridge, Massachusetts: Exact Change, 1993).

team away, he took his place for many people among the most hated men in history. As Dodger fan Bill Reddy said, "He did a terrible thing to the people of Brooklyn, because he took away part of the cohesiveness that held the borough together."[8] Bobby McCarthy put it more dramatically. "This was like seceding from the union."[9] Or as Peter Golenbock summed it up, "The heart had gone out of Brooklyn. The soul had fled. It's a place to live now, that's all."[10] For those fans and for countless others, Brooklyn stopped being Brooklyn the day the Dodgers left. It simply was not their home any longer.

For Bachelard, their sadness reflects his observation that "well-determined centers of revery [sic] are means of communication between men who dream."[11] That is, while we reflect on ourselves and on our world, we do so in a way that parallels other peoples' reflections. We will dream no matter what, because humans are dreaming animals, but when we do so within our individual homes and when we are conscious of others doing so within theirs, we come together as a community. A baseball stadium is one such "well-determined center" for dreaming. It is a place where 30,000 of us can come together wondering whether the manager should call a hit-and-run, whether Grady Little should have pulled Pedro Martinez in the 2003 A.L.C.S., whether the guy in the Bratwurst costume will beat the guys in the other three sausage outfits, or whether the traffic will be lousy getting out of the parking lot. It doesn't especially matter that we dream different daydreams. What matters is that we do it together, in a place that we have made our own, in a place that we share.

It's in that light that so many fans complain about the recent trend of teams selling off the naming rights to stadiums. For many people, accepting money from a large corporation to name a stadium or advertise behind home plate feels like putting a billboard in their living room. U.S. Cellular, First Union Bank, Qualcomm Communications, Safeco Insurance, and, most notoriously, the Enron Corporation have nothing in particular

---

[8] Quoted in Peter Golenback, *Bums: An Oral History of the Brooklyn Dodgers* (New York: Putnam, 1984), p. 447.

[9] *Ibid.*, p. 446.

[10] *Ibid.*, p. 449.

[11] *The Poetics of Space*, p. 39.

to do with the teams whose stadiums they "bought." Unlike Wrigley Field, owned for years by the Wrigley chewing gum family, or even the newer Coors Field in Denver and Miller Park in Milwaukee, named for long-established local breweries, such corporations' involvement makes baseball feel purely like a business, less comfortable. It is a business, of course, but it's one made possible by the illusion that each of us has a personal connection to the team and its place. The moment someone puts a price tag on that place, it ceases to be quite so personal: it ceases to be quite so much a home.

Safe at Home

When we use the word "home," we tend to mean more than simply our house, however. That particular house may be the heart of what we consider home, but our home generally extends to our neighborhood, city, and sometimes even our state or nation. We can draw concentric circles outward from wherever it is we consider ourselves most centrally at home to include larger and larger areas. For example, we can live at 1060 West Addison and be North-siders, Chicagoans, Midwesterners, and Americans all at the same time, with each area functioning in some ways as a kind of home within which we feel security by virtue of our shared experience with so many others. In a baseball stadium, there is only one home plate—the various bullpen plates don't count—but the entire stadium becomes home field for one of the two teams playing.

Most major league sports develop local followings and come to serve as rallying points for the community, but baseball has an advantage over all the others since it plays so many games. During the season, which runs from early April to early October, it generates news every day. Fans have to check stats in the newspaper or on the Internet each morning, and, in recent years, they've had the option of arguing on twenty-four-hour sports stations in most major league markets. Casual fans and even indifferent ones find themselves caught up in the fortunes of the local team; in most markets starting players are significant local celebrities, often endorsing car dealerships, banks, or grocery stores. One way you can recognize yourself and others as part of a shared community is that you have a common touchstone in the success or failure of the local team. "How 'bout them Royals?" announces you as a Kansas City-ian; it declares that you have a stake in at least some local affairs.

Benedict Anderson, a theorist of nationalism, argues that it takes such a shared sense of news in order to form a sense of nationhood. No community can emerge as a nation conscious of itself until after it regards the goings-on within part of it as news to all of it. For example, Boston is four times closer to Montreal than it is to Atlanta, but, to most Bostonians, news from Atlanta is more significant than news of equal weight from Montreal. That is so because the United States constitutes a community, a "home" in the national sense, and things that take place within it are more significant than things that take place outside it. As Anderson understands it, that community of interest comes before the political community.[12] One reason the United States survived as a nation was that the post-Revolutionary War generation already understood itself as part of a new nation; even after the Articles of Confederation fell apart, the people of the United States of America simply created a new government under the Constitution.

You may find yourself in Quincy, Illinois, but you know that you have entered "Cardinal Nation" because you can see pictures of red-and-black birds wearing baseball caps. Pick up the newspaper, *The Herald-Whig*, and you're likely to see the Cardinals getting bigger headlines and more photographs than the Cubs or the White Sox. The sports news that most people care about is news that comes out of St. Louis. Being a Cardinals fan announces both a loyalty and a kind of home. It says that even though you live in Illinois, a state with two perfectly good baseball teams, you understand yourself, in part, as connected to St. Louis, Missouri.

For Bachelard, such an understanding of your home changes the very way that you perceive the world. In the context of your entire life, a baseball team may not mean all that much. (In that case, you are clearly not a Red Sox fan, but that's another matter.) In the context of your sports life, however, it changes what you understand as significant. That Cardinals fan in Quincy may not care at all that the White Sox have signed Bartolo Colon yet

---

[12] Anderson elaborates his ideas in *Imagined Communities: Reflections on the Origin and Spread of Nationalism* (New York: Verso, 1983).

might regard with real anxiety that the Cubs, their division rivals, have a potent young pitching staff. A fan of either Chicago team would probably react to such news differently. He or she draws different boundaries around a different "home," and understands different news as relevant.

As Bachelard puts it, the philosophers who "know the universe before they know the house"[13] have it backwards. First we know the place we call home, for instance Yankee Stadium, and then we understand everything else through a "dialectics of outside and inside."[14] Yankee fans, and Yankee fans alone, cheered when Jason Giambi left the small-market A's to join what was already the best-funded team in the majors. Because they are fans, because they understand their baseball "home" (the house that Ruth built) as they do, they can look at the disparity in payrolls across baseball and understand it differently than most of the rest of us. They see what happens "outside" through a sensibility formed on the "inside." Yankee fans view all of baseball differently because they start out with a different sense of home than everyone else. Their home team benefits from the current payroll structure, so they are inclined to support it where, for instance, fans of the Pirates and Brewers, with different baseball homes, are inclined to call for wholesale changes.

Rounding Third and Heading Home

In the end, though, Bachelard's central point, and the point most relevant for baseball fans, is that he calls for a new understanding of small and local phenomena. He challenges us to take a new appreciation of the things that happen most intimately both because they inform our understanding of the world at large and because they contribute to who we are more subtly and more powerfully than we often recognize. In Bachelard's sensibility, the small and the concrete resonate more than the large and the abstract, and nuance is more powerful than bombast. He calls on us to consider what is right in front of us so that we can begin to understand how we understand everything else. He asks us to take a fresh look at the idea of home so that we can

---

[13] *The Poetics of Space*, p. 5.
[14] *Ibid.*, p. 211.

appreciate what is inside that home as well as appreciate what lies outside of it in all the directions of our imagination.

All of that is relevant because few sports turn on subtleties more than baseball does. In a tight game, the size of a runner's lead, the way the outfield shifts to play one hitter or another, the pitcher's delivery, and the third-base coach's pantomime all add to the tension and drama of the moment. It can take years of watching to learn what such tiny signs signify, but that's a part of what Bachelard is telling us. If you're someone who has made a home for yourself in a baseball park of America, you already understand that the details of that home matter even more than its overall shape. There is a plate right next to where the batter is standing. It takes an act of inspired imagination to transform it into something that we call home.

2 | Minnesota's "Homer Hanky Jurisprudence": Contraction, Ethics, and the Twins

PAUL HORAN and JASON SOLOMON

Hangovers were still fading in Phoenix on the morning of November 6th, 2001. It was only thirty-six hours after Luis Gonzalez's blooper had fallen over Derek Jeter's head in the ninth inning of game seven of the World Series, giving the Arizona Diamondbacks their first-ever world championship. Still fresh in the minds of baseball fans around the country were Barry Bonds's record-breaking seventy-three home runs, Ichiro Suzuki's MVP year in Seattle, and Curt Schilling and Randy Johnson's pitching performances in one of the most exciting post seasons ever.

But 1,500 miles from Phoenix, baseball's owners were meeting in Chicago, doing what they seemingly do best: putting the game's purportedly troubled business situation on the front page of every sports section in the country. The owners voted, twenty-eight to two, to eliminate two teams from the major leagues. Commissioner Bud Selig did not identify the teams to be eliminated, but did note, "The teams to be contracted have a long record of failing to generate enough revenues to operate a viable major league franchise."

It was a matter of hours before word got out on the two teams: the first, the Montreal Expos, an understandable and expected choice given their home in a town where the top three sports are hockey, hockey, and hockey. But the Minnesota Twins was a surprise. After all, in the last fifteen years, only the

New York Yankees had won more championships. And in two World Series victories, the Twins were a combined 8-0, playing in front of their home fans in the Metrodome.

What was going on here? Put simply, baseball was a business trying to eliminate two of its parts, purportedly because of business necessities. But though Selig told the public that twenty-five of the league's thirty owners lost money in 2001 for a total of more than $500 million, many disputed those figures. Baseball had near-record attendance in 2001—an average of almost 30,000 fans per game—and pulled in $3.5 billion in revenues.[1] *Forbes* magazine estimated that the Twins turned a $3.6 million profit.[2] The Twins had spent much of the season in first place, and their attendance had increased by 78 percent.

The public reaction to the announcement was fierce. The Twins had a long history and a loyal following throughout the Upper Midwest, not just in Minnesota, but also in states like the Dakotas where there are no major league baseball teams. On the airwaves and in the chat rooms, the story quickly morphed into a tale of betrayal, complete with villains like Bud Selig, baseball's commissioner and owner of the team next-door, the Milwaukee Brewers (a status which left his motives open to question), and Carl Pohlad, a multimillionaire banker who had bought the Twins just a few years earlier, tried and failed to get the taxpayers to pay for a new stadium, forcing him to spend his own millions. The story also featured a potential, if reluctant, hero, Jesse Ventura, a professional wrestler who had improbably become governor of Minnesota, and who had some experience in going to the mat in a fight. A grassroots movement began among Twins fans to "Keep the Twins At Home," with organized rallies and other media events across the state. But this being America, this morality tale played out in the courts. And so it was that within a few weeks, a lawyer representing the people of Minnesota stepped into a courtroom to advance the somewhat remarkable proposition, based more in ethics than in the law, that a team has an obligation to play baseball.

----

[1] www.kenn.com/sports/baseball/mlb. *USA Today* (December 7th, 2001).
[2] *Forbes* (April 15th, 2002).

Baseball's Special Place in the Law

Baseball has always had a unique place in the legal system, outside the rules that usually apply to a billion-dollar industry (though it is one). Instead, the game is governed by rules based on its mythic place in American society. Probably the most important example of this special status is baseball's exemption from the antitrust laws. Those laws are designed to protect consumers by preventing a company from exercising monopoly power, or engaging in unfair practices like collusion that restrict competition. Back in 1922, however, the Supreme Court first decided that the antitrust laws did not apply to baseball because the sport did not affect "interstate commerce." That notion quickly became silly as the business of baseball grew, of course, but the exemption has largely survived, most likely because of judges' and legislators' sentimental feelings about the national pastime and its place in society. Perhaps the exemption reflects the view that society has an obligation to protect baseball, a supposedly precious resource, from the vagaries and uncertainties of the market. Regardless, the exemption has been in place ever since Justice Oliver Wendell Holmes's 1922 opinion, and it possesses continued legal relevance today. For example, the reason that major league baseball owners can block teams from skipping town, without facing a lawsuit, is the antitrust exemption. And baseball owners were able to order contraction only because the exemption protected them from antitrust liability. In football, for example, the NFL cannot unilaterally order a team to stay in a city against its will, let alone fold up operations. Just ask Al Davis, the legendary Raiders owner who took his team down the West Coast from Oakland to Los Angeles, and then back to Oakland.

Contraction lays bare the contrast between the competitive ideal of baseball (closely paralleled by the logic of the markets), and the reality of the legal regime that governs the game. Unlike the theoretical competitive market, the owners decide who can enter, and now, for the first time, who must exit. Given baseball's "special place" in the legal system, then, it made sense that the lawyers for the people of Minnesota came into court, on the

---

[3] *Federal Baseball Club v. National League*, 259 U.S. 200, 42 S.Ct. 465, 66 L.Ed. 898 (1922).

surface, simply to enforce a commercial contract—the contract between the Metrodome, where the Twins play, and the Twins. But the lawyers' arguments were based more on broader notions of ethics than strictly on the law. Ultimately, the lawyers opposing contraction would successfully convince the Minnesota courts that they should consider not just traditional legal principles of contract law, but also broader notions of the public good: leading to the conclusion that the courts should, on behalf of the people of Minnesota, require the Twins to play baseball.

Ethics and Law

Utilitarianism is the philosophical school that emphasizes the public good. First systematized by philosophers Jeremy Bentham (1748–1832) and John Stuart Mill (1806–1873), utilitarianism teaches that, in making any decision, we should take the course of action that maximizes everyone's happiness. To measure this outcome, we should identify the happiness to each individual person that would result from a particular course of action, and then "add up" that happiness. We then deduct the total amount of collective misery that the same course of action might cause. Whatever course of action has the highest total accumulated happiness is the best utilitarian option. As the basic principle is often described, actions are right to the degree that they tend to promote "the greatest good for the greatest number."

This calculus should not be confused with deciding what would make the most people happy. If one potential course of action causes happiness in, say, one million people, and misery to only a half-dozen, it still might be a poor utilitarian option. If the happiness to each of the million people is almost infinitesimally small, and the misery to the half-dozen exceedingly great, then that option is likely have a net result of causing more misery than happiness, and is probably a poor utilitarian option (assuming there were other options that resulted in net human happiness).

It follows, then, that according to utilitarianism, a person should do that which would result in the greatest gain in human happiness: not just what would make her happy, or those around her happy, but rather that which would net the most total happiness. When it comes to fulfilling one's word, a utilitarian might say that a promise could be broken only if the breach, plus any alternative arrangements or damages ("I'll make it up to you by . . .") would result in more net happiness.

Utilitarianism is an ethical principle. And there has always been a connection between ethics and law, going back to the Babylonian Code of Hammurabi and the Ten Commandments. Ethically, we think it wrong to kill and steal, and that is reflected in our laws. If a college student steals a stop sign to hang in his dormitory room, this by itself is a relatively minor offense. However, if there is a car accident at the intersection with the missing sign, and people are hurt, then the punishment becomes much more serious. In other words, the consequences matter in criminal and other areas of law; the more harm that is caused, the more severe the punishment. In such circumstances, law reinforces utilitarian ethics.

But there are also times when law is distinct from the ethical principle of utilitarianism. We see this especially with legal obligations between private parties. If a company agrees to hire a group of employees for a year, it may be obligated to pay that group one year's salary. But maybe not, and certainly the company isn't obligated to continue employing them after that. Maybe a company that has operated a plant in a small town for fifty years, employing 200 people, shouldn't shut the plant down as a matter of utilitarian ethics, but it can do so under the law. Our free-market economy teaches that if it's cheaper to breach a contract and pay damages than fulfill the contract, you can go ahead and breach it, even if the other party and all affected parties would be less satisfied with the damages than with the performance. The fact that breaching the contract would involve breaking your word does not matter, nor does the fact that fulfilling the contract would mean "the greatest good for the greatest number," because such ethical concerns are not considered part of a legal obligation.

In a typical lawsuit, therefore, the concerns are pretty straightforward: did a party break a legal obligation it had to another party? And, if so, what damages—that is, what monetary payments—would be required to fully compensate the other party, to give him, as lawyers say, "the benefit of the bargain"? No thought is given to whether the breaching party should be punished for breaking his word, or to the non-economic losses that the other party might suffer. In other words, in the typical case, the Twins' community ties to Minnesota, and the heart-break of Twins' fans if the team were eliminated, wouldn't be very relevant to the team's obligations under their lease.

The Legal Obligation of the Twins

As a legal matter, then, the people of Minnesota were arguably on shaky ground. The Twins' landlord, joined by the state's Attorney General representing the people of Minnesota, had sued the team and Major League Baseball seeking a court order that would force them to fulfill their lease at the Metrodome—not by making payments to compensate for damages, but by actually playing their 2002 home schedule. In contract law, this kind of relief, called specific performance, is unusual. In fact, courts will rarely order specific performance even where it is explicitly provided for in an agreement, as it was in the use agreement between the Twins and the Metrodome.

The case was initially heard by Minnesota Superior Court Judge Harry Seymour Crump, who takes his place among base-ball's long tradition of great names. On November 16th, Judge Crump issued an injunction ordering the Twins to stay put for 2002. Importantly, Judge Crump said that one reason why he could force the Twins to play was the harm that would be suffered *by the fans*-not just the folks that run the Metrodome-if they didn't play. Judge Crump said:

> Baseball is as American as turkey and apple pie. Baseball is a tradi-tion that passes from generation to generation. Baseball crosses social barriers, creates community spirit, and is much more than a private enterprise. Baseball is a national pastime. Locally, the Twins have been part of Minnesota history and tradition for forty years. The Twins have given Minnesota two World Series Championships, one in 1987, and one in 1991. the Twins have also given Minnesota legends such as Rod Carew, Tony Oliva, Harmon Killebrew, Kent Hrbek, and Kirby Puckett; some of which streets are named.after. These legends have bettered the community. Most memorably, these legends, volunteered their time to encourage and motivate children to succeed in all challenges of life. Clearly, more than money is at stake. The welfare, recreation, prestige, prosperity, trade and com-merce of the people of the community are at stake. The Twins brought the community together with Homer Hankies and bobble-head dolls. The Twins are one of the few professional sports teams

in town where a family can afford to take their children to enjoy a hot dog and peanuts at a stadium. The vital public interest, or trust, of the Twins substantially outweighs any private interest. Private businesses were condemned to build the Metrodome. In condemnation proceedings, the building of the Metrodome was deemed to be in the interest of the public. The Commission, the State, citizenry and fans will suffer irreparable harm if the Twins do not play the 2002 baseball games at the Metrodome.[4]

The Twins and baseball quickly appealed, but found themselves in an ironic position. Having taken advantage for many years of the notion that baseball is somehow different or unique, they were now forced to argue that, in fact, baseball was just like any other business. Why? Because their argument boiled down to this: even if there was a lease between the Metrodome facility and the Twins, and the Twins were to breach the lease, the Metrodome would simply be entitled to money damages. Just like any storefront business that closed shop, the Twins might be responsible for making payments to fulfill their lease obligations, but no court should force them to stay in the Metrodome and play games any more than it would force the local business to stay open and service customers. Why? Because those obligations can be covered by cash payments to cover damages. Despite its apparent foundation in the law, at least one of the appeals judges seemed skeptical of this argument, asking the Twins' attorney: "Is there no difference between the Minnesota Twins and any other commercial entity as you described?"

The Attorney General, on the other hand, argued that a cash payment would not be enough because the Twins meant more to Minnesota than the mere revenue they produce through rent payments. He argued that the Twins were a "community asset" that provided substantial non-monetary benefits, such as "civic pride, economic stimulus, and social cohesion." By creating the Metrodome and setting up the lease agreement with the Twins, the state legislature made clear that it expected more from the Twins than money, giving the team very favorable terms. Indeed, the Twins pay no rent for use of the Metrodome, and

---

[4] *Metropolitan Sports Facilities Comm'n v. Minnesota Twins P'ship*, No. CT-01-16998, 2001 WL 1511601 at *1 (Minn.Dist.Ct. November 16th, 2001).

the stadium itself was heavily subsidized by public funds. As the Metrodome's attorney noted, the use agreement for the Metrodome was drafted to reflect the idea that the Twins were obligated to play baseball there. "The public enters into these use agreements and spends a lot of time and resources and, in fact, even subsidizes the use agreement, in return for an enforceable obligation to play games."[5]

In other words, the opponents of contraction used the very arguments that baseball had long invoked to benefit itself—that because of the sport's place in society, it could legitimately be held to rules that might not apply to other businesses.

When the Court of Appeals issued its ruling about a month later, on January 22nd, 2002, it was clear that it had bought the argument of the fans' representatives that the utilitarian "public interest" served by the Twins was a legitimate reason to force the team to play games in the Metrodome in 2002. The court specifically said that the public interest could be considered, and in a rather delicious moment turned Bud Selig's words against him: Selig had once testified that if Congress ended baseball's antitrust exemption it "could irreparably injure fans by leading to the removal of live professional baseball from communities that have hosted major league and minor league teams for decades." In other words, the court seemed to be saying, what's sauce for the goose is sauce for the gander. If baseball was going to argue that it should benefit from special rules, then those rules would apply to baseball's owners as well.

When the Minnesota Supreme Court refused to hear baseball's appeal of the case, the game was effectively up. The Twins would have to play in 2002. On February 5th, Major League Baseball announced that it was giving up its contraction plans— at least for 2002. And by October, local fans were cheering All-Star center fielder Torii Hunter and the Twins in the post-season.

Judge Crump's Utilitarianism

Judge Crump's decision, as upheld on appeal, seems to be based in large part on the idea that the Twins had an obligation

---

[5] All quotations from the attorneys and judges at the oral argument are taken from the reporting of Minnesota Public Radio, which can be found at http://news.mpr.org/features/200111/08_newsroom_twins.

to the community in which they played. But where does this obligation come from, ethics or law?

In large part, the judge's decision seems to rest on the idea of obligation to community—the obligation of the Twins to continue to provide certain intangible assets to a community that had given its support over several decades. For Crump, the team and its players are not merely an entertainment company and its employees, they are a part of the community and some players are among the community's role models. In upholding Judge Crump's ruling, the Court of Appeals cited intangible community benefits as one of the reasons why money damages could not fully compensate the Metrodome facility in the event of a breach by the Twins.

It's not so clear, however, that all this is true, that these supposed benefits are real. Economists have said that the benefits provided to a community by sports teams are often overstated.[6] In this situation and many others, it's about getting big public subsidies for stadiums, money that probably could be put to better use. While well publicized, the charitable efforts of athletes are really just a drop in the bucket, and the athletes are not the role models they might appear to be. Perhaps at the end of the day baseball is just another form of entertainment, with no more obligations than a band playing a concert or a theater group performing a play. If Dave Matthews cancels a show, people get their money back, but even the most rabid fans aren't going to get a court order requiring him to play in their hometown. Minnesota business leaders claimed that businesses considering moving to a city consider its sports and arts scene, for example, but many economists reject such arguments, saying the money spent on the Twins would be diverted to other forms of entertainment or other businesses.

The utilitarian idea that an organization has obligations to the community in which it operates is more radical than it might appear. Under the law, for example, businesses rarely have any obligations to the community, let alone their workers. In the movie *Roger and Me*, film-maker Michael Moore decried the fact that General Motors, at the time one of the largest employers in

---

[6] For the opposite view, see Albert Duncan's argument in this volume, Chapter 20.

the world, had not done more for its (and his) hometown of Flint, Michigan. But GM was not the exception; it was the rule. When it's time to move the factory to Mexico or China, just give the workers a little notice, and the business is fine, under the law. Legally, most employment in America is known as "at will." This means that the employee works at the will of the employer, and that the employer can choose to terminate the employment when it wants to and at its discretion. Most employers can fire their employees when they want to and for whatever reasons they want to, be they good reasons, bad reasons, or no reason at all.

For most businesses, utilitarian obligations to the community are rarely recognized. In fact, they're discouraged. During the boom economic years of the 1990s, "flexibility" and "free agency" were the watchwords of high-flying American businesses, particularly in the technology sector. Magazine covers trumpeted the latest whiz kid who started his own dot.com and struck it rich. Loyalty to the company that trained him? That's the old-school economy. And the lack of obligation goes both ways. Employees should act like "free agents"—like Alex Rodriguez—because businesses certainly do. When a big company moves a factory to China to cut labor costs, its stockholders jump for joy, even if thousands of American families dependent on the jobs are less enthused. If companies can look for countries with the cheapest labor, why can't the Twins look for cities that will give them the biggest public subsidy for the most luxury boxes? Utilitarianism is not part of the legal calculus; employees are expected to just move on, even if moving on means taking a huge pay cut to work at Wal-Mart. So were Twins fans expected to move on and root for the minor league St. Paul Saints?

Why, then, did Judge Crump order the Twins to play baseball, if traditional legal principles allow a typical business to close up shop with no problem? Perhaps because, throughout its history, baseball's relationship with the law has been uniquely tied to utilitarian notions of the public good. As far as the law is concerned, baseball has never been just another business. As Justice Holmes told us in 1922, and as Judge Crump confirmed in 2001, the law has always kept in mind broader questions of the public good when dealing with baseball. Such utilitarian concerns, frequently excluded from conventional legal consideration, are very much part of baseball's legal tradition.

The Obligation to Play Baseball

Maybe it does make sense, then, that there's an ethical and legal obligation to play baseball, if not other sports. Imagine someone in the very same community bringing a lawsuit to enforce the Minnesota Timberwolves' obligation to play the basketball season. The idea is absurd. Is it a part of the fabric of the community? An intangible community asset? Not quite. And it's not just about the Timberwolves versus the Twins; it's about baseball itself. As a game of mass appeal, basketball is young, on the move, the game of the hip-hop generation, where the most exciting plays take place, literally, in the air. A good basketball team, by definition, can't be tied down. In baseball, as Joe Kraus argued in the previous chapter, sense of place still matters: the ivy at Wrigley Field, the Green Monster at Fenway Park. Socks are still worn high, and for the most part, the manager, not the star player, is still in charge of the team.

Like the utilitarian mandate to consider "the greatest good for the greatest number," baseball is rather retro, even without throwback uniforms to take us back in the day. Basketball, football, hockey are part of the new economy, playing by the rules of the market, subject to the antitrust laws that promote competition, operating like the businesses that they are. Under those rules, obligations to others are for suckers. The self-interest by each leads to the best results for all, or so the theory goes. But baseball succeeded in setting itself outside those rules, and now has to live with the consequences.

Before the appellate court, the Twins' attorneys had argued that treating a baseball team differently than your typical business was enforcing the law based on emotion, not reason—that it was "Homer Hanky jurisprudence." "The fans are cheering and the Homer Hankies are waving, but there has to be some institution that applies the law," they argued. "It's like the umpires on the field. They've got to tune out the politics, the pragmatists and have got to call balls and strikes according to fixed rules. And we look to you—the men in blue—to establish the rule of law."

But these attorneys were in an odd position to complain, having successfully argued for many years, based on nostalgia and emotion, that baseball had a special place in society not subject to the usual rules governing market competition and creating a different set of obligations. When Justice Holmes was creating the antitrust exemption, baseball was more than happy to reap the benefits of the ruling that the game was more than just a business, and that its legitimate concerns were more than just economics. In 1972, when the antitrust exemption was challenged again before the Supreme Court, Justice Harry Blackmun, in an opinion upholding the exemption as an "established aberration," praised "the many names, celebrated for one reason or another, that have sparked the diamond and its environs and that have provided tinder for recaptured thrills, for reminiscence and comparisons, and for conversation and anticipation in-season and off-season: Ty Cobb, Babe Ruth, Tris Speaker, Walter Johnson . . ." This list, as Blackmun admitted, "seem[ed] endless."[7] Again, no objection was heard from baseball that utilitarian ethics was ruling the day, and not legal precedent.

So, even if "Homer Hanky Jurisprudence" did carry the day to some extent, it was an understandable result. The fans had attended the games, bought the merchandise, eaten the overpriced hot dogs, drunk the expensive beer, provided the team with the land to build their stadium, and offered favorable lease terms. In short, the people of Minnesota had provided the Twins with innumerable benefits. On top of that, Minnesota had made the Twins a part of its community life. In the normal course of events, if we were talking not about a baseball team but, say, a car manufacturer, all of these points might not have mattered. The state could have given the manufacturer tax breaks, land to build a new factory, and other forms of support, but no court would have required the company to keep making cars if it wanted to close. The Twins were treated differently because utilitarian consideration of the "public good" is a firmly rooted part of baseball's legal history. For many years, baseball took advantage of the courts' willingness to take utilitarian concerns into account; in 2001, baseball lost when the sport tried to act against the "public good."

Baseball once placed an asterisk next to Roger Maris's home run record because he had a longer season to pass Babe Ruth. Much like Maris's record, the Minnesota courts' contraction

---

[7] *Flood v. Kuhn*, 407 U.S. 258, 262–63, 92 S.Ct. 2099, 2103, 32 L.Ed.2d 728 (1972).

decisions belong to a long line of baseball cases that deserve an asterisk in the case books. These legal opinions are unique because of their utilitarian consideration of the public good. For Minnesota fans scoring at home, Judge Crump and utilitarian ethics combined for the save.

Second Inning:
You Gotta Believe!

"Just wait 'till next year," we tell ourselves at the end of yet another disappointing season. Why do we still have faith? Tom Senor argues that faith is rational, which should come as good news to Chicago Cubs fans. Willie Young explains how baseball and religion come together in the notion of sacrifice. In the game of life, sacrificing yourself for others is a lot more complicated than simply advancing the runner.

3 | Should Cubs Fans Be Committed? What Bleacher Bums Have to Teach Us about the Nature of Faith

THOMAS D. SENOR

You know the law of averages says that anything will happen that can. / But the last time the Cubs won the National League pennant was the year we dropped the bomb on Japan.

—STEVE GOODMAN, "A Dying Cubs Fan's Last Request"

Cubs fans love the Cubs, warts and all, no questions asked. This quality is called faith.

—PETER GLENBOCK from the introduction to *Wrigleyville: A Magical History Tour of the Chicago Cubs*

Spring is a time for fresh starts and blooming, a season when even the pessimist is tempted to dream of what might be. For Cubs fans, April is the month that brings with it the blessed guarantee that their team will be at least tied for first place for at least one day (Opening Day). Typically, the rest of the baseball season is not so kind to those who pull for the team from Chicago's North Side. The chilly winds of late September that blow across Lake Michigan not only tend to hold back long fly balls from hometown bats—they are also typically concurrent with both the dying leaves of autumn and the fading post-season dreams of the Cubs and their followers.

Yet it is spring and hope is alive. But should it be? Isn't there something positively irrational about believing, year after disappointing year, that *this* will be the season? Can hope in the absence of proof, in the absence of anything that even looks like good evidence, be rational? In short, should Cubs fans be committed?

This essay will attempt to answer this question. And in doing so we will, I hope, uncover something about the nature of commitment. We'll begin by considering what it means to be a fan and then apply these principles of commitment to the nature of religious belief and devotion.

What It's Like to Be a Cubs Fan

When you are a genuine fan of a team, you make a commitment. You like them, win or lose. A person who roots for whichever club happens to be winning is a true fan of no team. It goes without saying that Cubs followers are genuine fans. The same cannot be said, for example, for many Yankees fans. A team that has a great deal of success must look skeptically, maybe even cynically, upon those who fill its stands. For wide are the stadium gates of the winners but narrow is the way of true fandom. This, I suggest, is why the Cubs faithful are admired at least as much as they are ridiculed: no one can doubt their sincerity. With Yankees fans, no one can be sure.

To get a sense of the long-suffering nature of Cubs followers, one needs to recall a bit of baseball history. The Cubs didn't win the World Series for a century (give or take a few years) and they didn't win a National League pennant since 1945. Even the Cubs' championship in 1908 turns out to have been won only because of one of the most notorious mistakes in baseball history. The Cubs were trailing the New York Giants by a single game, having made up two games in the previous two days. (It might surprise contemporary Cubs fans to know that in the early part of the last century, the Cubs were a very successful club and winning and vying for pennants was a common occurrence.) But they were behind in 1908 and were trying desperately to overtake the Giants. The two clubs were playing in New York on September 23rd and were tied with two outs in the bottom of the ninth when Al Bridwell lined a single-scoring Moose McCormick from third base. The apparent success of the hometown Giants brought the crowd streaming onto the field and sending the players straight to the clubhouse. This would have been no problem except that Fred Merkle, a nineteen-year-old rookie who was the runner on first base when Bridwell hit his single, went directly to the locker room without touching second. Cubs shortstop Frank Evers noticed Merkle's mistake and, to make a long story short, retrieved the ball in the midst of the bedlam and touched second. The umpires convened and decided that Merkle was indeed out and that McCormick's run didn't count. With darkness coming, the umpires called the game a tie. The decision was appealed but the officials backed the umpires' ruling. Furthermore, it was decided that if the Cubs and the Giants finished the season tied, the game would have to be replayed. The Cubs and Giants did indeed finish with identical records and the Cubs won the tiebreaker. Thus, were it not for the mental error of a nineteen-year-old, the Cubs would never have won the 1908 World Series. They've gone nearly one hundred years without a championship and even that title was won only because of a rookie mistake.

There are those who maintain that the Cubs' haplessness is the result of a curse. In the '45 World Series, the Cubs were playing the Detroit Tigers. The owner of a local bar, William "Billy Goat" Sianis bought two tickets for game four. He wanted to take his Billy Goat, "Murphy," to the game and have him sit with him in a box seat. But Murphy smelled, well, like a goat, and the ushers refused to allow him into the park. Sianis was furious and left in a huff, placing a curse on the Cubs. As with most curses, this was not taken seriously. But when the next four seasons saw the Cubs struggling, team owner Philip Wrigley wrote to Sianis and asked him to have Murphy remove the spell. It took Sianis until 1969 to oblige, but one suspects that the curse removal didn't take. For it was in 1969 that the Cubs led the NL Eastern Division most of the season only to collapse in September and be overcome by the "Amazing Mets" who would eventually win not only the pennant but the World Series. In the 2003 post-season Sianis's curse resurfaced when a fan interfered in the eighth inning of game six of the NLCS, giving the Florida Marlins an extra out in the middle of a rally that turned a Cubs lead into an insurmountable deficit. Ahead in the series three games to one, the Cubs went on to lose the NL pennant in seven games.

Why Do People Struggle with Faith?

Cubs fans are tortured souls. Writer, political analyst, and baseball enthusiast George Will has claimed that "Cubs fans are ninety-three percent scar tissue." In the same way that Cubs fans hold on to hope even in the midst of a distinct lack of success on the field, the religiously devout hold onto their faith even as, in the western world, religious practices and faith seem to be in retreat. Certainly, the general cultural influence of religion in the United States is at an all-time low. Things are even tougher for the faithful in Europe. Increasingly, it seems to many believers that being a faithful member of a religious community is not unlike being a Cubs fan: it is a condition looked upon with equal parts pity and mystification.

So why do it? Why make a commitment to something that will bring heartache and disappointment (in the case of Cubs loyalty) and sacrifice and persecution (in the case of religious belief)?

Religious faith brings other objections as well. Many argue that faith in a benevolent deity is irrational, others claim that organized religion is a source of social and political stagnation that encourages the poor and displaced to be happy with their earthly lot (with the promise of a heavenly reward at the end of the road).

So how do we proceed? This is a hefty list of serious charges. Let's begin by looking first at the lighter issues—namely, those regarding commitment to the "lovable losers" of the North Side of Chicago. We'll then turn our attention to objections to religious commitment.

Commitment and the Cubs

Are there good reasons to be loyal to the Cubs? We can begin trying to answer this question by noting an important difference between religious institutions and baseball clubs. There is a clear measure of success for the latter: championships won. And it's precisely at this point that Cubs fans may feel particularly uneasy—indeed, even positively queasy. Is it, they themselves may wonder, rational to be committed to a team that has had so little success? We might get started by thinking about the nature of what it is to be a fan, or in other words, the nature of fandom.

Fans are the devotees (that is, the *devout*) of sport. A fan of a team, a genuine fan, has made a commitment. It is a commitment to support the team regardless of the team's success or failure. But it is more than that. It's also a conviction that the team is fundamentally *worthy* of support. While it is arguably inappropriate to quit supporting a team for the sole reason of lack of success, there are times when withdrawing one's support is not only allowable but perhaps even morally required. A recent example of this in sport can be found in professional basketball. Through the mid to late 1990s and the early 2000s, the Portland Trailblazers made a series of moves that not only stumped their fiercely loyal fan base but went so far as to alienate them. The Blazers appeared to go out of their way to sign players who had caused problems with other teams or had had scuffs with the law or both. (This tendency has led to the team's being dubbed the "Jailblazers.") While courting and signing such players as Rasheed Wallace and Isaiah Rider, they simultaneously traded or declined to re-sign solid citizens like Clyde Drexler and Terry Porter. They even fired their long-time and beloved radio announcer, Bill Schonely. Many basketball followers in Portland now think of themselves as former-Blazer fans. Should we say that the fans of the Blazers who have since jumped ship were not real fans? I don't think so. By recruiting the sort of players the Blazers recruited, they made themselves not worthy of true fanhood. They gave fans very good reason to quit supporting them. The problem wasn't that the team wasn't winning but that it became morally unworthy of having true fans. Those who continue to pay the players' salaries by buying tickets and attending games are those whose actions are questionable. Loyalty to Mother Teresa is a virtue; loyalty to Adolf Hitler is not. Indeed, it might be that those fans who maintain their support in the face of significant organizational wrongdoing exhibit the same vice that those who exhibit excessive patriotism are guilty of. "My team win or lose" is the declaration of the fan; "my team right or wrong" is the cry of the zealot.

We began by asking if there is reason to be committed to a team that frequently lets down its fans; is the heartache worth it? But in developing the beginning of an answer to this question (an answer we will give more fully in a moment) we have stumbled onto two other reasons people have for not being fans of some teams. The first reason for non-support is exemplified by the above example of the Portland Trailblazers: persistent wrongdoing by the players and a willingness of management to put up with such nastiness as long as the players who commit it can help the team win. So we will need to ask this question

about the Cubs: do they have the same kind of shady history as
the recent Portland Trailblazers have? The second new difficulty
is in a way similar to the original problem of supporting a team
that consistently loses; however, this second new difficulty is in
a way worse. It is one thing to be a team that has trouble winning championships or even making the playoffs; but it is
another thing altogether to be an organization that apparently
doesn't care to win.

A model of how to run a team if you want to drive off true
fans is baseball's Florida Marlins of the late 1990s. The Marlins
were willing to spend for a championship—for a year. The winter before the 1997 season, the Marlins signed a number of high-
priced free agents. They kept them for as long as it took to win
a World Series title. But when the Series of '97 was won, they
had the "fire sale" of the century. They dumped the big salaries
with even more speed than they had exhibited in signing them.
(Remarkably, as soon as the Marlins reversed their course, they
achieved great success, winning the 2003 World Series.)

In sum, then, it would seem that to be worthy of support, a
franchise must be committed to two things: winning and sportsmanship.

Should Cubs fans be committed? Do the Cubs fail either the
winning or sportsmanship condition of being fan-worthy? Let's
hear the bad news first. Many have claimed that the owners of
the Cubs (the Tribune Company) have no interest in spending
the money it takes to win as long as they can fill Wrigley Field
while they lose. More than one Cubs supporter has defended
the team against this allegation while worrying that there was
something to it. The Cubs are a big-market team with a large
and loyal national fan base, good TV revenues, and an owner
with deep pockets. Yet they do not have a record of regularly
pursuing the most valuable free agents. Indeed, they have sometimes not been willing to pay the going rate to keep players they
ought to try to keep. (The most egregious example of their letting a great player go is their failure to sign Greg Maddux following his Cy-Young-Award-winning 1992 season.) So this
criticism has some bite. It is one thing to be committed to a team
that regularly loses despite its best efforts; but an organization
that is more concerned with making a profit than with winning
is not keeping its end of the bargain. The good news for Cubs
fans is that it appears that the team is making progress. In recent

years, the Cubs have done more than they have in the past both to keep their stars in the Windy City and to attract high-priced players and managers. Signing Sammy Sosa to one of baseball's most lucrative contracts instead of trading him or losing him to free agency, and signing manager Dusty Baker are both indications that the team is learning that winning requires an investment of more than blood and sweat.

Now for the other possible reason to pull support from a team: bad sportsmanship. Is there any reason for a Cubs fan to feel qualms here? This question needs to be split in two: is the history of the team replete with bad characters? And does the team's current make-up provide reason to root against them? The answer to both of these questions is no. Any organization that has been around for more than a century will have some ruffians and even misanthropes. The Cubs are no exception. The man most closely associated with, and responsible for, the glory days of the Cubs in the late nineteenth century (actually, they were then called the *White Stockings*) was Cap Anson. Yet there is no one in the history of the game who bears more culpability for the exclusion of African-Americans from the major leagues until 1947 when Jackie Robinson broke in. In Toledo for an exhibition game in 1882, Anson demanded that a black player on the Toledo team be removed from the game. In 1887, the New York Giants made a deal for black pitcher George Stovey. When Anson got wind of this he rallied the other owners to insist that the transaction not go through and baseball's color line was thereby drawn.

While Anson's racism is an ugly scar on the franchise, the team's overall complexion is a good one. Ernie Banks is one of the most beloved baseball players of all time—and for good reason. "Mr. Cub" played the game with a joyous spirit that was reflected in his infectious smile. Indeed, Banks' friendly demeanor earned him a second nickname: "Mr. Sunshine." That Banks had such a gracious and easy-going attitude is made all the more remarkable by times. Today, it is easy to forget that African-American players of Banks's era often came to Major League Baseball via the Negro Leagues. Jackie Robinson had broken the color barrier only six years before Banks arrived in the big leagues in 1953. Banks himself endured the racist attitudes and practices of the times. Yet there was never a doubt as to why Banks played: for the love of the game.

Sammy Sosa may make one of baseball's top salaries but there is no doubt that on the field he plays for fun. His good-natured home run dual of 1998 with Mark McGwire captured the interest of the entire nation; and Sammy's grace and good sportsmanship when Big Mac finally broke Roger Maris's single-season home run record was everything one could hope for.[1]

So the Cubs are not guilty of the twin sins of fielding a team of charlatans and not being willing to pay for a winning team. Although the franchise has not always been as concerned with winning as one might hope, on balance, commitment to the Cubs is neither foolish nor morally suspect. But what of the heartache objection we began with? Isn't the Cubs' lack of winning (even if innocently 'achieved') reason enough to not be a fan?

Since the answer to this question so clearly mirrors the answer to a question about religious commitment, we will now have a look at objections to faith. In discussing the merits of belief in the face of suffering and persecution we will find our answer about value of commitment to a team that has trouble winning.

The Rationality of Religious Commitment

Is it irrational to believe in God and to commit yourself to a religious life? There are two distinct things the claim of 'irrationality' might mean. One concerns the *epistemic* (and perhaps social) acceptability of religious belief; the other matter is *prudential*. Religious belief fails to be epistemically acceptable if, on balance, there are good reasons for thinking it is false. The qualifier "on balance" is crucial in the previous sentence. For the mere fact that there is a reason, even a pretty good reason, to believe a claim is false does not imply that one is irrational in believing it to be true. For the totality of the evidence might nevertheless be in its favor. However, if the totality of the evidence clearly points to a proposition's being false, and if one is aware of this evidence and recognizes it for what it is, then one believes the claim at the risk of irrationality. Believing a propo-

---

[1] Sosa's bat corking controversy is discussed in Chapter 7 of this volume.

sition to be true if it has been shown or nearly shown to be false is to hold an irrational belief. So one way of understanding the charge that religious devotion is irrational is as the claim that religious belief has been intellectually discredited.

The second way the charge of irrationality comes in has little to do with the belief's epistemic credibility and more to do with the affect that holding it has on the individual. Remember Will's comment that Cubs fans are ninety-three percent scar tissue. You might wonder why the Cubs faithful do it to themselves. After all, aligning yourself with the Cubs is setting yourself up for pain and disappointment. So why do it? Similarly, being part of a religious community can be costly. The righteous suffer, and their expectation that God will rescue or heal them in this life is often frustrated. Jesus, for example, said to pick up your cross if you are to be his follower (Matthew 16:24); he also predicted that you would face persecution (Matthew 10:23). This is hardly the promise of sunny skies and worry-free life that many make religious invitations out to be. So why are they accepted as often as they are? Isn't it irrational to commit yourself to a cause that will take you down the road of self-sacrifice and suffering?

In a word, 'No.' Why not? Because, contrary to the teaching of the hedonist, life isn't all about smiles and pleasures. There is value in commitment to a cause and in the meaning that such commitment gives. The suffering experienced can be positive: not only because of lessons learned, but because it increases the joy one feels in the good times. No one doubts that the Yankees and their fans are made genuinely happy when they add to their bounty of pennants and championships. But does anyone seriously think that their joy has the height and depth which that of the Cubs or Boston Red Sox and their faithful will experience on that fine day when their droughts have ended? What will make the Cubs and Red Sox fans' rapture complete is not merely the fact that it has been so long since they've won; it is also the fact that they've so often lost, and so often lost after having their hopes raised throughout the course of the season only to have them dashed in September and, occasionally, October.

The religious analogue of winning the World Series is eternal life or union with the One. But it would be wrong to think that the sole reason for religious faith is the ultimate reward. The sincerely devout often say that the life of religious devotion is a sufficient reward of its own. Spiritual richness and an earthly life of meaning more than outweigh the hard-times and sacrifices. An eternal life of bliss is but icing on the cosmic cake.

So the life of faith is not irrational from the point of self-interest. But what about from the epistemic perspective? Faith has been defined as "believing what you know to be false." If that is correct, then faith is epistemically irrational. Even if one takes this definition of faith to be tongue-in-cheek, one might still think that there are good reasons for thinking that religious beliefs are false and that God doesn't exist. To believe in God is thus to believe what is false, and that begins to sound a lot like the above definition.

The first thing to notice is that, as far as rationality is concerned, there is an enormous difference between believing what is *in fact* false and believing what *you know* (or even just believe) *to be* false. I might have very good reason to believe that my car will start the next time I get in it even if, as it turns out, my battery has just died and the engine won't turn over. My current belief that it will start is not shown to be *irrational* (even if it is shown to be *false*) by my car's failing to start later. On the other hand, if I know that it doesn't even have a battery and that a car will start only if it has a battery, and yet I believe that when I go out to my battery-less car it will nevertheless start immediately, I believe irrationally.

So for religious belief to be irrational, it isn't enough that it is in fact false or even that there is, on balance, good evidence against it. The person of faith would have to have her religious convictions while at the same time believing that they are false or that her best evidence entails that they are false. While philosophers like Søren Kierkegaard (1813–1855) openly embrace faith irrationally, most believers have a different view. They accept that the evidence against God's existence is not *that* good and that they have reasons to believe in a creator, even if some of those reasons are hard to articulate. Whether they are right about where the preponderance of the evidence lies isn't really the point. To be epistemically irrational in the most straightforward sense is to hold a belief that even you recognize is not true. Religious believers, like unbelievers, are not often guilty of that.

Still, you might be thinking, isn't someone irrational if she believes what everyone else thinks is false? For instance, those who persist in believing that the earth is flat might really think the evidence is with them, but that doesn't stop the rest of us from viewing them as irrational. Might we not say the same of the devout?

This is a serious question and I haven't the space here to develop a theory of rationality—which is what it would take to put this issue to rest. But we can at least quiet this nagging doubt with the following point. What makes Flat-Earthers irrational is not that they are have a minority viewpoint, but that they reject the opinion of all experts and are fond of conspiracy theories to explain mountains of evidence against their position.

Religious believers, as a group, do neither of these things. That is, there is no group of experts who unanimously assert the truth of propositions they deny. True, there are fundamentalist elements that make claims about the origins of the universe that are routinely, and nearly universally, denounced by scientists (I'm thinking, for example, of claims that the universe is only six thousand years old and was created to be pretty much as it now is in six twenty-four hour days). However, these claims make up no part of the official theology and worldview of any of the major religions. And while some sects are fond of espousing conspiracies, such theories play no serious role in mainstream faith.

We've seen no overriding reason for eschewing either religious commitment or loyalty to the Cubs. But we have yet to understand the nature of the commitment we find unobjectionable. We'll first look at the nature of the loyalty of the true fan in the hope that we can also make a step toward better understanding religious faith.

The Nature of Commitment

What is a *true* fan? And what is the relation between being a true fan of a baseball team and being a faithful member of a religious tradition?

When it comes to having faith in a baseball team, the first and most obvious condition is that one must have a certain kind of pro-attitude toward the team in question. One must *want* the team to win, must have the *desire* that the team do well. Interestingly, being a fan of a team doesn't require that you want that team to win the championship. For if it did, no one could be a fan of more than one team. But surely there are fans of more than one team. Residents of New York City, for example, might be both Mets and Yankees fans (even if they are not in doubt about their ultimate allegiance). Perhaps, though, there is the need for the concept of super-fandom: one is a superfan of a team only if one desires that team win its championship. Be that as it may, standard fandom does require that one want the team to do well.

A true fan of a team is not someone who merely wants the team to win *today*. No, the genuine fan will be committed to her team, win or lose; she will be a supporter tomorrow even if the sun is not shining. We tend to think of true fandom as a virtue and of bandwagon-jumping as a vice. But why? What's so great about pulling for a team even when it does poorly? And what's so bad about pulling for any team that is doing well?

Humans rightly value loyalty. Being a loyal friend means being a friend even in the bad times. Fair-weather fans are like fair-weather friends. They display a culpable lack of fidelity. Conversely, one who exhibits genuine fanhood displays the exact same virtue as the good friend. In fact, the true fan can be seen as exhibiting this virtue more selflessly. For the good friend has a reasonable hope and expectation that the friend to whom she is being faithful in the tough times would do the same for her. Even if this expectation is not her motivation for being a true friend, the fact is that she who is loyal is more likely to find friends around during her darkest hour. But the true fan expects nothing of her team in return, or at least nothing that is directed at her. The fan expects her team to be dedicated to excellence and sportsmanship but these virtues are not directed at her.

An unexpected point here is that attitudes toward teams are not voluntarily chosen. While this fact is not often recognized it nevertheless can be understood with only a little reflection. Being a fan of a team, really *wanting* it to win is an attitude that is not under direct voluntary control. If you have doubts about this try this experiment: think of a team you generally root against (for most of us that would be the New York Yankees). Can you now, by a simple act of will, (that is, by just now choosing) decide to become a fan of that team? No, you can't.

You can decide now to *act like* a fan. You can cheer and tell people you are pulling for them, but you can't just choose to like them starting *now*. This doesn't mean, however that you have no control at all.

For example, suppose you grew up in San Francisco and were naturally a Giants fan. To your initial chagrin, the company you work for has transferred you to Chicago where you will reside for many years. Being a baseball fan but having no prior interest in the Cubs, you nevertheless decide to make the best of it and begin regularly attending Cubs games, watching them on local TV, and even listening to them on the radio. You get to know quite a bit about the ownership, the manager, the players, and even the farm system. And the more you know, the more the names, faces, and history are familiar to you, the more you like them. Eventually, you are a Cubs fan. You now pull for the Cubs without trying, and you find yourself disappointed when they don't do well. Although you weren't able to just get up one morning and decide to become a fan, you were able to directly do things that would make this likely. You went to Wrigley Field, you watched games on TV and listened to them on the radio, and you learned about the players and the ballclub. But of course while doing these things will often lead to becoming a fan, such is not always the case. Recall the example of the recent Portland Trailblazers. The regular bad behavior both on and off the court made the team unlikable to many. A person might have moved to Portland expecting to become a Blazer fan but been so put off by both players and management that the more she knew the less she liked them. When it comes to knowing a scoundrel, familiarity rightly breeds contempt.

If it is surprising that one can't simply choose to become a fan of a team, it might be downright shocking to realize that religious belief is also beyond our voluntary control. The reason for this is that belief in general is, like desire, a mental state that is not truly chosen. For example, you undoubtedly believe that Abraham Lincoln was President of the United States during the Civil War. Now if belief is under direct voluntary control, you should be able to stop believing that and to start believing instead that Franklin Roosevelt was. So here's a challenge: give it a try. Try ceasing to believe that Lincoln was President during the Civil War and beginning to believe that FDR was. You can't do it, can you? The reason is that, again as with our desires, we have only indirect control over our beliefs. You can't come to have a belief just by deciding to. However, as with being a fan of a team, you do have a certain amount of indirect control.

Choosing Faith?

A philosopher who is often misunderstood but who makes an important point relevant to this discussion is Blaise Pascal (1623–1662). Pascal is famous for his "wager." Crudely put, his argument is this. When you sort through all the reasons for and against God's existence, you'll find that there just isn't compelling evidence for either theism or atheism. The evidence is split; reason can't decide. Yet religion (and he was thinking primarily of Christianity) makes certain demands. Now if you positively disbelieve, then of course you won't heed its commands. But equally, if you don't make up your mind, if you are an agnostic and live out your convictions (so to speak), you won't heed religion's commands either. And if you fail to live a life of religious commitment and devotion, and there is a God, you will miss out on the ultimate good: union with God. So, practically speaking, atheism and agnosticism come to the same thing. And the outcome is possibly even worse than the loss of the greatest good. For according to some religious traditions, rejecting God can result in a hell of an afterlife.

So, Pascal claims, here is your situation: You have your life to bet, and the way you live your life determines where you lay your bet. You must either bet on God or against God; there's no in between. If you bet against God (if you live a nonreligious life) and you are right, what do you gain? Not much. Maybe you have a little more fun for your three score and ten on earth—or maybe you don't. Actually, Pascal thinks that a life that emphasizes the values of religious commitment will be happier in the here and now. But let's suppose that you'd be a little happier if you bet against God and God doesn't exist (than you would be if you bet on God and God doesn't exist). That's your best payoff. But if you bet against God and you are wrong, what is the outcome? Well, at least the loss of an infinite good (eternal union with God) and maybe also the gaining of an infinite "bad" (eternity in hell). Now suppose you bet on God and lose. What does it cost you? At most, a little fun during the earthly life. But suppose you place that bet and win;

suppose that God exists. Then you hit the jackpot. An eternal life of infinite bliss.

Pascal argues, then, that the rational person will bet on God. Since one can't make up one's mind on religious matters by grounding belief on good evidence (remember, according to Pascal the evidence for and against God's existence is split) a rational person will go elsewhere to make up his mind.

Pascal has been unfairly criticized by William James (1842–1910) and others who claim that he presupposes that belief is under direct voluntary control, and that one can choose to believe in God as one can choose to lay a bet. If philosophers like James are right, Pascal's wager will be undercut. For it clearly does suppose that laying the wager is up to us; but if laying the wager amounts to immediately choosing to believe in God, then we aren't in a position to place the bet.

So does Pascal presuppose that belief in God is under our direct control? No he does not; Pascal was not nearly so naïve. Pascal's advice was that once you see that believing in God is in your rational self-interest, then you should do what you can to bring it about. So he recommended going to Mass and "taking holy water" as a way of generating belief. What does that mean? Did he think that somehow holy water could work magic? Not at all. He thought that being part of a religious community and taking part in the religious life could bring about belief in just the same way that going to Cubs games and listening to them on the radio, and reading the sports pages of the Chicago newspapers could bring about Cubs fandom. Once you see the rational preferability of belief in God, you'll want to lay your bet on God. This means living a life of religious commitment. So you'll begin to do what the committed do: that is, go to the church, synagogue, or mosque and start to live according to religious principles. And even if belief in God is an integral part of religious faith, and even if it is not under direct voluntary control, belief will come if you take part in the religious life. As with being a fan of a particular team, you can't simply decide to believe in God, but there are steps you can take that will tend to bring it about.

Baseball and Religious Commitment

Being a fan is oftentimes more an activity than attitude. A true fan must be a *follower of the team*. Just what being a follower of a team comes to will vary depending on one's circumstances. For example, a true Cubs fan who is a resident of the Windy City and who is of at least moderate means will be disposed to attend a number of Cubs games each year. This condition of fanhood isn't strictly necessary: one who has a strong dislike of large crowds or who has physical limitations that make attending a game very difficult can be excused. But one who lives in Chicago, has a reasonable amount of disposable income, attends Bulls and Bears games, but who never goes to see the Cubs is not a true fan. One who lives a great distance from Chicago, in Arkansas, say, and is of modest means might never attend a game and yet still be a true fan. Even so, fandom has its demands. Being a fan requires at least keeping track of the team via the sports page, the Internet, or games on cable.

So a fan will want the team to do well and will follow the team's performance. Are there other attitudes or activities that being a fan entails? In particular, one might wonder if being a fan of a team doesn't require being disposed to believe that team will do well. Can one be a fan of a team even if one believes or expects the team to lose most of its games? That seems possible. Indeed, in most of the past fifty years, Cubs fans have generally expected that their team will not win the pennant. Indeed, there have been years when the general make up of the team in early April gave Cubs fans reason to believe the team would lose the great majority of its games. So then is there no requirement of positive expectations for fandom? This is perhaps a harder call than the other conditions we've been considering. Still, I think this much can be said with confidence: a true fan will tend to look favorably on her team's chances for success. By this I mean that she will tend toward optimism. While it might be that even the best fan will not believe that her favorite team will have a successful season when all the experts predict disaster, she will be inclined to accept favorable predictions of her team's success over less favorable predications. So when, for example, the opinion of experts is split, she will pay heed to the voices predicting a good season over those who predict disaster. That is to say, she won't let objective probabilities dictate her attitudes and activities. She'll look positively on her team's post-season chances. But this doesn't mean she'll be blind to the facts or that she'll drastically over-estimate the probabilities.

There is an obvious parallel between fandom so understood and religious commitment. While a religious skeptic will generally be inclined to be unimpressed with anything less than conclusive or at least overwhelming evidence, the believer will tend to put a positive spin on the data. While this distinction between the skepticism of the unbeliever and the epistemic optimism of the devout can be see in corresponding attitudes toward arguments for God's existence and other sorts of public evidence, I think it is clearest when religious experience is at issue. Suppose two people, a believer and an agnostic, are separately going through difficult times. Each is borderline desperate and feeling at the end of his rope. In the grip of this despair, the believer has a sudden rush of comfort and joy; this experience seems to him to be God reaching out to him and holding him in God's loving arms. The agnostic has a similar experience—this is, a sudden rush of comfort and joy—but being of a skeptical cast, he is inclined to think that this feeling of being comforted is illusory and that the comfort and joy he feels is grounded in a psychological defense mechanism.

Let's play out these respective mindsets a little more. Suppose that the agnostic is asked why he thinks that the feeling of being comforted is illusory. At first puzzled, he says, "Oh, you mean why don't I think that it is God comforting me? Well, I suppose I can't rule that out, but why in the world would I make that assumption? I don't have any evidence of that; in fact, I don't even have anything I think is good reason to believe in God's very existence. Every decent piece of positive evidence seems offset by a negative one. No, while I can admit the bare possibility that my experience is caused by God, I see no good reason to accept that and so I don't."

Now let's ask the believer the parallel question. How do you know that the experience is not just illusory? "Well, what reason do I have for thinking it is illusory? I have a general habit of accepting what seems to me to be true unless I have some good reason not to. The experience I had seemed to me to be the experience of being comforted by God. Could I be wrong? Of course. I don't take myself as being certain that what I experienced is God comforting me. But my lack of certainty here doesn't make this belief any different from most of my other beliefs. In short, I don't see any reason not to accept that things are the way they honestly seem to me."

There is yet another striking parallel between a fan's commitment to her team and a believer's commitment to her faith. We've seen how the true fan does not only pull for her team when it is doing well. Even in a year when projected outcomes are dismal and the team is precisely living up to expectations, the true fan is committed and awaits better days. Things may get so grim that for a time, she may not even like her team much. She will feel frustration and perhaps even disgust. Yet if she is virtuous and she is a true fan, she will continue to support her club even when she doesn't feel like it. She will have what philosophers sometimes call a second-order attitude: she'll believe that her current bad attitude is only temporary, that tomorrow or the day (or week or month) after that she'll feel differently. Second-order attitudes like this are familiar enough: a fight with a friend might cause you to feel as though you never want to see him again, while all the time you recognize that after your anger subsides you will feel differently than you do now.

The parallel between this aspect of fandom and religious commitment is close. There are dark days for the devout, days when joy is gone and peace is not found, when even the eyes of the faithful see a world that appears without meaning and mercy. During these times the faithful who are virtuous do not lose hope. Rather, the devout recognize that feelings and emotions can be fickle and that they can unduly influence our perceptions and beliefs. The importance of this point can scarcely be exaggerated in the realm of religious commitment. What makes someone committed to a faith is not the feelings she has at the moment; it is the course of the person's life and what she values and cherishes in the long run that determine her faithfulness or lack thereof.

Who Should Be Committed?

So what are we to conclude? Should Cubs fans be committed? Of course, that question is partially a joke: there is no reason for your average Cub fan to be institutionalized. But neither is there a reason for a Cubs fan to not be a Cubs fan. The organization has not committed the atrocities against sportsmanship that basketball's Portland Trailblazers have. It has also recently been committed to adding players and managers that can help it win.

We've seen that to be a true fan requires both an attitude and action. It requires commitment and perseverance. In this, genuine fandom and religious commitment are alike. In closing, I'd like to point out one more similarity between the two. In committing yourself to a cause, you reach out to something beyond yourself and thereby form a bond with others who are similarly committed. If the nature of the organization or institution to which one is committed encourages loyalty from a homogeneous group, then this commitment likely does no more than duplicate already existent ties. However, baseball is not like this. Baseball fans come from all walks of life, are of all ages, and are an increasingly international group. In the Friendly Confines (a nickname for Wrigley Field), CEOs sit next to short-order cooks, plumbers sit next to professors, octogenarians sit next to eight-year-olds, and recent immigrants sit next to the native born. All are equal as fans of the national pastime.

The same kinds of cross-cultural and trans-class bonds are found in religious institutions as well. In most of the major religions, the fundamental equality of humankind is a basic tenet of faith. Humans of all ages, backgrounds, nationalities, and genders are unified in their faith. In the Christian tradition, this point is made clearly by St. Paul in his letter to the Galatians. "There is no longer Jew or Greek, there is no longer slave or free, there is no longer male or female; for all of you are one in Christ Jesus" (3:28).

If fidelity to something larger than yourself, and shared with people from all walks of life is a virtue, and if loyalty is also of moral value, then by all means, let Cubs fans and believers of all stripes be committed.

4 | Taking One for the Team: Baseball and Sacrifice

WILLIE YOUNG

Football has hitting, clipping, spearing, piling on, personal fouls, late hitting and unnecessary roughness. Baseball has the sacrifice.

—Comedian GEORGE CARLIN

It's a cool Saturday afternoon in June, with several high-profile interleague matchups on television. Two of these games provide a study in contrast. In the Yankees-Mets game, Alfonso Soriano reaches base to lead off the game. The next batter, Derek Jeter, lays down a perfect sacrifice bunt: the ball deadens on the dirt in front of home plate, easily advancing Soriano to second. When Jason Giambi bloops a single to left, just out of the shortstop's reach, Soriano races home from second. The "Bronx Bombers" open the scoring thanks to two at-bats that together travel about 120 feet.

A couple of hours later, in the ninth inning of a ballgame that they would win in extra innings from the Red Sox, the Philadelphia Phillies get their leadoff batter to first base. With the heart of the order coming up, getting him into scoring position is of paramount importance. The next batter, Placido Polanco, is a rising star, but in this case he pulls the bat back on the first strike, and then pops the bunt up to the first baseman on the next pitch. The sacrifice fails; the runner remains at first, and is still stranded there when the inning ends.

Ultimately, neither sacrifice decided the game's outcome (the Yankees-Mets game was suspended by rain, and Polanco later scored on a passed ball to win the game). Nevertheless, both plays evoked strong reactions: shame that Polanco should have been able to lay down the bunt, and admiration for Jeter who made the play that had to be made. Together, these plays suggest that sacrifice is closely connected with the "ethics" of baseball. Sacrifice provides a window on how baseball relates to ethics, and on some of the questions philosophy can raise about the place of baseball in our culture. For sacrifice is something we do both on the field and in our daily lives; how one thinks about sacrifice in baseball may help us to think about it elsewhere as well.

The Nature of Sacrifice

In baseball, sacrifice is central to teamwork. As Yogi Berra is believed to have said, "When you sacrifice, you stand beside your teammates, by putting them in front of yourself." When writers extol the virtues of baseball—its team concept, its demand for trust and cooperation—sacrifice comes to the fore. Philosophically, sacrifice has meant to give oneself up on behalf of others, for the sake of a good. As Julia Kristeva writes, "Sacrifice is an offering that, out of a substance, creates Meaning for the Other and, consequently, for the social group that is dependent on it."[1] Sacrifice is an act by which someone renounces something, so as to achieve an end, thereby also forming a social group. In baseball, such sacrifice can take many forms: a sacrifice fly, advancing to draw a throw so a runner may score, or pitching deep into a ballgame to let the bullpen rest. A batter may let himself be hit by a pitch, to give his team a baserunner; or, if an opposing team pitches the batters inside, a pitcher may throw at the opposing team, risking ejection or retaliation to protect the other players. While these many forms of sacrifice are all part of baseball, the most central sacrifice in baseball is the sacrifice bunt, which embodies all the dimensions of Kristeva's above definition. First, a sacrifice bunt is performed

---

[1] Julia Kristeva, *Tales of Love*, translated by Leon Roudiez (New York: Columbia University Press, 1987), p. 142.

for the sake of a social group–the team. Giving up the at bat, the batter creates "meaning" by creating a greater probability for his team to score a run by advancing the runner, and thereby a greater chance for the team to win (sacrifice makes no sense when the game is out of reach, or if there is a need for many runs).

One would be wrong, however, to restrict the meaning of the bunt simply to run production, or the goal of winning. A sacrifice bunt is also a communicative event involving understanding and trust; only if it enacts these qualities will it be successful. Much like a friendship, it "forges a unity of minds," in the words of St. Augustine (354–430). The manager or base coach must communicate to both the runner and the batter. The runner must trust that the bunt will be laid down, so as to properly advance on contact. In the case of a suicide squeeze, the baserunner must *believe* that the bunt will be laid down, in order to break for home during the windup. The bunter promises to lay down a sacrifice, and the runner reciprocally promises to run the bases. To keep this promise requires excellence on the part of both players: a popped-up bunt or poor baserunning will kill an inning, with no good achieved for the team. If one doesn't know what one is doing, the promise is empty. A failed sacrifice is much like a broken promise, as one not only fails on this occasion, but also diminishes the team's trust in one's ability.

There is another dimension to sacrifice as communication: its deceptiveness. Deception is especially important in the suicide squeeze, which must be a surprise in order to work. The sacrificer must know what he is to do, but he must keep this secret. His body language must signify that he will hit the ball, thereby deceiving the other team. While this is most obviously an issue with the suicide squeeze, it is important for other sacrifices as well; National League pitchers, and other weak hitters who frequently show the bunt early, often have the most difficulty successfully completing a sacrifice, because the other team expects it. If the opposing team knows a sacrifice is coming, they can charge from third or first base, or use the "wheel" play. Occasionally, when a team anticipates a bunt and the infielders close in, the batter may show bunt and then swing, so as to terrify the fielders. A sacrifice bunt thereby signifies trust and communication for one team, and deception for the other.

The communicative dimensions of sacrifice highlight its complexity; it involves much more than just moving a runner over. Given this complexity, the sacrifice bunt can help trace some of the differences in different philosophical positions with respect to the various aspects of sacrifice. Central issues in the philosophical discussion of sacrifice are: 1) the relationship between sacrificing *for someone* and sacrificing *for something*; 2) the relationship between the individual and the common good; and 3) whether sacrifice is voluntary or involuntary. In both ancient and modern philosophy, the language used says a great deal about one's views on how one should sacrifice. Thus, while ancient philosophers such as Aristotle (384–322 B.C.E.) and Seneca (around 4 B.C.E–A.D. 65) discuss sacrifice as a feature of friendship, and thereby emphasize its voluntary nature and its contribution to the common good, modern philosophy describes sacrifice as mechanical, highlighting the impersonal generality of sacrifice. Let's square around and see what they throw our way.

The Ancient Virtue of Sacrifice

The central features of Kristeva's definition of sacrifice—establishing a community, and acting for the sake of a meaning or purpose—can be developed by exploring the connections between sacrifice and friendship in classical philosophy. Sacrifice differentiates Aristotelian and Stoic philosophy in several important ways, particularly regarding the relationship between virtue and community. For Aristotle, a friend is willing to sacrifice for the sake of virtue, *and* personally for the sake of a friend. This has several dimensions. First, one is willing to give up pleasure, comfort, and material goods for the sake of the good that one seeks. In extreme circumstances, one should even give up one's life for the sake of a good, such as justice. Acting for the sake of the good will also involve acting for the sake of a friend; one may give up food, or lay down one's life, to protect or care for a friend, as an act of love for his sake:

> Besides, it is true that, as they say, the excellent person labours for his friends and for his native country, and will die for them if he must; he will sacrifice money, honours and contested goods in general, in achieving what is fine for himself . . . This is presumably

true of one who dies for others; he does indeed choose something great and fine for himself. He is ready to sacrifice money as long as his friends profit; for the friends gain money, while he gains what is fine.[2]

For Aristotle, one sacrifices both for someone and for something, acting for the sake of the good and the sake of friends; both dimensions demonstrate that one chooses "something great and fine" because one is choosing the life of reason as opposed to pleasure or passion. Think of Texas third baseman Hank Blalock hitting the key home run in the 2003 All-Star Game. Though the Rangers had virtually no chance of playing in the World Series, and thereby benefitting from home field advantage, Blalock claimed he was happy "especially for the guys in the clubhouse who might be in the World Series."

In sacrificing for a higher good and for friends, the exercise of virtue brings a greater, more noble friendship than one would receive from material goods. However, in friendship, you don't only want to do what is excellent for your friends, you also want your friends to excel at virtue, so that it becomes reciprocal. True virtue will share the spotlight, because this is how one develops a virtuous community centered on the common good: "It is also possible, however, to sacrifice actions to his friend, since it may be finer to be responsible for his friend's doing the action than to do it himself."[3] For Aristotle, while one seeks to be virtuous individually, the primary unit of virtue is the community (*polis*), and therefore true virtue will seek to cooperate in developing the virtue and heroism of others. Blalock was likely hoping for personal accolades as he stepped up to the plate in the All-Star Game, but he was also hoping to help his new teammates in the dugout. One sacrifices to cultivate friendships, as well as to achieve a good. As David Bowie sings, "We can be heroes," but the emphasis is as much on the "We" as on the heroism.

For Stoicism, by contrast, friendship is an occasion for sacrifice, but one does not sacrifice for the sake of a friend. One has friendships so that one can show loyalty, fidelity, and courage,

---

[2] Aristotle, *Nicomachean Ethics*, translated by Terence Irwin, in M. Pakaluk, ed., *Other Selves: Philosophers on Friendship* (Indianapolis: Hackett, 1991), p. 62.
[3] *Ibid.*, p. 63.

but only for the sake of virtue itself. As Seneca writes, "For what purpose, then, do I make a man my friend? In order to have someone for whom I may die, whom I may follow into exile, against whose death I may stake my own life, and pay the pledge, too."[4] One has friends for the sake of exercising virtue; one does *not* exercise virtue for the sake of friends. Friendships are important because they provide ways to train oneself not to value external goods, which may be lost or shattered as easily as Sammy Sosa's bat. However, one should not become too attached to friends, because they too can be lost to fortune, like a utility infielder sent to the minors in the middle of a double-header; therefore, a Stoic does not act for the sake of friends, strictly speaking. Virtue, as the act of reason, is the only thing worthy of love, since it is all that is in one's power. Stoic virtue is therefore individual; one will sacrifice to exhibit virtue, but the relations of trust and communication that grow from sacrifice have no inherent value.

The differences between these two approaches to sacrifice becomes apparent in how we talk about sacrifice in baseball. First, sacrifice is essential for the development of civic excellence, as one acts for the sake of others. In baseball, Aristotle would be willing to sacrifice, so that his teammate would have an opportunity for virtue, becoming the hero by driving in a winning run. By not swinging for the fences, but laying down the bunt, one helps the whole team to excel. Aristotle even suggests that renouncing the heroic long ball, so that others will be heroes, actually gives the David Ecksteins of the world a greater happiness than Bonds, Sosa, and McGwire will ever know. Furthermore, if we look at sacrifice in the broader sense, different players will make different, reciprocal sacrifices, much as friendship is reciprocal. Teammates will sacrifice not only by bunting, but also by the sacrifice fly, swinging through a pitch on a steal, or throwing at an opposing batter who took out the second baseman. In all of these cases, the players give up material rewards or risk injury so that the team will profit, and each of them will profit with the team: "when everyone competes to achieve what is fine and strains to do the finest actions,"

---

[4] Seneca, *Epistulae Morales*, Letter IX, translated by R.M. Gummere, in *Other Selves*, p. 121.

Aristotle writes, "everything that is right will be done for the common good, and each person individually will receive the greatest of goods, since that is the character of virtue."[5] Ultimately, each player finds his or her true good in the friendships of the team; as all players enact this mutual commitment to winning, and to playing team-oriented baseball, each of the players benefits. In this shared commitment to a common end that transcends each individual, each player finds a greater reward than isolated, personal excellence could provide.

By contrast with Aristotle's synthesis of individual and team excellence, the Stoic conception of virtue radically divorces the two. One does not sacrifice for the sake of one's teammates, but rather because that is what reason requires in this situation, as a manifestation of one's detachment from external goods. It's as if one plays only for the sake of one's internal broadcaster, the baseball gods within us, and when one ought to sacrifice, one will. Acting on behalf of the team may be necessary, but it is not the end that motivates one's action. To sacrifice only for virtue affects not only how one sacrifices, but also when. For example, a Stoic would not sacrifice so that the next batter would personally exercise virtue and receive glory. He would do so because it is the virtuous thing to do, whether the man on deck is his best friend, Cal Ripken, Jr. or John Rocker (okay, he doesn't hit, but you get the idea). Moreover, if a Stoic pitcher's teammate were hit, he might not retaliate and hit an opposing batter. It's not that he's selfish, but rather that he thinks it contrary to reason, even if it would build community with his teammates. As citizens of the world, Stoic players would have different, less attached commitments to the team than their Aristotelian counterparts, leading to different versions of sacrifice.

The Vice of Involuntary Sacrifice

What both the Aristotelian and Stoic views share is that sacrifice is a component of virtue when it is *voluntary*. The one sacrificing must be the agent of renunciation, and she must understand both the act and its goal. The model for such sacrifice would be Socrates, who lays down his life out of fidelity to philosophy as a way of life, and for his friends. For someone to be sacrificed

---

[5] *Other Selves*, p. 62.

without understanding or consent is immoral for both the victim and the sacrificer: the victim neither shares in the good achieved, nor is treated as rational, and the sacrificer acts neither for the sake of the good, nor for the sake of the victim. Destroying the common good, involuntary sacrifice also destroys virtue.

One such involuntary sacrifice is found in the story of Iphigenia, the daughter of Agamemnon, the famous Greek king and warrior. In order for the Greek fleet to sail to Troy, an oracle declared that Agamemnon would have to sacrifice his daughter. Iphigenia has no share in the victory that comes to Greece; her father is briefly hailed as a conquering hero. Iphigenia, then, does not share in the good that comes from her sacrifice; it is not the greatest good for her. As Seneca's Clytemnestra describes the horrific sacrifice:

> Oh, shameful thought! That I, the heaven-born child
> Of Tyndarus, should give my daughter up
> To save the Grecian fleet! . . . O bloody house,
> That ever wades through crime to other crime!
> With blood we soothe the winds, with blood we war.[6]

Iphigenia's death "saves the fleet" in allowing them to go to war. Neither she nor Clytemnestra shares in the good achieved by the sacrifice; Agamemnon's vice is to destroy his fidelity to both wife and daughter, for the sake of gain and civic honor. Moreover, Iphigenia's sacrifice is involuntary; even if, as in some versions of the tragedy, Agamemnon tells her what is to be done, she has no choice, and does not understand what is being done to her. The breach of trust, rousing of passion, and violence of Agamemnon all come home to roost on his return, and these vices continue to haunt this family into their next generation.[7] When Clytemnestra says, "with blood we war," she speaks

---

[6] Seneca, *Agamemnon*, in George Eckel, ed., *The Complete Roman Drama*, translated by Frank Justus Miller (New York: Random House, 1966), p. 720.

[7] In some versions of the story, Iphigenia is rescued at the last moment, and she is carried off to a faraway land. This accentuates the vicious nature of Agamemnon's action—on the bloody stage of Greek tragedy, it's too terrible to contemplate his murder of his daughter for military gain. In Seneca's *Agamemnon*, however, this does not happen, and modern philosophical discussions of the myth (in particular, explanations by Kierkegaard and Franz Rosenzweig) treat the sacrifice as if it actually happens. My thanks to Greg Bassham for reminding me of this variation of the story.

both of the war on Troy and the sacrificial blood, as she and her lover will murder Agamemnon. As Iphigenia does not share in the good, and it is not a voluntary act, this sacrifice is vicious on both Aristotelian and Stoic terms, a violence that can only breed more violence. Such sacrifice destroys the very trust and community voluntary sacrifice seeks to establish.

In their violence, such stories of sacrifice seem far removed from the peaceful greenery of the baseball field. Yet if we consider not only baseball as it is played by gods and wizards, Jeters and Ecksteins, but also as it is played and coached by mere mortals, these distinctions strike closer to home. Let us switch from the fields of men to the games of children. In little league, the manager makes the decision for a player to sacrifice. He may expect certain players to lay down bunts, while other players will not; most often, it is the weaker players who will be told to sacrifice. They are deprived of a baseball life, as their very opportunity to develop as hitters is sacrificed for the sake of victory. This may help the team to win, but it will not help the players' development, as it takes away their opportunities to hit and to learn. Such sacrifices, gaining short-term victory at the cost of children's dreams, certainly seem to be involuntary, and thus immoral for either a Stoic or an Aristotelian.

To make such sacrificing voluntary, and truly a common pursuit, one must teach it well, so that the players really understand what they are doing, and better appreciate the workings of the game, rather than simply following what the adults tell them to do. Moreover, one should make sacrificing a common endeavor, such that the players understand that they can all do this for one another, and it should be practiced toward their excellence as players, and their growth as friends, helping in the cultivation of a *polis* of virtue.

The Spirit of Baseball: Hegel and the Reds

Whereas ancient philosophy stresses the voluntary nature of sacrifice, in modern philosophy sacrifice is described as self-renunciation. In the quest for action that strives for universality, the ethical action is seen as the one that gives up its individuality, and particularity, for the greater good. As J.R.R. Tolkien writes, "The greatest examples of the action of the spirit and of reason are in *abnegation*."[8] Abnegation, here, is the giving up of oneself, not only external goods, nor one's life, but even one's reason, personal relationships, and individuality. Whereas ancient philosophy emphasizes that one must make certain sacrifices, modern philosophy stresses that one must sacrifice *oneself*. According to German philosopher G.W.F. Hegel (1770–1831), one must give up the particular, distinctive features of one's selfhood in order to participate in something greater than oneself, such as universal reason; one embodies "spirit," in Tolkien's words, through self-sacrifice.

The rhetoric of self-sacrifice leads to a strange, almost paradoxical, coincidence: to become the embodiment of the universal spirit, one must become like a machine. Giving up all emotions, community, and reason, is not only to give up one's individuality, but to be stripped down to a mechanical rationality that will not be interrupted or disturbed by specific relationships or commitments. Hegel, for instance, describes real individuality as existing "only as a *cog* playing its part in the *mechanism* of an external organization,"[9] when one blindly and fully obeys the dictates of the state. This highlights the way that active freedom demands commitment to something greater than an individual, and participation in a project that involves others. It is often said that there is no "I" in team; here, Hegel negates the "I," so the team can emerge. One sacrifices so as to help the whole run smoothly, in a way that can be generalized: one's sacrifice should be what anyone, in the same position, would do, to help the whole to succeed.

The generalizing, team-oriented, and mechanical character of baseball sacrifice fits very closely with this modern conception of sacrifice. Excellent teams aspire to play with mechanical efficiency, as with the 1970s Cincinnati powerhouse, the "Big Red Machine." To sacrifice well is to be a cog in a well-oiled team machine, helping it to be a productive, unified whole. When a player sacrifices in this way, his action should be generalizable: it should be a sacrifice that any other player would offer in that same situation. Individuality is absorbed into the whole of the

---

[8] *The Letters of J.R.R. Tolkien*, Humphrey Carpenter, ed. (Boston: Houghton Mifflin, 1981), p. 246. My thanks to Greg Bassham for this citation.
[9] G.W.F. Hegel, *The Philosophy of Right*, translated by T.M. Knox (New York: Oxford University Press, 1967), p. 211.

team. Moreover, baseball does require a teammate to renounce his ego and his reason; he follows the manager's orders, renouncing his own will and reason, and he should be willing to sacrifice for the team, rather than for any particular relationship with another player. The manager's decision also represents a Hegelian "universal," as it absorbs the individual into the whole of the team. Baseball, therefore, fits very closely with the mechanical sacrifice of modern philosophy.

Kierkegaard Lays It Down

Beginning with Søren Kierkegaard, a strand of postmodern philosophy has questioned the ethics of such a general conception of sacrifice. As Kierkegaard describes it, general, mechanical sacrifice precludes the possibility of *singular* responsibility to another. Take, for example, Abraham's "absolute" responsibility to God in the binding of Isaac. Abraham fascinates Kierkegaard because he does the unthinkable. On the one hand, he undergoes "infinite resignation," as he is willing to sacrifice his son Isaac, for God's sake, thereby renouncing his fatherly, ethical duty. On the other hand, he also believes he will get Isaac back, and continues to love Isaac, remaining faithful in his particular fatherly duty. Absolute duty, then, requires *both* singular responsibility to one (for Abraham, to God) and to all others (for Abraham, his general duty as a father). As Kierkegaard admits, such sacrifice flies in the face of reason, and is absurd. Still, it is precisely in holding his individual and universal responsibilities together that Abraham, or any "knight of faith," becomes "higher than the universal,"[10] and transcends the general, mechanical responsibility we find in Hegel and in baseball. To remain at the level of generality, as Hegel does, forgets that one may have an exceptional duty that overturns ethics, a paradox where reason "wills its own downfall."[11]

---

[10] Søren Kierkegaard, *Fear and Trembling,* translated by Howard and Edna Hong (Princeton: Princeton University Press, 1983), p. 81.

[11] As Jacques Derrida writes of Kierkegaard, "Paradox, scandal, and aporia (which are central to *Fear and Trembling*) are themselves nothing other than sacrifice, the revelation of conceptual thinking at its limit, at its death and finitude. As soon as I enter into a relation with the other, with the gaze, look, request, love, command, or call of the other, I know that I can respond only

Given the parallels between baseball and mechanical sacrifice, Kierkegaard's work raises important questions about the
ethics of baseball. First, since baseball conceives of sacrifice in
general terms, Kierkegaard forces us to ask, does sacrifice teach
us to forget the exceptional, individual responsibility that one
may have to other individuals? Baseball does develop trust and
community, and players do become responsible for one
another, but its abstraction may also limit this responsibility: one
is only responsible as anyone else would be. Furthermore, baseball players are taught to accept the manager's calculations that
they should sacrifice, without question and without say, giving
up their individual reasoning and particular attachments. This
creates a relationship to authority that is, at least, in tension with
democratic society, as it creates one class of people who decide
who should sacrifice, and another class that undergoes those
sacrifices. Does baseball train us to be obedient soldiers and citizens? What should we make of how baseball trains us to think
of sacrifice as something *some* people must do, on the orders of
others, for the sake of the whole, simply based upon their place
within the social group, without reference to either the end they
seek or for whom they sacrifice?

To be willing and able to sacrifice demonstrates a devotion
to the craft of baseball and to one's team that is honorable in
the eyes of the fans. Yet, it is not enough to say that sacrifice
creates relationships and commitments, and enables the pursuit
of a good. Sacrifice, as we have seen, may make us friends, or
it may make us simply cogs in a machine. How one sacrifices,
and why, are the questions that philosophers must ask, so as to
determine if the sacrifice is voluntary, if it is for the common
good, and what mode of responsibility to others it entails.

These questions, however, are not questions that *only*
philosophers must ask. The beauty of baseball is that it is only
a game; the sacrifices we make on the field are not costly,
except when one risks injury. There's always another game to
play. Baseball can therefore serve as a field for mental as well
as physical play, where players can learn how to sacrifice, and

---

by sacrificing ethics, that is, by sacrificing whatever obliges me to also
respond, in the same way, in the same instant, to all the others." See Derrida,
The Gift of Death, translated by David Wills (Chicago: University of Chicago
Press, 1994), p. 68.

begin thinking about the implications of the sacrifices that they make. The game can thereby serve as a vehicle for developing the *understanding* that is necessary for sacrifice to contribute to friendship and the pursuit of the common good. As it captures and stimulates the imagination, it can serve as food for thought, whether one is in the dugout, on the field, or in the stands. If baseball becomes a way to philosophy, then in the words of Ernie Banks, let's play two.[12]

---

[12] My thanks to the following teammates for their comments, suggestions, and general conversation regarding drafts of this essay: Joe Kraus, Greg Bassham, Eric Bronson, Bill Young, Peter Eash-Scott, Kevin Dyer, Anthony Chiu, Ted Sherman, and Melissa Sherman, my eternal teammate. Errors remain my own.

Third Inning:
The Umpire's New Clothes

"He missed the tag! He missed the tag!"
It seems as if everybody thinks he knows
better than the umpire. The good
news is the umpire really isn't blind.
The bad news is that some rules are so
ambiguous, the umpire may as well be
blind. Ted Cohen challenges the
baseball rule committee to clarify
when a tie really does go to the runner.
J.S. Russell draws on legal philosophy
to encourage umpires to make their
own rules, when all else fails.

5 | There Are No Ties at First Base

TED COHEN

I. Thoughts on the Wonder of Rules

If you look closely enough at a rule, the cosmos will appear in all its physical, metaphysical, moral, and spiritual aspects, presenting you a life's work.

I wouldn't like you to think these characteristics are found only in American games. Consider the least American game we know (except, perhaps, for tossing the caber)—cricket. Here is part 10 of its Law 42, which is the law concerning Unfair Play:

10 TIME WASTING
Any form of time wasting is unfair.

On the not unreasonable assumption that playing cricket is itself a form of time wasting, what are we to make of this law? Is it that there is a proper way to waste time, in contrast to wasting time in a time-wasting way? It would not be such a remote observation that this chapter is a waste of time, but now we are wasting time while we waste time. These are very, very deep questions.

This observation about the cricket rule is only a jest, poking gentle fun at our British friends and their wonderful game, whose rules are subtle and fascinating. But there is a serious question about rules.

The common understanding of sports is that they are, as the saying goes, "rule-governed." And surely it must be correct to suppose that there are rules involved. How else could we explain our expectations of one another when we engage in these games? And yet—you may take my word for it—two puzzling facts threaten this idea: 1) Very few of the participants in these games really know much at all about the rules; 2) The rules themselves seldom withstand much serious scrutiny.

Let us turn away from cricket, for a time, and have a look at a rule from that game whose rules are more comprehensive than any other I know. Of course this is baseball. Here is an example, from the section of the rule book concerning the pitcher:

> *The pitcher shall not . . .*
>
> (2) *Apply a foreign substance of any kind to the ball;*
> (3) *expectorate on the ball, either hand or his glove;*
> (4) *rub the ball on his glove, person or clothing;*
> (5) *deface the ball in any manner;*
> (6) *deliver what is called the "shine" ball, "spit" ball, "mud" ball or "emery" ball.*

When we first read this rule we may imagine it to be needlessly verbose, redundant in fact. It says, first, that the pitcher may not expectorate on the ball, but then, later, it says that the pitcher may not deliver a spit ball. If the pitcher may not spit upon the ball, then why bother to prohibit his throwing a spit ball, you may ask. But then we realize the need to prevent the pitcher's securing "expectoratory assistance" from a team-mate or anyone else. Suppose the ball comes into the possession of the shortstop. If he spits upon the ball before returning it to the pitcher, then we will indeed require part (6) of the rule in order to prevent the pitcher's delivering the ball even though the pitcher himself has not spat upon it.

This seems the proper exegesis, and yet there is this question. Suppose the batter hits a slow grounder foul up the first base line. The ball is picked up by the first base coach. This person, a team-mate of the batter, not of the pitcher, slyly spits upon the ball before tossing it back to the pitcher. When the unwitting pitcher delivers his next pitch to the batter, the batting team protests that the pitcher has thrown a spit ball. What now?

I will not go into this: I leave it as an exercise. Nor will I take up the question of whether the rule is intended to prohibit the pitcher's spitting on the ball in all possible circumstances.

Suppose that the umpire has decided that the ball should be removed from the game, but before the umpire could confiscate the ball, the pitcher spits on the ball. What's wrong with that?

For some time I have offered a bet, perhaps rashly. I bet that if we observe as many as a half-dozen major league baseball games, we will see at least one indisputable indication that the participants do not know the rules. I have never had to make good on the bet, but during the second game of the 2000 World Series between the Yankees and the Mets, I had an encouraging moment. The Mets were batting, with fewer than two out and a runner on first. The batter struck out, but the ball went by the catcher. The batter ran toward first, the (Yankee) catcher retrieved the ball, and as the runner already on first base ran to second, the catcher made a poor throw to first base, but a throw good enough to beat the runner. So the batter was out, and the runner had advanced to second base. I believe that most observers, and many players, thought that this had happened: having struck out, the batter was entitled to try to get to first base but was out because the throw beat him. The runner on first had been forced to try advancing to second base because the batter was coming to first, and he did indeed wind up safe at second. But that is not at all what happened. In fact the batter was out, even though the catcher could not catch the third strike, and his running to first base was pointless. The runner at first in fact succeeded in stealing second base: he did not have to run. And, in fact, if the catcher had been able to get the ball to second base in time for the advancing runner to be tagged, both the runner and the batter would have been out. This was later explained by one of the television announcers, Tim McCarver, and he certainly knew the appropriate rules. But there can be no explanation of the behavior of the batter or of the catcher other than that they did not know the relevant rule, and surely the runner on first base did not know. It is marginally possible, I suppose, that the batter knew the rule but was trying to confuse the fielding team. If so, it was an ill-advised ruse because it could well have resulted in a double-play (because of the mistake of the runner on first), and there can be no explanation of what the catcher did besides his ignorance of the rule.

You will long since have grasped the main theme of this short disquisition: the fact that usually we don't know what the rules are, and the fact that when we do know a rule we discover that the rule makes little sense, are two of the main facts about life. And what are we to make of that?

II. There are No Ties at First Base

Even if it is now an obsession with me, it did not begin as one. That was many years ago, early in June, the beginning of the summer, during a family picnic held to mark the end of the year's Sunday school. A softball game was under way, one with too many players even though sixteen-inch softball accommodates ten players on each team. We had more: there were a handful of adults and a dozen children on each team. My team was at bat; a small child was at the plate. I can't remember who the child was, not even whether it was a girl or a boy, but someone hit a slow roller toward the left side of the infield. The batter first hesitated, as children do at the plate, and then tackled the infinite distance to first base, running with a child's desperate, furious slowness, while an infielder triangulated carefully and came together with the ball. It was probably the third baseman, although I am not sure of that, and he heaved the ball to first, where it was caught on the bounce. The ball and the runner arrived together, and immediately every child on my team yelled "Safe" while every child on the fielding team yelled "Out." There arose that wonderful American polyphony: "Safe," "Out," "Safe," "Out," overlaid with "He didn't have control of the ball," "He turned the wrong way," "He never touched the base" (said by both teams), and the other initiatory chants of serious ball. Then an adult loped in from the outfield and with calm, good sense, and an intention to soothe, spoke softly but firmly, commanding immediate quiet and attention. "It was a tie. Let's let him be safe."

It was a perfect remark. It was generous and also fair. It was paternal but not patronizing. It satisfied all the children: the batting team was given a runner at first, the fielding team was given respect.

But it was wrong. I alone knew it was wrong, and had anyone else known it, I would have been alone in feeling the necessity of saying so. "If it was a tie," I said, "then you don't have to *let* him be safe; he *was* safe."

The other adult turned his calm on me: "I know it's a convention in baseball that ties go to the runner." With that remark he put me with the children, I suppose, as if I were a perverse child and perhaps a bright one, but a child still. I had a brief thought of letting it go at that, but that thought faded like a weak throw from the outfield, and I became the kind of child-adult who is too much for a sensible man to handle. "It's not a *convention*," I said. "The rule says that the runner is safe unless the ball arrives before him. If the ball arrives at the same time, then it doesn't arrive before him, and so he is safe."

The other adult was silenced. The older children were in awe. I was trembling with a sense of moral triumph. I can remember nothing else from that game.

A few weeks later some men asked if I would help to organize a weekly softball game during the summer months for children and their parents. I have superintended that game ever since. The children are mostly boys and almost all the adults are men—fathers. I show up every Sunday morning from June through August or early September with my son. We bring a plate and bases and a one-hundred-foot measuring tape for laying out the infield. Everyone is grateful to me for maintaining this institution, but the children regard me with a steady ambivalence. On the one hand, I see that the game is played properly and I give good instruction to very young children who have yet to learn how to bat or field or throw the ball. On the other hand, I am insufferable. I control the tempo of the game, refusing to allow the children to dally on their way to the plate; I insist on sensible, attentive play in the field; and I compel a dedicated attention to the rules. On one occasion, a girl hit a ground ball that got through the infield. When the ball was retrieved, she was at second base and the second baseman was her father. He was playfully tagging her with the ball and pretending to push her off the base while a runner at third sneaked home with an important run. I delivered a quick lecture on the need to bring the ball all the way into the infield, to be aware of all the baserunners, and to attend to everything, and finally the second baseman's father said to me, "You're being obnoxious." All the children who play regularly know this about me, and especially my son knows it. But they sense that this goes with the order I give to the game. We play in a large athletic park that holds four ball fields along with other facilities, and many people wander by on Sunday mornings. Some children who live in the neighborhood often come by, and those who have played in our game once usually come back, choosing it over the more informal pickup games elsewhere in the park. They seem to like the structure I supply, the umpiring and the authoritative commentary on the rules, and I think they are entranced by my obtuse scholasticism.

The Shock of Contradiction

After that initial overture, in which I assessed the value of a tie at first base, I was immediately aware that I must consult the rules. I had spoken with confidence but I was not really sure. I thought I must be right because, like everyone, I have absorbed an encyclopedia of sandlot lore, but unlike almost everyone, I have turned it over in my mind thoroughly enough to force it to make sense. For instance, I never believed that runners were to be called out for leaving the base paths. That doesn't make sense. They transgress only if they leave the path in order to avoid being tagged, or if they are being obstructive-which is altogether a different matter. If a runner is casually, whimsically running outside the path, he is increasing the distance he must run. Why penalize him for that? So if a runner is to be called safe if he ties the ball, this cannot be a convention: it must be the rule. But I was not sure, and so I checked. There it was, and is: Rule 6.05(j):

> *A batter is out when after a third strike or after he hits a fair ball, he or first base is tagged before he touches first base.*

This rule does not say that the runner is safe unless the base is tagged first, but that is its import because the other rules do not give any other reason for calling him out. So I was right. The tie goes to the runner because he has not been put out.

For months after I'd found Rule 6.05(j) I delighted in exhibiting my verbatim acquaintance with it. My delight increased as I discovered that no one but me actually knew the rule, really knew it. People began to solicit opinions and information from me. I would receive calls asking what happens if the pitcher falls dead during his windup or if the ball becomes stuck in the umpire's mask. I had to make clear that I was no authority on the history of baseball and knew little of its infinite tables of figures, and that I had no particular knowledge of the rules of other games; but I cultivated my position as authority on baseball's rules. In fact, I continued to peruse the rule book and became a genuine authority. And then I found Rule 7.08(e):

Any runner is out when he fails to reach the next base before a fielder tags him or the base, after he has been forced to advance by reason of the batter becoming a runner.

This was stupefying. The anomaly seemed marvelous. For some time my son and I pondered this odd reversal. This rule says, for instance, that when a runner is at first base and the batter hits a grounder, the runner advancing to second will be out if he doesn't beat the ball to second base. And that means that if he ties the ball, he will be out. Why, we wondered, was this tie at second base being called against the runner, while the tie at first base was being called for him? My son produced a brilliant exegesis, speculating that the authors of the rules had attempted to compensate for the greater difficulty in calling force plays at second base. I was wondering whom to consult to learn whether my son was right, when I was struck by the hitherto seemingly trivial 6.09(a):

The batter becomes a runner when he hits a fair ball.

My God. I saw at once that with 6.09(a) in the works, it was not merely an anomaly that had been uncovered but that 6.05(j) and 7.08(e) are inconsistent with one another. I cannot help putting it this way; I am a philosopher. These two rules together are contradictory. You see it, don't you? The rules in Section 6 concern the Batter. Section 7 is about the Runner. This had led me to believe that they could not ever be in conflict. But 6.09 tells us that under certain circumstances the batter is a runner, or has become one. This will happen if a batter hits an infield grounder, and if he then arrives at first base simultaneously with the throw, 6.05(j) says that he's safe, while 7.08(e) says that he's out.

My feelings were very strong, but they were ambivalent. I was deeply troubled by this logical rot in the Official Baseball Rules. I had become extremely fond of the rules. They have charm and, so I had thought, precision. They do not have logical elegance, but that is part of their charm. They have the appearance of having been written by journeymen lawyers. This is the kind of lawyer who has enough experience to be able to imagine most of the cases that his contract or statute will have to comprehend, but who does not have the analytical power necessary to divine a few simple principles that will do the trick, and so he enumerates the cases, one by one, seemingly as he thinks them up. There is a charm in that. The rules have the further charm of their turn-of-the-century idiom. For instance, Rule 5.03:

> *The pitcher shall deliver the pitch to the batter who may elect to strike the ball, or who may not offer at it, as he chooses.*

With all that charm, and with their natural appeal for my philosophical sensibility, the rules had won me over. Now I found them wanting at their core.

On the other hand, I anticipated the statutory immortality that would be due me. I would effect a change in the rules. It was unlikely that I would be given a footnote in the rule book itself, but I might well find myself in a Roger Angell essay, and I would certainly let my ball-playing friends know. I imagined myself apologizing to all those I had persuaded of the correct ruling when ties occur at first base, and then going on to inform them that I had seen to it that the rules were rectified.

Is the Umpire Blind?

As I planned how to proceed, I became bolder in announcing my discovery and even in predicting the change it was sure to bring. I told my friends, ballplayers I knew, and even students in my classes, especially students who found me wonderfully eccentric, except for the few, always a few, who find me tedious and irrelevant.

I did not know what to do next until I thought to call a sportswriter at the city newspaper. It is from my wife, whose father was a newspaperman, that I learned this device. It's amazing what one can learn by calling people who work on newspapers. They know an immense amount, and they know how to find out an even greater immensity, and they genuinely enjoy imparting this knowledge. They are true professors, practical professors. The senior sportswriter whom I called seemed moderately interested in my claim, although I sensed that he did not find it easy to believe that the rules could be axiomatically defective, but he did tell me what I needed to know. He didn't have the address of the rules committee, but he did have the name and address of an executive in the office of the president of the National League. This man had formerly worked for a Chicago baseball team and was known personally to the sportswriter.

Now I knew whom to write, but I was not sure just how to compose my letter. I was on the verge of writing on my own stationery, when my wife made the first of two excellent suggestions. Guessing that the baseball people must receive reams of frivolous mail, she advised me to write on my university letterhead. That would add weight and, perhaps, command the brief attention necessary for my profound purpose to become evident. I worried about compromising my university and my philosophy department, but my wife saw the truth, that my case was proper and urgent, and indeed the university should be proud that another of its faculty was entering history.

Her second suggestion was that I write with no attempt at humor or irony, but that I just do the job.

I took both suggestions, and thus began my correspondence with baseball by way of the Administrator of The National League of Professional Baseball Clubs. As a matter of fact, I am an American League fan primarily, and it was the accident of my sportswriter's acquaintance that led me to the National League. No matter. Both leagues use the same rule book, and that book is seen to annually by the Official Playing Rules Committee. I was certain that I could persuade that committee of the need for revision, and I even entertained lavish hopes of being invited to attend one of its meetings.

I wrote seriously and carefully, and with all the lucidity I could manage. Despite that, and despite the acuity of my point and the gravity of my letterhead, I feared that my letter would be consigned to the buckets of crank mail. But no: within a week I had a wonderful reply from the Administrator (from whose letterhead I have learned to call it "The National League of Professional Baseball Clubs"), thanking me for my letter and my interest in baseball, and telling me that I was the first to find this interpretation of the rules, and also informing me that both rules were meant to say that the runner is safe unless the ball beats him, but that because of my interpretation the rules committee would look into the matter at its winter meeting.

Now I was energized and, above all, truly hopeful. Before it had been a lark; now it was serious: a serious lark. In my excitement, I nearly reverted to professorial pedantry--which may be the best part of me anyway—and thought of writing back that it was not a matter of "interpretation," because the only significant term was the word *before* and its meaning was clear and unambiguous. But I restrained myself, realizing that it had been my wife's fine advice which had gotten me this far, and I drafted another sincere, unargumentative letter. I thanked the Administrator for taking me seriously, and added only that it might be of help to the rules committee to note that the current rules had been written as if either the runner beats the ball or the ball beats the runner. That is—although of course I did not write this in the letter—as though the runner beats the ball if and only if the ball does not beat the runner. (In logic, that might be put "*rBb iff −bBr*," but that kind of flourish would be of scarcely more use to baseball than it is to philosophy.)

All those letters went through in the autumn of 1982. The following December, the time of the winter meeting of the rules committee, came and went and I heard nothing. Six months later, in June, well into the next baseball season, I finally wrote again, asking what had happened. The reply has left me dispirited and confused—permanently, I fear—for I can't think what to do next.

The umpires present at the rules committee meeting told the committee that in their opinion there never are any ties. Therefore, said the Administrator, "To set up a special rule, which in effect would allow for ties, we felt would be extremely confusing."

What am I to say to that? I have thought of many things, but none of them will do. I have thought of asking why such a rule would be confusing. Why not humor me and put in a rule which would cover these cases that never arise? If some biologist produced a scientific classification for unicorns, would that be confusing just because no one ever found a beast to apply it to?

Is it that a rule to cover ties would induce unwary umpires to look for ties when in fact there are none to find, and that would be a waste and a shame?

The heart of the matter, of course, is the business about there not being any ties. Why do umpires opine that there are no ties? When they seem to see one, what makes them sure that things are not as they seem? I have heard television and radio baseball announcers also declare that in truth there are no ties, saying this as if it were an arcane scientific fact known only to those who really know baseball, and these announcers are former players. But I really know baseball, and I don't know this fact.

I have toyed with the idea that we are dealing here with difficult matters of modern physics, but I have consulted a good friend who is a philosopher of relativity physics. He has explained that once we restrict attention to the context of special relativity, and take as a background standard the uniform motion of the playing field (and if we don't do that, imagine the problem of umpiring), it is perfectly possible for a foot to touch a base at the same time as a ball touches a glove. At about the same time, I learned a miracle of umpiring from another friend, a philosopher of cognitive psychology. When the umpire is making a close call, particularly at first base, he sometimes looks for the runner's foot to touch the base while he listens for the ball to arrive in the baseman's glove. This has always bothered some of us, because, after all, light travels much faster than sound, and this means, for instance, that in the case of a genuine tie, the umpire will see the runner arrive before he hears the ball. But my friend tells me that recent research has shown that the human brain processes its auditory stimuli much more rapidly than its visual stimuli, just enough so that the look-and-listen method gives very accurate results, and it does that because the distances are right. In football the distances are wrong if, for instance, you're trying to tell whether members of the punting team cross the line of scrimmage too soon while watching from fifty yards away and listening for the punt. It's no surprise that even nature contributes to the perfection of baseball.

I cannot write any of this to the Administrator or to the rules committee. They would take me for a crank. But I cannot rest. If anything in this world could be right, it is baseball; but baseball isn't right with its current rules. I cannot stand it.

The Ambiguous Consolations of Philosophy

I have been reminded, with pain, melancholy, and sweetness, of my personal discovery that I could never play baseball at a high level. This news came to me, as it does to many boys and young men, when I was a high-school player. My daughter has complained bitterly that baseball cannot have this place in the lives of girls and young women: because women do not play professional baseball, although girls can learn the game, become significant fans, and even play, they cannot connect these themes with an ambition to play forever better. This saves them some pain, but it costs them the humanity it brings.

Had my daughter had the chance, perhaps the realization would have come to her as a high-school player. It comes to some at an earlier age, and to others it doesn't come until later, in college or the minor leagues; but to many it comes, as it did to me, when one must try to bat against an impossible pitcher. Mine was a fastball pitcher, faster by far than any I had seen or imagined. And he was wild. The first pitch came right across the plate and was gone before I even thought to swing. I attempted to adjust, to accelerate my mind, my eyes, my arms—everything—and I did swing at the second pitch, but only when it was already in the hands of the catcher. Strike two. Now I wanted desperately just to be able to touch the ball with my bat, and I stood tense and rigid in the box. The third pitch was wild, coming right at my head, at least as I saw it, and I leaped backward in terror. That terror is still with me. It is permanent. And it was with me then, when I stepped up with the count one-and-two. It made no difference whatever where the pitcher might have thrown the next ball. I was backing away from the instant his arm came forward, and although I swung, I could not have reached the ball.

So I struck out, and I knew I would always strike out against that pitcher. And that was painful, but it was not the occasion for the metaphysical pain I recalled when I struck out with the rules committee. That pain came the second time I batted against the same pitcher, two or three innings later. That at-bat began with two quick strikes, both swinging, and with me flailing as I bailed backward out of the box. The third pitch, which I foresaw as the inevitable third strike, was another wild one. This time the ball sailed at least five feet over my head, and I swung. I did not swing involuntarily, nor was I enfeebled by fear. I did it on purpose, with calculation, and I immediately dashed for first base. I was safe by a mile. The ball had gone by well above the reach of the catcher and it nearly cleared the backstop. Had it done so, and gone on into the cornfield behind the diamond, I was ready to go on to second base. The catcher did not even make a throw.

I had never been as proud of myself athletically as I was in that moment, in which I had overcome the finest pitcher I knew. I could not do it by hitting, but I had done it by knowing the rules and thinking fast despite a nearly paralyzing fear. And then my soul was squeezed. By my teammates. They did not care for what I had done. I did not receive even grudging admiration. I barely got grudging acceptance. It was not that they found me unmanly, although perhaps they did do that. They regarded me as someone who did not really grasp the nature of the game. I thought that in knowing the rules I knew the game; they knew the game in some other way. It was this ache that reappeared when I heard the last word from The National League of Professional Baseball Clubs.

There have been two sequels, one cosmic and one personal. The cosmic one has to do with Chicago baseball. In an effort to add a slight light touch, I ended my first letter to baseball with this jest: "I am very fond of the rules of baseball (perhaps partly because we in Chicago have been driven to a somewhat academic interest in the game)," and that was during the 1982 season. In 1983 the White Sox won the Western Division championship of the American League. The Cubs won the National League's Eastern Division championship in 1984, and did it again in 1989. The 1989 win was sweetly unexpected, humble and inspiring, truly cosmic in the way in which only gentle things can be cosmic, without the irrelevant distractions of sound, fury, and apocalypse. In the interim the Bears had one magnificent, terrorizing season, during which they won every game but one, an insignificant one, usually not only winning but winning easily, often giving up no points, and almost always hurting their opponents. Football does not engage me much, nor do its rules. It has some interest as a struggle to determine whether it will be a game of players or a game of rules, much like the epic struggle in modern states to decide whether they will be societies of men or societies of laws. And its racial features may be interesting. But I have found nothing in football approaching the metaphysics of baseball.

In all, Chicago sports swung up during the 1980s. My logic was offended, but my world improved.

The personal note is sad. My confidence in the order of our summer softball games has been shattered. My heart is no longer in it when I articulate and administer the rules, and that leaves me with nothing to dwell on but the rate at which the children in the game have overcome the strength and speed of us adults.

What good are the rules if no one knows them? What good is it to know the rules if no one believes you? And what if they believe you but just don't care?[1]

---

[1] "There Are No Ties at First Base" first appeared in *The Yale Review*, 79.2 (Winter, 1990), pp. 314–322. "Thoughts on the Wonder of Rules" is taken from sections of an unpublished essay, "Playing by the Rules," and appears here for the first time.

6 | Taking Umpiring Seriously: How Philosophy Can Help Umpires Make the Right Calls

J.S. RUSSELL

> When I'm right no one remembers. When I'm wrong no one forgets.
>
> —Umpire DOUG HARVEY

There's an old baseball joke that tells a lot about why umpires find themselves in this unhappy position. The Devil challenges God to a baseball game between the residents of heaven and hell. Puzzled, God asks the Devil: "Why would you want to play me at baseball? I have all the greatest players at my disposal." "I know," responds the Devil, "But I have all the umpires." Jokes like this one, and remarks like umpire Harvey's, readily attest that baseball umpires lay sad claim to being the most under-appreciated and disrespected participants in sport. Indeed, anyone who has ever spent time in the stands watching ballgames has seen the contempt that is freely heaped on umpires: the boos and catcalls, the kicked up dirt, close up views of oral hygiene, and even at times common assaults.

All this merely recaps what everyone already knows: umpires deserve better. But there is another less obvious, though just as compelling, reason for treating umpires with more serious respect. What umpires do is *philosophically fascinating*. This is a novel concept for the sporting public or, indeed, for umpires themselves, since they are not usually trained philosophers. But as we shall see, a philosophical treatment of umpiring is no mere academic exercise. It can have important practical implications for determining what umpires actually do on the field. Thus, philosophy and practice cannot be separated here. Taking umpiring seriously means taking philosophy seriously, too.

What philosophy shows us is that umpires have more discretion to change calls and even the rules of the game than is commonly recognized. That umpires could have any significant discretion in either of these areas will seem heretical to many students of baseball. But today's heresy can be tomorrow's orthodoxy, and recent philosophical contributions to our understanding of language and law can now help us to see clearly how this might be true even in baseball. It is convenient, too, that baseball history provides ample resources to illustrate and support these philosophical claims. We shall see that controversies like the justly famous "pine tar incident" (involving George Brett and Billy Martin) and debates over calls absorb much of our attention precisely because they raise interesting philosophical puzzles and problems that call for careful philosophical treatment.[1]

Making the Calls

In baseball, as everyone knows, the umpire makes the calls. But this apparent truism raises interesting metaphysical puzzles. Metaphysics is that branch of philosophy that investigates the nature of reality. As such, it sounds too lofty to be connected with baseball or calls. But in fact the study of metaphysics is not only about lofty things. In its broadest sense, metaphysical inquiry is about understanding all the things that make up the furniture of the universe, those that are profound (what is time, matter, love, justice?) and those that are rather more mundane (what is a call?). Baseball, fortunately for us, is part of the furniture of the universe, and calls are part of baseball. Hence, a complete metaphysics of the universe would be able to explain what sort of thing a call is.

The best way to begin is to look at a bad call. Consider the oft-heard rationalization of a bad call: "The umpire makes the

---

[1] Many of the ideas presented here draw on and are developed at greater length in my "The Concept of a Call in Baseball," *Journal of the Philosophy of Sport*, Vol. 26 (1997), pp. 21–37 and "Are Rules All an Umpire Has to Work With?" *Journal of the Philosophy of Sport*, Vol. 26 (1999), pp. 27–49.

call." One way of understanding this is that the umpire, *by his call*, literally makes the person out or safe or the ball fair or foul, and so on. As Bill Klem, unofficial dean of umpires and Hall of Famer, once said, expressing this idea with particular succinctness and clarity, "It ain't anything 'til I call it."[2]

Now there is something puzzling about this view. Yet it is not entirely wrong, for the umpire by his call will indeed make it the case that a player is safe or out. Thus, another Hall of Fame umpire, Bill McGowan, expressed the same idea when he reportedly said to a skeptical player, "If you don't think you are out, read the morning newspaper . . ."[3] Both Klem and McGowan seem to agree on a piece of metaphysics, namely, that it is their pronouncements as umpires that in some sense create the main events of baseball, the outs, safes, fair and foul balls, runs, and so forth.

Odd perhaps, but there is an important element of truth to these claims. A call in this sense is what the philosopher of language J.L. Austin (1911–1960) termed a "performative utterance." These are uses of language that bring particular facts, events, or states of affairs into being.[4] The standard example is making promises. When you say that you promise to do something, you perform an act that makes a fact—the promise that you will to do something. Similarly, when two parties to a wedding ceremony say "I do," they create the fact that they are married. Or when someone says "I'm sorry," they make an apology. Words thus can be used in certain circumstances to make important facts—promises, contracts, marriages, apologies, and so on. A similar point seems true about calls. When the umpire calls a strike, it creates a new event or state of affairs, namely, that the batter has another strike added to the count. The idea that the umpire *makes* the calls, then, reflects what seems to be a clear performative element to calls. A call by an umpire is a verbal utterance that, given his role in the contest, brings it about that you are out or safe, or behind in the count 0-and-2. Thus, language in this case begets metaphysics, and Austin's analysis helps us understand this.

---

[2] Cited in G. Sullivan and B. Lagowski, *The Sports Curmudgeon* (New York: Warner, 1993), p. 164. Often quoted as "It ain't nothing 'til I call it."

[3] *Ibid.*, p. 165.

[4] J.L. Austin, *How to Do Things with Words*, J.O. Urmson, ed. (Oxford: Oxford University Press, 1962).

So far so good, but we should press the analogy with performative utterances further. Austin also held that performative utterances were unique in that they can't be considered true or false. The statement, "Sosa's bat is corked" is either true or false. Thus, philosophers say that it has a truth value. By contrast, the utterance "I promise to meet you at Fenway Park at 2 o'clock" uses language to bring about the event or fact of making a promise. Facts or events themselves do not have truth values; they are "out there," they exist. A promise, then, is simply a fact, as a corked bat is a fact. Neither is true or false. We don't talk about corked bats or promises being true or false. Philosophers clarify this by observing that only *statements about* facts (like "Sosa's bat is corked") can have truth values–that is, be true or false. Another way of making these points, then, is to say that a promise is not a statement about a fact. It is itself a fact created by language, just as the umpire's saying "you're out!" creates the fact that a player is out.

This clarifies the idea of performative utterances, but it has troubling implications for baseball. For if a call is a pure performative utterance, it cannot be true or false. This is too convenient for umpires. It means they can never make bad calls. It is never the case that an umpire ever mistakes a ball for a strike, an out for a safe, a fair for a foul ball, and so on, for the idea of making true or false statements about events on the field does not apply. Of course, it also means that we can never criticize an umpire for missing a call (or praise him for getting a difficult one right). This would undermine the very idea of a contest as involving the accurate assessment of the relative skills of the competitors.

Philosophically minded persons love paradox, sometimes too much. I have heard both competent professional philosophers and non-philosophers seriously defend this account of calls. And who knows? Umpires, like Klem and McGowan, perhaps overly impressed by the importance of their roles, may even have been tempted to take this idea seriously. But there is clearly confusion here. Umpires do make mistakes—they express false statements about whether someone is safe or out, for example—and good umpires are good because they make the fewest mistakes. The puzzle is how to explain this phenomenon while retaining an obvious performative aspect to the language of calls.

The solution, as Austin himself came to realize, involves recognizing that language can combine both performative and descriptive functions in the same utterances. The example of baseball umpires at work neatly demonstrates this. What is distinctive about umpires in baseball and in other sports, as compared with judges in most other contexts, is that umpires are *witnesses* to, as well as judges of, the events they preside over. As a result, a call in baseball is also a witness's report or description of events. It is, in effect, a first-hand statement about a fact or an event, as well as a call.

The umpire rightly says "I call 'em as I see 'em." A call, then, is not, strictly speaking, a performative utterance in the sense in which Austin originally used that term. It is also a witness's statement about what actually occurred. Thus, it creates an event (the out or safe call), but as a witness's report or statement it can also be either true or false. This is fortunate. For we have seen that to preserve the game, we must be able to say that whether you really were out or safe depends ultimately on how accurately an umpire is able to report a witnessed event. Tom Connally, another philosophical Hall of Fame umpire, speaking for judges of every kind, got it right then when he said, "Maybe I called it wrong, but it's official!"[5]

A number of important practical implications follow from this analysis. The first one is that if a call is conceptually understood to be a witnessed event, then an umpire has no business making calls that he does not see. Yet in fact this happens often enough in baseball, even in the major leagues. Ron Luciano admitted that he sometimes completely missed calls but made them anyway on the basis that he usually had a fifty-percent chance of being right.[6] Luciano was a good and unusually candid umpire. There is no reason to think his behavior is unique. Indeed, lapses of attention, distractions, and being out of position are all inevitable. For example, in the first game of the 1970 World Series between the Baltimore Orioles and the Cincinnati Reds, umpire Ken Burkhart was knocked out of position during a critical play at the plate. Recovering, Burkhart called Cincinnati's Bernie Carbo out, though replays showed that Orioles catcher Elrod Hendricks never tagged him out with the ball. Because of the collision, Burkhart was unable to see the missed tag. But it was actually worse that this. Not only was

---

[5] Cited in *The Sports Curmudgeon*, p. 164.

[6] This is an oft-repeated statement in Ron Luciano and David Fisher, *The Umpire Strikes Back* (New York: Bantam, 1982).

Carbo not tagged out, he never touched the plate. So the proper call in this case was no call at all. The "Old Perfessor" Casey Stengel wryly remarked about this play that "it was a dead heat: Carbo missed the plate, Hendricks missed the tag, and Burkhart missed the call."[7]

Such missed and guessed at calls are only calls in a merely technical sense. They are not fully-fledged instances of calls because they are not witnessed events; and the very idea of an umpire's call is that it is a witnessed event. In these circumstances, umpires have no responsible alternative but to look for, or accept, help and to consider whether it is possible to revise a mistaken call. Or at any rate, they should be encouraged to do so. Admittedly, sometimes it will not be possible to revisit a blown call, particularly if it occurs during continuous play, since the call may affect subsequent play and it may be impossible to say what would have happened if the right call had been made. But there will be many other cases where a game can be improved by going back and correcting a bad call.

Another example occurs when players deceive umpires into making bad calls, for example, when a fielder feigns cleanly catching a trapped line drive or fly ball or makes a phantom tag. Here successful efforts are made by players to prevent umpires from being effective witnesses to events, for example, by blocking their views or manipulating or intimidating them into wrong decisions by their behavior, including lies ("Look blue! I made the catch!"). Thus, the umpire can be prevented from performing his role as an effective witness through the player's intentional efforts to deceive. Again, this is a good reason for umpires to look for or accept help, even after a call has been made. There is another compelling reason for reconsidering calls in these cases, for the players' attempts to deceive umpires create a type of *anti-game*. Here, the contest is settled not just by who is best according to performances of skill that take place within the rules, but also by discovering who is best at deceiving umpires for their own advantage by trying to gain advantages that are clearly not permitted by the rules, for example, by gaining outs on dropped balls.[8]

---

[7] Cited in John C. Skipper, *Umpires* (Jefferson, North Carolina: McFarland, 1997), p. 90.

[8] More about this below. A similar analysis can be extended to failures of impartiality by umpires. Except perhaps at recreational levels, this obvious anti-game behavior is undoubtedly of academic interest.

The *Official Rules of Baseball* are, unfortunately, silent on these specific matters. They do say that an umpire should be prepared to change "a *manifestly wrong decision* when convinced that he has made an error."[9] Obviously, such calls should be changed to maintain the integrity of a game as a fair contest of skills. But a deceived call or one that is not witnessed may not be manifestly wrong, although the judgment of other umpires who were able to see the play properly may be that it was mistaken. The integrity of a game can be undermined in these circumstances as well. Unfortunately, the rules pose further impediments by requiring that no umpire may seek to criticize or reverse another umpire's decision unless his advice is sought (Rule 9.02(c)). Thus, an umpire can easily remain in ignorance of his being deceived, and someone who merely guesses is not likely to seek help on his own. Umpires should have a system of signals in place to alert each other to manifestly wrong calls, but again this may be of no help in these specific situations.

What should umpires do when confronted with the uncertain and to some extent contradictory advice of the rules on these matters? The arguments are compelling that umpires should be prepared to work together collegially to review certain calls to preserve the integrity of games. Can umpires, then, in effect revise the rules so that they conform to these arguments? Where is the authority for umpires to do so if, contrary to the Old Perfessor, you could not "look it up"? What is the relationship, if any, of the notion of integrity to this authority?

Are Rules All an Umpire Has to Work With?

There is a conventional view of umpiring that I wish to challenge. It is the idea that, as major league umpire Joe Brinkman once put it, "rules are all an umpire has to work with."[10] The idea expressed here is that the rules of a contest are fully authoritative. They are the only legitimate source of umpires' authority and action; and, since they are *all* an umpire has to work

---

[9] See "General Instruction to Umpire" in *The Official Rules of Baseball* (emphasis added), available at http://mlb.mlb.com/NASApp/mlb/mlb/baseball_basics/mlb_basics_umpire.jsp (July 6th, 2003).

[10] Joe Brinkman and Charlie Euchner, *The Umpire's Handbook*, revised edition (Lexington, Massachusetts: Stephen Green, 1987), p. 6.

with, he is never to step outside the rules that are officially laid down to govern the conduct of games.

This is a deeply cherished popular view of the nature of rules in sport and of the adjudicative role of umpires. But it is also an erroneous, hopeful illusion. We need to recognize that rules are not so tidy, not in games nor in life more generally. It is not difficult to demonstrate that rules in sport face the same indeterminacies that rules do in other contexts. Once this is recognized, the issue of the proper nature and extent of umpire discretion in amending the rules cannot be ignored.

Baseball's most famous rule dispute occurred in July 1983, in Yankee Stadium, when George Brett of the Kansas City Royals had a potentially game-winning two-run home run disallowed with two out in the top of the ninth after it was discovered that pine tar resin had been spread over more than the bottom eighteen inches of his bat. Brett was called out (the third out) for using an illegal bat, and so the Royals lost the game to the New York Yankees 4 to 3. Yankees manager Billy Martin successfully argued that: Rule 1.10(b) stated (then) that such extravagant use of sticky substances like pine tar shall cause a bat to be removed from the game; Rule 2.00 implied that a ball hit with a bat not conforming to rule 1.10 is an illegally batted ball (it defined "illegal" as "not conforming to these rules"); and Rule 6.06 stated that a batter is out when he hits an illegally batted ball. The logic of the rules seemed inescapable. Brett was out, the game was over, the Royals had lost. But Brett had just as clearly gained no special advantage from having the extra pine tar on the bat (if anything having sticky substances high up on the bat would be a disadvantage), and so it was just as inescapably clear, including to the umpires, that Brett had earned his potentially game-winning home run without the benefit of any undue advantage, and that, therefore, it was "unjust" to call him out.[11]

Did the umpires make the right decision in calling Brett out? American League President Lee MacPhail thought not. He later reinstated the home run and ordered the rest of the game, which was a crucial one in a tight pennant race, to be replayed from

---

[11] See the account by Joe Brinkman in *The Umpire's Handbook*, pp. 2–12 and in Ron Luciano and David Fisher, *Strike Two* (New York: Bantam, 1984), pp. 212–18. See also Richard Goldstein, *You Be the Umpire* (New York: Dell, 1993), pp. 99–105 for a careful discussion. Brinkman reports the scores of this protested game incorrectly (as 3–2 and 4–3 respectively).

that point on. The rules were evidently lacking (they have since been amended). Even the umpires agreed that it seemed unjust to take away Brett's home run but felt they had to apply the letter of the law. "It didn't seem right to take away Brett's homer because of a little pine tar, but rules are rules. Rules are all an umpire has to work with," wrote umpire Joe Brinkman in a manual for umpires (Brinkman was crew chief for this game). League President MacPhail accepted that the umpires' decision was "technically defensible" but held that their ruling was not in keeping with the "intent or spirit" of the game itself, declaring that "games should be won and lost on the playing field--not through technicalities of the rules." The Royals eventually won the game 5 to 4 on Brett's reinstated home run.

Brinkman and other umpires understandably received MacPhail's decision as a rebuke for failing to make the correct decision in this case. What was puzzling to them was where they could go to find direction in making the correct decision if they could not find it in the rules themselves. MacPhail justified his decision by acknowledging that the rules looked as if they supported the umpires, but he asserted that following the rules was not in the spirit of the game in this case. But this looks vague and unhelpful. Is there some way to clarify and explain the exercise of umpires' authority and discretion in these sorts of "hard cases," or is Brinkman right to think that the rules are the only source of an umpire's authority?

The noted contemporary philosopher of law R.M. Dworkin has developed an account of legal obligations that is helpful here as well.[12] Dworkin claims that there are authoritative resources outside of the written rules that may be used to resolve legal disputes. His approach represents another, perhaps deeper, way of understanding some of the problems that might arise in sport adjudication. Indeed, Dworkin's views may apply more straightforwardly in this context.

Dworkin has developed two main criticisms of purely rule-oriented approaches to legal reasoning: 1) that a body of moral principles is part of law in addition to its rules, and 2) that such principles must be applied in hard (or controversial) cases to resolve them. The second point implies Dworkin's idea that the

---

[12] R.M. Dworkin, *Taking Rights Seriously* (Cambridge, Massachusetts: Harvard University Press, 1978), and *Law's Empire* (Harvard University Press, 1986).

supreme virtue of law is *integrity*. Roughly, integrity requires that the law speak in a coherent and principled way. In municipal legal systems, integrity implies that law must be interpreted to aim ultimately toward "some single comprehensive vision of justice."[13] To achieve this vision, judges must interpret rules in a way that gives them a principled rationale that coheres with a comprehensive conception of justice. In so doing a judge must also participate in the progress of a legal system toward this goal. He does this by taking account of what went before, by providing the best moral interpretation of previous judicial decisions, in particular by showing those earlier decisions in the best light he can. Moreover, the constraints imposed by moral principles and the notion of integrity mean that judicial officials exercise discretion in only a limited "weak" sense. They cannot simply act arbitrarily or merely as they see fit, but are bound to act according to the relevant underlying principles and an ideal of integrity.

Dworkin and the Pine Tar Controversy

What is the relevance of all this for adjudication in sport? What might the relevant underlying principles be in baseball or sporting games generally? Could they be shown to support the justness of MacPhail's decision in the pine tar controversy? Can the notion of integrity be applied to sporting legal systems to show games in their best light?

Consider the following principle as fundamental to all sporting games:

> *Rules should be interpreted in such a manner that the excellences embodied in achieving the lusory goal of the game are not undermined but are maintained and fostered.*

The "lusory goal" (or playing goal) of the game is winning, or attempting to win, by overcoming certain obstacles or inefficiencies that the game sets in its participants' path. It is a fundamental feature of sporting games that they establish physical obstacles to achieving certain goals. Thus, in baseball the test is not merely "can the batter hit a ball?" but "can the batter hit a *pitched* ball, a ball with late movement or real pop?" The com-

---

[13] *Law's Empire*, p. 134.

petition in a game is designed to test how well participants are able to demonstrate their physical and mental skills in surmounting such obstacles. The rules set those obstacles and determine the related skills or excellences (the "lusory means") that are available to overcome them.[14]

The principle just described requires us to recognize and respect this fundamental feature of games. It forces us to recognize and respect that the very idea of a game requires setting obstacles which must be overcome through the development of skills that are permitted by the rules. Call this "the first principle of games adjudication." There are undoubtedly other principles of games as well, but many can be shown to flow from this basic principle.

In the pine tar controversy, MacPhail justified his decision to reinstate Brett's home run with the oft-stated but vague chestnut that games should be won and lost by events on the field, not by mere technicalities of rules. It should now be evident that the authority for MacPhail's decision was drawn from the first principle of games adjudication. For since Brett's excellence in using a wooden bat to hit a ball, surmounting the substantial physical obstacles of major league pitching and a 300-to-400-foot distance to the fence, was achieved without any extra advantage conferred by the pine tar, the role of the pine tar is simply irrelevant from the point of view of this principle and the competition itself. That is, since the basic idea of a game is to create a context for the establishment of such obstacles, and the development and exercise of related excellences in surmounting them, the umpires' decision to discount Brett's home run undermines the very goals and purposes of the game. MacPhail's decision is compelling when viewed in this context.

Perhaps it will be argued that part of the obstacles that are to be overcome in some games is the strategizing that may be employed to come up with picayune rule interpretations (à la Billy Martin) that would give one participant an advantage over another. Here, then, is another sort of excellence that is involved in playing certain competitive games. But games do not set out to create a context for this type of rule quibbling to flourish. On

---

[14] I borrow the terms "a lusory goal" and "lusory means" from Bernard Suits's classic discussion of games, *The Grasshopper, Games, and Utopia* (Toronto: Toronto University Press, 1978), pp. 36–37.

the contrary, they do their very best to anticipate and eliminate such possibilities. This is because employment of such stratagems amounts to another instance of an anti-game, in this case a game played with the rules of the game as a way of circumventing the lusory goal.

Such stratagems should rarely, if ever, be given serious weight, since their aim is to evade facing the very obstacles and related excellences that define a game and without which there would be no game at all. The strategems aim to succeed in a game by not playing it, attempting a sort of free-ride to the game's goal. Again, the first principle of games adjudication opposes such stratagems by insisting that games be run so that the excellences they embody are maintained and fostered, not evaded.

The Integrity of the Game

We can see that the first principle of games adjudication clarifies and provides a reasoned justification for MacPhail's decision to reinstate Brett's home run. In fact, looking at the history of baseball, it is easy to find instances of this principle and other related principles of games at work qualifying and amending rules in a typically Dworkinian fashion. Baseball is a fertile ground for demonstrating these ideas, given the complexity of its rules and the prominent role that umpires play. Take the decision of umpire Wes Curry from the early days of baseball.[15]

In 1887, in an American Association game between Louisville and Brooklyn, a Louisville player, Reddy Mack, who had just safely crossed home plate, turned around and interfered with the Brooklyn catcher, preventing him from making a tag on the next runner. While the jostling continued, another runner made use of the opportunity to cross the plate. The umpire, Curry, called the runner out who immediately followed Mack and disallowed the next run. Curry's decision occasioned much controversy among the baseball public, for the rules at the time stated that no *baserunner* may interfere with a fielder, but when Mack crossed the plate he was, of course, no longer a baserunner. The

---

[15] David Nemec, *The Rules of Baseball: An Anecdotal Look at the Rules of Baseball and How They Came to Be* (New York: Lyons and Burnford, 1994), p. 174. (An official publication of Major League Baseball.)

rules said nothing explicitly to prohibit non-baserunners from interfering with fielders.[16]

Did Curry make the right decision? His decision was not explicitly covered by the rules at the time, but his actions seem irreproachable, were not overturned, and were the basis for a subsequent rule change (now Rule 7.09(e)). The offensive player's interference had prevented a runner from being tagged out. That runner should be out. The interference made the play dead from that point on, and so the next run should have been disallowed. Any other decision would have invited a nine-inning-long wrestling match.

Umpire Curry's exercise of discretion, in effect, adding a rule to regulate the behavior of non-baserunners, seems justified by the way it preserved the opportunities for fielders to demonstrate their skills in fielding and throwing balls and tagging out runners. It's also a nice illustration of the idea of integrity. The principle of integrity attempts to portray the rules governing a legal system and the practices they embody in their best light. The first principle of games adjudication does the same: it directs adjudicators to interpret rules in a way that maintains and fosters a context for games-specific obstacles and related excellences to be realized. But there is an important backward-looking aspect to integrity. Integrity is committed to making the best of a practice, taking account of what went before, and showing that practice in its best light. This prevents adjudicators from making wholesale revisions to a practice. They do not start with a clean slate, but must try to show the practice, as it has emerged to a particular point in history, in its best light. Umpire Curry did this with his decision as well.

Tackling of fielders by non-baserunners (how about flying blind-side tackles from the bullpen?) would hardly be baseball as we know and think of it. It would not be the same game at all. As early as 1887, the rules went to considerable lengths, as they do today, to prevent actions by offensive players that interfere with defensive players' abilities to field balls and to make plays. The fact that the rule was so quickly changed and has occasioned no subsequent controversy is compelling evidence that Curry's decision respected the integrity of the game.

---

[16] I discuss other examples in "Are Rules All an Umpire Has to Work With?"

Talk about the integrity of games is common when it comes to umpiring controversies, and Dworkin's theory nicely clarifies this idea. Baseball's strike zone is one of the better on-going examples. Although there have been many official efforts to change the size of the strike zone, umpires themselves have rarely, if ever, followed the letter of the rules, preferring instead to call the strike zone "according to what the game demands."[17] This particular use of discretion by umpires has often seemed arbitrary and unjustified to fans and others, but it has produced exceptional consistency in one respect. It is a remarkable fact that despite the many changes to the strike zone, the creative tension between official changes to, and umpires' interpretations of, the strike zone has resulted in overall major league batting averages at around .260. This average has remained constant for about 100 years.[18]

The principal anomaly over this period occurred in the 1990s, primarily in the American League, when batting averages zoomed into the .270s. Averages are now coming down somewhat. This is due in part to recent official efforts to change the strike zone. But it remains true that essentially no umpire calls the strike zone as it is written in the rules (it is generally called smaller). If we assume that league batting averages of around .260 represent something close to an optimum for testing and displaying the skills of the game, umpires have evidently interpreted and adjusted strike zones with astonishing consistency so that the skills of the game can be demonstrated to best advantage. Thus, the strike zone has changed many times, officially and non-officially, during the course of the history of the game, and there is apparently remarkable integrity in this. What this also means in practice is that, as batters, pitchers, and fielders develop new strategies, it will be important to preserve the nature of the contest as a meaningful opportunity for the exercise and display of relevant sport-related skills.

---

[17] Attributed to major league umpire Jim Evans in D. Tuttle, "Zoned Out," *Inside Sport*, Vol. 19, No. 6 (1997), pp. 24–28.

[18] See American and National League statistics at Baseball-Reference.com, available at http://www.baseball-reference.com/leagues (July 5th, 2003). For discussion of the .260 average statistics, see Stephen Jay Gould, *Tragedy and Triumph in Mudville: A Lifelong Passion for Baseball* (New York: Norton, 2002), pp. 163–66.

The evolving nature of sport implies another principle of games adjudication, namely, that *rules should be interpreted to achieve an appropriate competitive balance.* I do not mean that umpires should set out to ensure a basic equality of skill among participants in a contest. Rather, there is a more formal idea of competitive balance that is fundamental to games and that umpires should seek to preserve. If we think of sports as games involving the mastery of certain physical excellences in the pursuit of a lusory goal, then competition should be designed to provide fair and meaningful opportunities for participants to exercise such skills. The opportunities should be fair in the sense that the rules should not unduly prejudice the outcome from the beginning in favor of some of the participants. And the opportunities should be meaningful in the sense that they genuinely allow for the exercise of sport-related physical skills by participants. To the extent that either of these conditions fail, competition will be undermined along with the opportunity that it affords for the development, mastery, and display of a game's distinctive physical excellences.

Finally, an obvious principle of games adjudication is that *rules should be interpreted according to principles of fair play and sportsmanship, and so that the good conduct of games is maintained.* Again, this is evident from the first principle of games adjudication, for failures of fair play, sportsmanship, and good conduct all have the potential to undermine the opportunity for a game to be a contest that compares competitors' physical excellences in overcoming common barriers.

Examples abound here. Interventions to prevent the intimidation of players so that a contest does not become a melee—or so that a player has no fair opportunity to demonstrate his skills—are instances of this principle at work. Another common violation of this principle in baseball is the use of delaying tactics. For example, this principle is violated when a manager of a team that is ahead in a game engages in delaying tactics hoping that a rain delay will bring an early end to a game. Umpires should intervene in these contexts, even though the rules may appear to permit such practices, since these actions are an attempt to evade the game as a contest of athletic skills. Again, this can be another type of anti-game strategy, and it should not be permitted for that reason.

And lastly, participants' disrespect toward umpires cannot be tolerated. Roberto Alomar's expectoration on umpire John Hirschbeck is one of the more vile examples of player misconduct toward umpires from recent baseball history, but Billy Martin kicking dirt, Lou Piniella throwing bases, and Earl Weaver refusing to return a base are over the top as well. These antics are great theater, but they are also intimidating and disrespectful, and cannot be tolerated if umpires are to uphold the good conduct and fairness of games.

Umpires often say that theirs is the only profession where you have to be perfect when you start and then improve from there. Enough has been said here to explain how umpires can perfect their activities through the application of certain principles that are fundamental features of games. By now, it should also be evident that there is a compelling principled basis for umpires to interpret the rules of baseball to permit review of bad calls on more occasions than is now the case. Indeed, the argument could undoubtedly go further to defend the use of video replays on calls in some circumstances, for example, for certain crucial plays like tags at the plate or for suspected cases of deceiving umpires. However, this is not something umpires could put into effect themselves. The basic criterion to apply to any suggested rule change concerns whether the integrity of a game will be upheld. Will the change maintain or foster the display of excellences that are the basis of the competition, while preserving the good conduct of the games themselves? All the principles of games adjudication play a role in addressing these issues. Given the complexity of the rules in baseball, there are many hard decisions waiting to be made (as thoughtful umpires know). Also, a myriad of hypothetical situations and the principles that underlie them not only provide for lively conversation but also for education and enlightenment about the goals and purposes of the game.

Will my proposals give umpires too big a role in determining the rules and terms under which baseball is played? I doubt it. Umpires, like judges everywhere, are by nature conservative and will generally act with restraint. They are also constrained by the idea of integrity. This leads me to finish with one last heretical idea. It is likely that misunderstandings about umpiring and the principles that lie behind games adjudication contribute to participants' and fans' frustration with umpires who themselves fail to recognize the real nature and limits of their role. If so, taking umpiring seriously from a philosophical perspective cannot be separated from improving the status and respect that umpires are due. In this respect, responsibility for reform lies not only with fans and participants, but also with umpires themselves. Let's "play ball!" for the game itself.

Fourth Inning:
Fair or Foul?

Everybody knows that lying, cheating, and stealing are selfish and unethical. So why do we reward these acts on a baseball field? Randolph Feezell claims that there is a tradition of cheating in baseball that many fans are quick to overlook. But does that make it right? Mark J. Hamilton believes that deceiving the opponent is part of the game, but deceiving the umpires is not. A better understanding of ethics and the nature of rules can help us learn the difference.

7 | Baseball, Cheating, and Tradition: Would Kant Cork His Bat?

RANDOLPH FEEZELL

Nobody denied that Sammy Sosa corked his bat. The evidence was in the shards of his bat that had splintered on a routine groundout, in a game against the Tampa Bay Devil Rays, June 3rd, 2003. Bob Watson, Major League Baseball's vice president for on-field operations, said the bat was "illegal," and suspended Sosa for eight games. Sosa called his action a "mistake." After his appeal, baseball's president and chief operating officer, Bob DuPuy, reduced Sosa's suspension to seven games, citing Sosa's exemplary "sincerity" and "candor." Throughout the brief investigation, none of the principal people involved dared to use the word "cheating."

Long before I became a philosopher and a coach, I played on a summer semi-pro team in a league primarily made up of college players, some of whom would go on to play major league baseball. (The competitive details may be relevant.) Here's the scenario. We're playing an excellent team coached by a former major leaguer (who remembers Bob Cerv?) and our starting pitcher is a crafty little lefty with a good curve and a mediocre fastball. I suggest to him that he might add a couple of feet to his fastball in crucial situations by stepping in front of the rubber, to shorten the distance to home plate. When you step up, be sure to put the ball on the batter's hands, I suggest. Great idea! He uses the "strategy" effectively in the early innings until the voluble third base coach (Cerv) notices a hole dug in front of the rubber in a very unusual place. He blows up and

creates quite a memorable scene. Our little lefty sheepishly continued, unsuccessfully as I recall, against a more highly moti-
vated opponent. Imaginative strategy or cheating?

Another former major league player, notoriously pugnacious
Eddie Stanky, coached in college late in his career. He developed a unique home field advantage for his team, filled with
left-handed hitting speedsters. After one of them beat out a routine grounder to shortstop for an infield hit, an opposing coach
demanded that the distance from home to first be measured.
Oops–eighty-eight feet! Imagine the scene at the ballpark that
day. Was Stanky a cheater?

Among contemporary sports, baseball may not be unique in
offering numerous opportunities to cheat, but it has certainly
developed in such a way that all kinds of subtle and questionable actions and illegalities have been used to gain a competitive edge—or dull the opponent's edge. Some examples
have become part of the lore of baseball. The Giants watered
down the basepaths to slow the prodigious base-stealing
efforts of Maury Wills, and the Cubs did the same for Vince
Coleman. The Dodgers changed the height of the mound,
while other teams kept their infield grass high for their sinker-
ball pitchers. Supposedly, if you roll a ball down the third base
line in Boston's Fenway Park, it always goes foul. Watered
base paths and sloped foul lines are merely the beginning
entries in a long list of irregularities for discussion: batters set
up with their back feet outside the legal batter's box, runners
go outside of the baseline to break up double plays, left-
handed pitchers artfully perfect their balk pick-off move to
first, players steal signs, perform hidden ball tricks, pretend to
catch trapped balls in the outfield, decoy runners, and fake
tags. These plays of deception are discussed in the following
essay by Mark Hamilton. In this essay, I will explore questions
of outright cheating by people like Hall of Fame pitcher
Gaylord Perry, whose autobiography is titled *Me and the
Spitter*, and hitters like Sosa and Albert Belle who have been
caught corking their bats.

No wonder questions are intermittently raised about the ethical atmosphere of baseball, like a recent edition of the Dan
Patrick show on ESPN radio. "Tony Gwynn says over fifty percent of major league players cheat," Patrick says to Cal Ripken,
Jr. "Do you agree?" Patrick offers his own examples for consid-

eration, like an infielder who tries to return a scuffed or torn baseball to the pitcher, or a baserunner who tries to steal signs from second base. Brainy co-host "nasty boy" Rob Dibble chimes in: "Everybody cheats in baseball." Ripken's response? Much to his credit, he responds as Socrates might have,[1] not by offering precipitous judgments but by asking the key philosophical question. What is cheating? How do you define cheating? Ripken's response suggests that we can't make headway, that is, we can't be confident about our judgments of particular cases until we address the general issue, and to do that we need to engage in philosophical thinking.

Dibble's comment, "everybody cheats," already assumes some understanding of what counts as cheating and the nature of cheating, but it may express an overly simple view. It's not clear that some examples mentioned as instances of cheating (for instance, stealing signs), are really examples of cheating at all. We first need to return to Ripken's question and be reminded of the importance of Socrates's approach to such matters.

Socrates, impassioned seeker of truth, has been one of the most influential philosophers in the western philosophical tradition, not so much for the specific beliefs or positions he happened to hold (for he seemingly held few), but for the questions he asked, the value he put on them, and the way in which he tried to answer them. Socrates has been called the "father of moral philosophy" not because he produced a systematic ethical theory but because he attempted to answer such fundamental questions as "How should I live?" and "What is virtue?" by using his reason in a new and sometimes unsettling manner. Plato's admiring portrait of Socrates is offered especially well in the early dialogues,[2] in which we find Socrates often engaged in critically examining some important ethical concept, attempting to find its definition, its very nature. We find him talking with others whose character and approach to the issues strikingly contrast with his.

---

[1] Most of Plato's writings are known as dialogues, conversations between Socrates and others. Socrates, who had been Plato's teacher, left nothing in writing. It is not known for sure how much of what Socrates says in Plato's dialogues is really what Socrates said and how much is Plato's own ideas. Socrates was executed in 399 B.C.E. and Plato died in 347 B.C.E.

[2] In the *Euthyphro*, for example, Socrates addresses the question of piety. In the *Crito*, Socrates investigates reasons for breaking the law.

The conversations are far from academic and abstract discussions, for they are occasioned by real-life situations that demand some serious thinking, of which his interlocutors are initially incapable, requiring Socrates's skillful questioning, ironic goading, and insightful direction.

In the spirit of Plato and Socrates, I would like to examine the issue of cheating and baseball by offering a brief dialogue as an appropriate way for the reader to engage in thinking about these issues. Plato's dialogues show that philosophical problems are complex and difficult, so facile answers are to be avoided. There are no easy answers to the question of "What is cheating in baseball?", so perhaps a dialogue can convey the sense that philosophical reflection often begins and ends with some intellectual humility.

The Meaning of Cheating

In the following dialogue, Abbey will defend a position I will call "absolutism," while Trev will defend "traditionalism." Ron, the defender of "realism," will at first be a skeptic about answering the question of cheating. Although the meaning of these terms will arise in the context of the conversation that follows, it might be helpful to first make some brief clarifying comments.

In sports and in other contexts, cheating is often understood in relation to the status of rules. In ethics, an "absolutist" holds that a moral rule like "Do not steal" applies equally to everyone everywhere in a relevantly similar situation. In this sense, moral rules are universal. In the second sense, an absolutist holds that a moral rule is exceptionless. For example, stealing or lying is always wrong, period. As the reader will see, the great eighteenth-century German philosopher Immanuel Kant insisted that moral rules are absolute in both senses. In the following dialogue, Abbey, the absolutist, argues that the rules that define baseball are absolute in the sense that such rules apply equally to every participant and a player or coach ought not to intend to break any explicit rules. The rules of baseball bind all participants without exception. To break a rule with the intention of gaining an unfair advantage is to cheat.

On the other hand, the traditionalist believes that such strict obedience to rules is unrealistic and ignores how games like baseball are actually played. Strategic rule-breaking is "part of the game" and not necessarily the attempt to cheat or to gain an unfair advantage, since opponents expect each other to engage in such strategies and umpires are available to preserve the competitive equality defined by the rules. In the language of the tradition of virtue ethics, the fair or just player may break certain rules without cheating.

Finally, the realist view of cheating in baseball is a more extreme version of the insistence that strict obedience to rules is unrealistic. What I will call realism appears to ignore the ethical view altogether. According to the realist, the point of participating in competitive sports is to win, so whatever is required to achieve that end is permissible, even if it involves cheating.

ABBEY (absolutist): There is one obvious way that baseball raises philosophical questions. It raises various ethical questions, like the question of sportsmanship or the ethics of using performance-enhancing drugs. In particular, I'm interested in the question, "what is cheating?"

RON (realist): But everybody has his own definition of cheating. People don't have the same definition. What's cheating for some people may not be cheating for others. People may disagree with your examples.

ABBEY: I would admit that there's disagreement about some of the examples, but that doesn't mean there's *no* agreement about others, or that there's no central meaning of cheating. We seem to have some publicly shared meaning in mind when we talk about cheating.

TREV (traditionalist): Your point is well taken. Instead of looking at disputed or difficult borderline cases, we should look at central, undisputed examples of cheating in order to develop a general definition and an explanation for why we make such judgments. Then we can return to our borderline cases and base our judgments on a better understanding of the concept. This is a good response to those skeptics who think it is impossible to define cheating.

ABBEY: If we start with examples outside of sport, it's natural to think of the tax-cheat or someone cheating at cards. Or think of a student cheating on an exam by having someone else take the test or by bringing in hidden notes to class. In these cases there are rules that apply to everyone in the relevant situation and the cheater wants to make himself an arbitrary exception to those rules in order to gain some advantage. The cheater has an advantage in relation to others who are acting by the rules. The advantage is unfair because everyone else is seeking the goal in question only by the means allowed by the rules. There seems to be an implied agreement in place that the rules apply to everyone equally and the cheater breaks the agreement. A clear example of injustice is when two individuals are treated dissimilarly in similar circumstances, for no good reason. For example, some people argue that people like Mike Tyson and Winona Rider get special treatment when they break the law. Similar treatment of similar cases means that rules apply to everyone equally. Since the cheater wants some unfair advantage that others in the situation wouldn't agree to, the cheater will usually engage in deception. I conclude that the concept of cheating usually involves breaking rules with the intention of gaining an unfair advantage, since others involved are seeking their goals according to the agreed-upon rules. Cheating is wrong because it's a form of injustice or unfairness.

TREV: What about sports? What about baseball?

ABBEY: If you look at obvious, undisputed examples of cheating in sports, they don't seem to be matters of strategy. They involve things like keeping score fairly, playing only eligible players, using unbiased officials, and using legal equipment. It would be fairly easy to find specific examples of cheating in baseball for each of these categories. If you look at these paradigm cases, they have something in common. They involve the deliberate attempt to gain an unfair advantage by altering the conditions of competitive equality as defined by the rules. Since cheaters don't want their competitors to find out, they will usually engage in deception.

An Interlude on Kant

The strategy so far is reminiscent of Socrates's approach to philosophical inquiry: the search for a definition that will help us explain our judgments of particular cases. We have encountered an approach that is incompatible with taking seriously the task of such an inquiry. As we have just seen with Ron's first comment, the relativist's assertion that "everyone has his own view of cheating" can't take seriously the goal of finding the central meaning of such fundamental concepts. If you think you already have the truth (as the dogmatist does) or there's no truth to be found , then there's no point in looking for it. The suggested truth about the core meaning of cheating is reminiscent of another philosopher's views: Immanuel Kant (1724–1804).

Kant's thinking has a reputation for being extremely difficult. Yet Kant's ethical theory in his *Groundwork of the Metaphysics of Morals* (one of the most important books in the history of ethics), expresses some elements of our common, everyday moral thinking that are clearly occasioned by the attempt to understand cheating. Kant called his fundamental moral principle the "Categorical Imperative" and he formulated it in a number of different ways. (How these different formulations relate to each other is a question that has kept scholars busy for a long time.) For our purposes, his first formulation is most relevant: "I ought never to act except in such a way that my maxim should become a universal law." While his formulation is rather obscure, the basic idea is not. Kant stressed that the moral evaluation of an action should focus on our intentions or "maxims," that is, what we take ourselves to be doing when we act. Kant supposed that we could always describe our actions in terms of some general principle, and if a general principle was acceptable from the standpoint of morality it must be "universalizable." In other words, what if everyone acted that way? Would it be acceptable? Moral rules must apply to everyone equally. If you are acting, implicitly or explicitly, on the basis of a "maxim" or general principle that cannot be universalizable, your action is morally wrong.

One central example of this thinking is when someone is doing something that she would not want others to do. Consider the tax-cheat, the person who rolls back the odometer before selling the car, or the person who gossips. We naturally respond:

What if everyone did that? The Kantian interpretation of this common rhetorical question is to understand it as a piece of moral criticism. If you are acting in a way that you wouldn't want others to act, then you shouldn't act that way yourself. You should not make yourself an arbitrary exception to moral requirements. If you are acting on the basis of a principle that may be formulated as "I may do this but others may not," then when the principle is universalized it becomes incoherent. (Since everyone would be the exception, no one would be.)

Kant argues that morally acceptable action requires that our intentions (our will), our underlying principle of action, be consistent. When Mom and Dad respond to the child's hurtful behavior by asking, "How would you like it if someone did that to you?" they respond as instinctive Kantians, pointing out that right action requires consistency, and reasons for action should be based on whether they are acceptable from the standpoint of equality or universal application.

Despite much controversy, most philosophers have agreed that moral rules must, in some sense, be equally applicable, as laws are if they are to be considered fair or just. Kant's stress on universalizability is simply the recognition that rules bind equally those to whom the rules apply. Since sports are rule-governed activities, the rules that define the very sport in question apply to everyone equally, and the decision to play the sport is based on the agreement that all participants will act according to the rules that define the game and make its very existence possible. The ethical evaluation of cheating in sports, including baseball, is naturally understood in terms of the requirements that are central in Kant's ethical theory and apply outside of sports as well. Let's return to our dialogue.

Cheating and Tradition

RON: So if a player breaks a rule, then that's an example of cheating?

ABBEY: Not exactly. A player might break a rule without intending to do anything wrong. As a pitcher I might hit a batter without intending to or I might trip someone in football or basketball or soccer without deliberately trying to get a penalty or foul.

TREV: I believe we're in the right ballpark, but we haven't yet successfully defined cheating. I don't believe that deliberately violating a rule is sufficient for cheating or for unsportsmanlike behavior, because the core meaning of cheating as the attempt to gain an unfair advantage over the opponent isn't necessarily represented when a rule is deliberately violated. A good example comes from basketball. It's late in a close game, your team is behind, and the opponent has the ball. If you can't steal the ball, you should foul. Send the other team to the foul line to make free throws. It's a strategy that is universally taught by coaches. Here's an example of deliberately committing a foul, that is, breaking a rule, and I don't consider it an example of cheating because I don't believe there's anything unfair about it. You expect the opponent to do the same thing in the same situation. There's the "similar treatment of similar cases" requirement for justice. It's strategy, not cheating. The person who commits the foul is a *strategic rules breaker*, not a cheater. Notice also that there's no deception involved, but deception, by itself, certainly isn't wrong in sports. Fake right, go left. Fake the reverse, throw a long pass. Throw a changeup. Deception is often a crucial part of strategy in sports.

ABBEY: But when someone cheats there's unethical deception taking place. Give me some more examples.

RON: Well, when I played in the outfield, I wasn't afraid to do little things to get an edge. I always faked out umpires on trapped balls. When I played first base I might drop a ball on a tag but act like I caught it if the ump didn't have a good view of the play. If I was at the plate I sometimes tried to peek at the catcher giving signs. You do what you have to do to win. The better you become as a ballplayer the better you become at knowing what you can get away with.

ABBEY: That is, you become better at cheating.

RON: If that's what you want to call it, fine. Everyone cheats in baseball and in other sports.

TREV: I disagree. That attitude comes about because your notion of cheating is too loose. I wouldn't call all of these examples cheating. You expect the opponent to be well-coached and to do some of them. Pretending to catch a trapped ball is part of the game. Also, there's an umpire to enforce the underlying agreements expressed in the rules and to make the correct call. If a hitter tries to peek at the catcher's signals he may get plunked. That's a lack of respect for the traditions of the game, but it's different. The opponent enforces the unwritten rules, not the umpire. When you set a screen in basketball, you may move a little to set an effective one. If you move too much, a foul may be called. That's not cheating. There's nothing unfair about it. It's good strategy. The game hasn't broken down because of a moving screen.

ABBEY: You are breaking rules deliberately. How about subtly grabbing the opponent's uniform as she drives, or pushing off on a rebound, or pushing off with the non-shooting hand as you're going up for a lay-up, or flopping as if you've taken a charge when the offensive player has hardly touched you?

TREV: But there's a big difference between playing an ineligible player, like the 14-year-old pitcher who dominated the 12-and-under Little League World Series, or hiring a biased official, or not keeping the score fairly, as opposed to the things you've mentioned. I think there is a *prescriptive atmosphere* associated with most sports, an *ethos* associated with how rules are interpreted, what you can and cannot fairly do as you compete for victory within the context of the rules. It defines an atmosphere of competitive expectations in which opponents can gain a competitive advantage only in the context of agreements about the underlying equality expressed in the written rules and in the so-called unwritten rules.

ABBEY: I don't find your appeal to "unwritten rules" particularly persuasive. You seem to use this notion to preserve the sense that agreements are being kept or that the advantages that arise from strategic rules breaking aren't unfair.

TREV: The prescriptive atmosphere of a sport is partly constituted by the central, explicit rules of the sport and partly by the unwritten understandings that arise in the historical development of a sport. I confess that I've come to this position by reflecting on baseball, but I would also say it applies to other sports.

RON: During baseball season there's usually some discussion on ESPN about unwritten rules. Remember the controversy when Ben Davis of the San Diego Padres broke up Curt Schilling's perfect game in the eighth inning by bunting for a hit? For some people, that was a big no-no.

TREV: Precisely. That's not an example of cheating, but it's a great example of what I've called the "prescriptive atmosphere" of professional baseball. Some things you can do, other things you're not supposed to do. In baseball, at least at the higher levels, you can steal signs, (but not peek), break up a double play at second base by going slightly out of the basepath, pitch inside by brushing people away from the plate, quick-pitch, step out of the batter's box to disrupt the rhythm of the pitcher, dig up the chalk line in the batter's box to set up as deep as you can, and so on. On the other hand, there are things you shouldn't do, like steal, or hit and run, or squeeze when you're crushing another team. You shouldn't show up your opponent. You don't stand at home plate and admire your towering home run, even if you're Barry Bonds. And you don't prance around the bases and then jump on home plate. That shows up a pitcher.

ABBEY: But some of your examples aren't matters of breaking rules; they're more like matters of etiquette.

TREV: Some are related to the strategic breaking of rules, others are not, but they're all related to the notion of sportsmanship as respect for the game, respect for the traditions and customs that have developed in a sport, and respect for your opponent. Cheating fails to respect your opponent. Here's an example that shows the problems for your view. One of the most important skills for a young catcher to develop is called "framing": catching the ball in such a way that the umpire might call a close pitch a strike, even one that is outside of the strike zone. The rules defining the strike zone, walks, and strikeouts are fundamental to baseball, but catchers like Ivan Rodriquez are taught to deliberately receive a ball in such a way that it looks like a strike. Do you really think that's cheating?

ABBEY: Is the intention to deceive, or is it to increase the likelihood that close pitches that are strikes will be called strikes?

TREV: It doesn't matter, but probably the former.

ABBEY: Yes, it matters, because the intention to gain an unfair advantage matters, ethically.

TREV: Again, good framing isn't unfair. The opponent's catcher has the same opportunity and the umpire is available to ensure that calls are fairly made.

ABBEY: What about doctoring baseballs? Some pitchers in professional baseball put different substances on the ball to make it move more, or they have been known to cut and scuff balls, gash them with something sharp to make them dart and dive. That's cheating.

TREV: I'm not so sure. That's been part of the game for a long time.

ABBEY: That's cheating. You're not telling me that throwing spitballs is not cheating, are you?

TREV: It depends. In high school and college baseball you don't expect pitchers and coaches to be so artful.

ABBEY: You mean "dishonest."

TREV: But the prescriptive atmosphere in professional baseball is more flexible, in a sense, in terms of the expectations involved. Umpires look out for pitchers doing it, opponents are aware that it often occurs, and penalties are invoked—or balls are tossed out of the game. I'd say it's more like holding by an offensive lineman in football or setting an illegal screen in basketball.

ABBEY: You appeal to some mysterious unwritten rules or latent agreements that allow people to break rules, but who decides what are the unwritten rules? What if one opponent is ignorant of the assumed understandings, or what if someone is aware of the so-called unwritten rules and simply thumbs her nose at them? Then you have competitive inequality—unfair advantages.

RON: Abbey, you need to be more realistic. Sports are about competing and attempting to win, and to do that you try to find any edge you can. Everybody cheats in sports; that's why officials are necessary. You know your opponent is doing everything he can to win the game, just like you are. I hate to say it, but it looks to me like the old saying is true: It's not cheating unless you get caught.

TREV: That's not my view. I think cheating is wrong and that cheaters lack integrity and violate the integrity of the game. There are certainly many people in baseball, for example, who are extremely competitive but don't think of themselves as cheaters. They want to think of themselves as fair and they want to compete and win fairly.

RON: Some don't care. Sammy Sosa used a corked bat. Gaylord Perry threw spitballs.

TREV: But Perry's spitballs or vaseline balls or whatever he threw were a part of a tradition, in front of opposing players and umpires. Yes, he broke a rule, for strategic reasons. It's like a left-handed pitcher using a pickoff move to first base that is actually a balk, but he hopes he will not be caught by the umpire. Using a corked bat is different. It's not strategic; you don't expect many others to try to get away with it. The deception is more hidden and it's harder for the officials to protect the integrity of the game while it's being played. It's not an established part of the tradition of the game, in terms of expected permissible strategies. I'd say Sammy Sosa is a cheater.

RON: I'd say he's a competitor who wanted to win and he got caught. If you want to call him a cheater, that's fine. Whatever. I call him a competitor.

ABBEY: What has happened in our society? Studies show that an amazingly large number of students cheat in high school and in college. Plagiarism from the Internet is an increasingly major problem in colleges and universities. To say that "everybody cheats," in sports or in life, is for me a major indictment of our ethical life. It's as if the term "cheating" no longer has the same negative ethical force it once had.

TREV: I agree with you. I want the term "cheater" to retain its negative moral force. If Sammy Sosa is a cheater, then what he's doing is wrong. He shouldn't cheat. Ron, you seem to be using the term differently, as if it just describes breaking rules, and everyone breaks or stretches the rules. No big deal. But it is a big deal. People shouldn't cheat, and we shouldn't be teaching our children that it's *acceptable to cheat.*

ABBEY: Trev is forced to accept traditionalism. The traditionalist holds that a player is both required and permitted to follow the traditions of the sport, which includes both written rules and unwritten rules and, of course, some unwritten rules allow for a player strategically, but fairly, to break a written rule. The standard justification that the good sport, the non-cheater, gives when breaking a written rule is "it's part of the game." The central ideal for this approach is *conforming to a tradition,* or "respect for the game," and the wise but fair player needs historical awareness of her sport and insight into its customs. This is the basis for the latent agreements that preserve the competitive equality so valued by the absolutist. Rules must always be applied and interpreted, according to the traditionalist. But I see a big problem for this approach.

TREV: You probably don't find the appeal to the unwritten rules of a tradition very clear.

ABBEY: No, I don't. Not everyone agrees to or is even aware of the same unwritten rules that are the basis for the latent agreements to which you appeal. Where and how do you draw the line between corking a bat and throwing spitballs? Framing is permissible, but what about trapping a ball in the outfield and pretending that you have caught it? Why not just be honest? There is a slippery slope that leads directly from your traditionalism to Ron's realism, where everything is permitted as long as you don't get caught.

TREV: Just because a distinction is difficult to make doesn't mean it's impossible to make. I believe the appeal to tradition, experience, good judgment, and good intentions can help us. Corking bats is different from pretending that balls are strikes, or a trapped ball is caught. Why do you call Ron's position "realism"?

ABBEY: As I understand it, you want to distinguish your appeal to tradition from the view I've called realism. When someone starts talking about being "realistic," about conduct being "part of the game" and what she expects other competitors to do, she will end up with the view that the ultimate purpose of sport is simply to win. In discussions of the ethics of war, or war and morality, realism is contrasted with pacifism or just war theory. It's the view that moral guidelines are irrelevant in the conduct of war. By analogy, the realist approach to cheating in sports seems to be that a player is allowed to do whatever it takes to win and she expects her opponents to do likewise. It's cheating only if you get caught, but that merely describes the fact of rule-breaking, and the term ceases to have its moral force.

TREV: I don't accept it, either. But my view of cheating is not as narrow as the absolutist's. I want to avoid cheating and I want to preserve the integrity of athletic competition, of competitive *play*. I believe good judgment is possible and the appeal to tradition or custom is crucial.

RON: Who cares about tradition? Traditions change. You do what you have to do to win, and absolutism is for losers. Just win, baby!

ABBEY: I disagree. We should avoid cheating, and the best way is never to intend to break a rule—any rule.

Kant, Aristotle, and the Cheater

I leave it to readers to decide for themselves what are the best arguments concerning the ethics of cheating in baseball. At least one discriminating reader (my wife) finds Abbey's absolutism most compelling. My hunch is that no amount of argument will convince a baseball person to give up at least some of the rule-breaking strategies associated with Trev's traditionalism. The question is whether the arguments that attempt to distinguish framing, deceptive trapping, and even scuffing baseballs from corking bats, playing ineligible players, or changing the distance to first base are strong enough to sustain the notion that the player or coach who wants to compete fairly or justly is still allowed to break certain rules.

The issues involved here are big ones that are of continuing interest to philosophers engaged in ethical theory. Let me conclude by briefly describing an approach to moral life more in line with the classical Greek tradition in ethics. Whereas Kant's ethical theory provides a plausible model for the absolutist's emphasis on rule-following, Aristotle's approach might be used to defend traditionalism. Modern ethical theories, like Kant's are attempts to provide an account of the underlying nature of right and wrong action in terms of moral principles or rules. The focus in classical ethics is on traits of moral character, virtues that are praiseworthy and contribute to a good or flourishing life. For Aristotle (384–322 B.C.E.), the central ethical question is not, "What should I do?" Rather, it is, "What kind of person shall I be?" The stress in classical ethics is not on generating basic rules or principles of moral obligation, but on recommending excellences of character that are essential for living a good life in communities. For Kant, truth-telling is an absolutely binding obligation prescribed by a fundamental moral principle—no exceptions. For Aristotle, truth-telling is a character trait (honesty) that involves a range of qualities that might be involved in situations in which the person must decide whether the best or wisest choice is to tell the truth. When Aunt Alice walks into the room and asks, "How do you like my new hat?" the honest person need not say that it is an ugly monstrosity. Aristotle holds that virtue requires finding the "Golden Mean" between excess and defect. Deceptive truth-telling is characteristic of the liar and the deceiver; but excessive truth-telling may express defective character traits like tactlessness or boastfulness. Likewise, courage is a mean related to dangerous situations involving emotions like fear and confidence, in which the coward is disposed to act in light of excessive fear and the rash or foolhardy person is one who acts too confidently without proper regard for appropriate fear. For Aristotle there are no precise rules or algorithms that show the person who is honest or courageous how to act. Good judgment based on experience and wisdom is possible, yet there is no precise decision-procedure to follow in every situation.

The traditionalist might conceive of the just or fair player or coach as one who strives to find the mean between an excessive rule-follower (probably quite rare in sports) whose conscientiousness towards the rules is expressed in Abbey's absolutism, and an excessive rule-breaker, the ruthless win-at-all-costs player or coach who cheats in order to win. Armed with a notion of cheating as the attempt to gain an unfair advantage, the Aristotelian traditionalist denies that ethical judgments are always precise and clear-cut, but insists that one can make good judgments about appropriate rule-breaking that do not violate the competitive equality that must be preserved for fair competition to take place.

Much more would have to be said here to explain and defend the Aristotelian model, yet enough has been said to suggest that traditionalism might invoke the philosophical resources and insights of classical Greek ethics to defend its position. Absolutists like my wife may be unconvinced—other interested fans should turn off ESPN and read Kant and Aristotle!

8 | There's No Lying In Baseball (Wink, Wink)

MARK J. HAMILTON

In the film *A League of Their Own*, team manager Jimmy Dugan (played by Tom Hanks) tells an upset right-fielder Evelyn (played by Bitty Schram), "There's no crying in baseball." But how about lying, Tom? Is there lying in baseball?

It has been said that good sport maximizes effort, skill, and strategy. But what should be included in strategy? Many sports, and baseball may be the best at it, provide great opportunities for deception and lying. How has lying as a form of deception been mastered in the art of baseball strategy? To what extent should deception be an acceptable part of baseball and are there forms of deception or lying that are permissible, and other forms which are illegal to the game or immoral in their practice? Are plays of deception good strategy or bad sport? This examination of these questions begins by meeting up with Diogenes and his lantern in the fourth century B.C.E., plunging through the darkened streets of Athens looking for an honest person.[1] Let's transport him to the twenty-first century to see if he can find an honest person in the dugouts of Fenway Park, Jacobs Field, Yankee Stadium, or your local sandlot.

Is honesty an essential part of good sport? If good sport is simply following the rules of the game, then ideas like honesty,

---

[1] Tradition has it that Diogenes, an ancient Greek Cynic philosopher, traveled around even in daylight with a lit lantern searching for an honest man.

character building, or virtuous sport are irrelevant. Good sport and ethical behavior, however, require more than simply following the letter of the law. In the previous chapter, Randolph Feezell dealt with explicit rule breaking and examples like using corked bats, pitchers who doctor baseballs, or coaches who teach players to intentionally break the rules. My favorite example of explicit rule breaking was a high school coach who once told me he successfully used the double squeeze to score runners from second and third by teaching the second runner to cut fifteen feet inside of third base on his way home. So while all of the action occurred on another part of the diamond, with the fielding of the bunt and the runner scoring, neither umpire in a two-umpire system watched the runner going to third and so no one noticed his cutting of third base. It is illegal because the essential rule of advancing from base to base in baseball is violated; and it is immoral because it is an attempt to gain an unfair advantage to win the contest. Feezell elsewhere has also argued that this coach is no longer playing the game of baseball because of his overt violations of the rules.[2]

The coaches and players who participate in this type of double squeeze play pretend that nothing seriously immoral is involved. They fail to face up to the harsh reality that it is cheating and may even hold the false belief that this is an acceptable strategic play in the game. This inner lie of believing something one knows to be false (that this type of cheating is morally permissible) is similar to white-collar crime or taking everything not glued down from one's motel room. The moral liabilities are not even taken into account. Being driven by the motive of victory and fear of losing, a coach may believe that his plays are technically illegal but not significantly wrong or unethical. Worse still, not only are these types of double squeeze plays practiced, but there is also hearty approval or acceptance of the behavior by others in the game. This creates an atmosphere where there is no disgrace or shame among those who practice this type of cheating or immorality in the game. The burden of proof certainly rests on these deceivers to justify the morality of these actions, which they cannot do.

---

[2] Randolph M. Feezell, "On the Wrongness of Cheating and Why Cheaters Can't Play the Game," *Journal of The Philosophy of Sport*, Vol. XV, pp. 57–68.

Once this distinction between the legal and the moral is made, and good sport is considered to be both legal (following the rules) and demonstrating good character, then there is the possibility of an action that is legal but not moral. In this chapter, I will present examples of strategic deception in baseball where the deception is technically legal, that is, where no overt rule of the game is being violated. But I will argue that these deceptive attempts at strategy are not moral and therefore, not good sport.

Plays of Deception

What are some of these plays that may be technically legal but not moral and by what criteria can we evaluate their morality? The oldest baseball play of deception must be the traditional hidden ball trick in its numerous forms. This can be when an infielder bluffs throwing the ball to the pitcher and tags out the runner as he begins his lead, usually as the pitcher moves toward the mound (if he gets too close a balk can be called). This is one of the first plays learned by 13- and 14-year-olds who first begin to lead off base. It is clearly an act of deception where there is a bit of acting, but no rule is being violated and no umpire is being deceived.

Mike Hegan, a former big-leaguer and current Cleveland Indians announcer, tells the story of his first year in professional minor league baseball when he hit a ball off the fence and slid into second safely. The shortstop asked him to step off the bag so he could brush it off. Hegan stepped off and was tagged out by the infielder, thus becoming a victim of this variation of the hidden ball trick. Or one might find a first baseman walking the ball back to the pitcher several times after pick off attempts but finally as he does so he keeps the ball, goes back to first, and then tags the runner out when he begins leading off. A few years ago, when Boston Red Sox Manny Ramirez ran to second base on a pitch, one of the opposing middle infielders told him that it was a foul ball even though it wasn't. So as Ramirez began to return to first base, he was tagged out. Not only was Ramirez deceived but the infielder had lied. How awful! Didn't he know that it is wrong to lie and that telling an opponent it was a foul ball when it was not a foul ball is a blatant lie? Doesn't this violate those absolute prohibitions against lying made by numerous moral philosophers? Is this an act of immorality?

Occasionally a big league middle infielder will act as if he is fielding a ground ball when there has been a base hit with a runner moving. The intent is to get the runner to slow down and slide at second instead of continuing. Omar Vizquel is a master at this. At the high school level, this type of fake is often out-lawed to prevent injury from an unnecessary slide and umpires are given the authority to throw this player out of the game.

One of the plays sometimes used by boys and girls just learning the game is when a pitcher, not on the rubber, fakes a throw toward first base. The first and second basemen turn and scramble down the right field line acting like an overthrow has been made. The ruse draws the runner into breaking toward second only to find that the pitcher still has the ball. The run-ner is then tagged out. This play of deception had an additional element added to it in the College Division I World Series some years ago as the players in the right field bullpen scattered as if they were avoiding an overthrow on the fake throw from the pitcher.

But an Ohio College coach in the 1980s added an even more outlandish twist to this traditional play. He would signal a pitcher to warm up in the right field bullpen and on cue the player would throw the ball he is warming up with past the bullpen catcher. At the same time the pitcher on the real mound faked a throw to first. So now the runner sees a loose ball rolling in the bullpen and thinks it was the one thrown by the pitcher who actually still has the game ball. Another popular play has the pitcher fake a pick off throw to second with middle infield-ers diving and acting like they had missed the throw behind sec-ond. The pitcher still holds the ball and then throws to third to nail the runner who has been deceived into thinking the ball has been thrown into center field.

A Florida university used what I consider one of the most innovative trick plays. There was a runner on third, less than two out, and the defensive team was in the third base dugout. When the batter struck out, the catcher immediately rolled the ball toward the mound and broke toward the dugout. The pitcher, third baseman, shortstop, and first baseman also quickly moved in that direction, acting as if it was the third out. But while heading toward the third base dugout the first baseman picked up the ball and fired it to the shortstop. Passing by third, the baffled runner straying off third was tagged out. This crafty maneuver of deception could fool the smartest of base runners and third base coaches if done with zeal and the runner lets down his guard for just an instant. However, the runner would have no one to blame except himself and his third base coach, for both should have known better.

Can these plays be morally justified? Can principles be found to guide behavior in these areas? What criteria or guidelines can be followed that give a clearer understanding of the morality of these plays in order to separate the ones that are acceptable from those that are not? And what about the possibility of plays that are moral at one age level but are immoral at another level?

Is There an Ethicist in the House?

First, we must define what a lie is and whether these deceptive plays fit that understanding. What does it mean to tell the truth and what obligation is there to tell the truth on the ball field?

The most demanding understanding of truthfulness is presented by philosopher Immanuel Kant. As Feezell explained in the previous essay, Kant believes there is a moral obligation or duty not to lie. Truthfulness is owed to all men at all times in all situations. Kant insists that "every man has not only a single right but the strictest duty to be truthful in his statements, and this duty he cannot avoid whether it harms him or others."[3] Kant even rejects lies for altruistic reasons (for example, telling your boyfriend he looks great in that awful Hawaiian shirt). "Little white lies" are not acceptable.

Kant's moral test of any action is whether it can be made universal, holding true of all rational beings. One must not do an action unless everyone would be permitted to do so. What if I consider breaking a promise? Can I then universalize it into a maxim so that anyone can break promises whenever it is advantageous, and do I want to live in such a world? This would be absurd and irrational, and thus immoral. If everyone broke promises at will, then no one could ever believe anyone. So

---

[3] Immanuel Kant, "Concerning a Pretended Right to Lie from Motives of Humanity," *Ethical Choice* (New York: The Free Press, 1970), p. 22.

truthfulness is the formal duty of everyone. A lie "always hurts another; if not another (particular) man, at least mankind in general by making the source of all right (law) useless."[4] The liar also destroys his own dignity. "The essential evil of lying therefore lies in the maxim itself, regardless of motives for and consequences of telling lies."[5] But Kant's conception of lies is too broad. This understanding of lies and deception would make all of the previously described baseball plays immoral.

Augustine and Thomas Aquinas (1225–1274) are among those theistic thinkers who completely ban all falsehoods without exception because of injunctions against lying, but they make important distinctions among lies. Aquinas differentiates between lies, defining three types with only the last one constituting the traditional understanding of the lie. They are officious or helpful ones told for our neighbor's good, jocose ones told in jest, and mischievous or malicious ones told to injure another.[6]

Jocose lies are told for amusement, without malice, so they are falsehoods that do not really count as lies. Lying to opponents as a form of strategic deception in an artificial recreational context is not a lie in the traditional malicious understanding of an immoral lie. It is to be expected in the context of a game. These plays of deception, though taken very seriously by those, especially, who are fooled, must fall into the category of jocose lies because the game itself is an activity of amusement. The artificially created competition in sports allows the opponents to deceive one another within the rules and no one is injured. The player who uses the various forms of the hidden ball trick, the play where the defense pretends a strike out is the third out when it is not, the fake throw to a base, or the infielder who fakes a pop up when a runner is stealing is playing the actor.

In the movies Vin Diesel may lie and deceive but in that context no one is actually injured or harmed. Similarly, in baseball the jocose lie should be expected from opponents, but the intentional lie to the umpire is another story. The play which attempts to distort the truth and deceive the unbiased officials is

---

[4] *Ibid.*, p. 20.

[5] Roger J. Sullivan, *An Introduction to Kant's Ethics* (New York: Cambridge University Press, 1994), p. 58.

[6] Thomas Aquinas, *Summa Theologica*, at http//www.newadvent.org/summa/311002.htm.

mischievous because it tries to get an undeserved advantage. A runner intentionally shortcutting a base, a catcher pulling a pitch, a first baseman coming off the bag early to get a call are examples of mischievous lies. The following examples further demonstrate this difference.

In the first situation there is a fly ball to left field in Pac Bell Park. The Giants leftfielder, Barry Bonds, sprints in, dives for the ball and rolls over coming up with the ball. He actually traps the ball but the umpire cannot see the trap, and Bonds is so quick and masterful at acting like he has made the catch, he sells everyone in attendance, including the umpires, that he has caught the ball. This is a common occurrence and occasionally the deceptive fielder gets the call due to his quick thinking and acting. Compare this to the play where there is a runner on second base and there is a deep fly ball to Ramirez, the leftfielder in Fenway Park. In this case Ramirez runs toward the Green Monster turning his back to home plate and looks up, acting as if the ball is going to hit high off the wall and bounce back. But as the ball descends, he quickly turns toward the infield and with his back to the wall catches the ball on the fly. He then rifles it to second to double off the runner who has been decoyed into believing the ball was going to be off the wall.

What is the difference between these two plays of deception? In the first, the outfielder is trying to deceive the umpires and really is lying by his actions that he caught a ball that he did not catch. This is a mischievous lie. By the rules of the game he is trying to gain credit for something he is not worthy of claiming. In the second case, Ramirez is trying to trick the runner into going when he should not. He is not trying to get away with anything illegal, nor is he trying to deceive the umpires. And anyone who has played the game a few years should be aware enough of the game not to be caught by this type of trickery that is parallel to a hidden ball trick. A player fooled in this manner has no one to blame but himself. He has been "gotten." He is caught by a jocose lie.

The nature of competitive sport should teach the participant that the opponent is not to be trusted in the game, but that does not diminish the character of the person. It is not the same thing, however, to intentionally attempt to deceive the umpire for the purpose of gaining an advantage or to get a call in one's favor. This is a case of dishonesty and should create a sense of guilt and shame in the athlete who attempts to gain an undeserved call. The lie to the opponent could be described as a jocular lie and thus not really a lie while the lie to the umpire is a mischievous lie and therefore immoral.

Dietrich Bonhoeffer (1906–1945), a theologian who was martyred in Nazi Germany for plotting an assassination of Hitler, writes that truth-telling "depends on the situation in which one speaks and acts." He believes that often our definitions of lies are improper.

> The usual definition of the lie as a conscious discrepancy between thought and speech is completely inadequate. This would include, for example, even the most harmless April-fool joke. The concept of the 'jocular lie', which is maintained in Catholic moral theology takes away from the lie its characteristic features of seriousness and malice (and, conversely takes away from the joke its characteristic features of harmless playfulness and freedom); no more unfortunate concept could have been thought of. Joking has nothing whatever to do with lying, and the two must not be reduced to a common denominator.[7]

Bonhoeffer also says that when evaluating truth, three things should also be considered. They are: perceiving who causes me to speak and what entitles me to speak, perceiving the place at which I stand, keeping the context in mind as one speaks. All speech is subject to certain conditions: meaning its place, its time and its task, and consequently also its limits.[8]

Can we apply this distinction to faking an injury? Faking an injury to gain an advantage is a form of deception which occurs in a variety of sports, particularly in sports that are governed by a clock and the injury serves the purpose of stopping the clock or delaying play. This does not happen often in baseball because there is no clock. But there are times when it can be advantageous in baseball. Occasionally a coach or player delays the game either to give a relief pitcher time to warm up or to stall for a rainout. To fake an injury is an immoral mischievous lie, but an umpire should be able to recognize and control this

---

[7] Dietrich Bonhoeffer, "What Is Meant by 'Telling the Truth'?" in *Ethics* (New York: Macmillan, 1960), p. 331.

[8] *Ibid.*, p. 333.

behavior. Faking a leg injury might be used in baseball to decoy the other team into thinking a person is hurt and thus unable to run. This might cause the defense to let down its guard, allowing the runner to steal on the next pitch. But in this case the defense should expect something and if they are caught letting down their guard, then it is their own fault. This type of deception is a jocose lie.

A more serious form of faking an injury is when a batter falls to the ground, pretending a fair ball actually hit his foot. He is hoping to persuade the umpire that it is a foul ball instead of a potential ground out. This, too, is attempting to gain what does not rightfully belong to the hitter and is thus a mischievous lie.

Five Questions about Good Sportsmanship

The following are five questions that should be asked when evaluating the morality of strategic plays of deception in baseball.

1. Are the Constitutive Rules of the Game Being Broken?

It's wrong to use plays that violate the written rules of the game. Cheating by using corked bats, illegal substances on the ball, and teaching runners to cut bases are quite obviously illegal and immoral. But rule breaking should also include plays where those not actually playing in the game attempt to directly influence the outcome of the game. This would include the players scrambling in the bullpen on the fake overthrow, the third base coach breaking toward the batter with a runner on third attempting to draw a balk on the pitcher, or a person stealing signals from the centerfield bleachers using binoculars. These examples should be viewed as illegal activities and umpires and league officials should not permit them.

When a coach teaches these types of rule-breaking plays the player should keep his integrity and refuse to cheat. Cleveland sports writer, Hal Lebovitz, tells the story of pitcher Al Worthington who was sitting below the outfield scoreboard in the bullpen in San Francisco and noticed that his team was stealing signs from the bleachers. Worthington went to his manager, Bill Rigney and said, "This is against all that I believe and if you do not stop I will have to leave the club." Rigney knew that if

Worthington left the club he would have to provide an explanation and the spy story would become public.[9] Those in positions of authority, whether they are owners, administrators, or parents should never tolerate rule breaking. A player should disobey a coach who gives an illegal directive and thus suffer the fate of the whistle-blower in business. It is an illegal order and just as a soldier must disobey an illegal order, so this coach should be disobeyed when directing an illegal order.

2. TOWARD WHOM IS THE DECEPTION DIRECTED?

If a play is designed to fool the umpires rather than the opponents, then it is an immoral play. There is no moral justification for deceiving the unbiased arbitrators. Therefore the double squeeze example where the baserunners take advantage of unsuspecting umpires is dishonest and bad sportsmanship (as is the deceptive trapped ball, the infielder's fake tag, and the batter pretending a ball has gone off his foot). Even if these are accepted practices in the game, there is no moral justification for them. The burden of proof is on the one attempting this type of play to justify its morality. These are all cases where a player is attempting to deceive the officials as a method of strategy in order to gain an advantage in the contest. These deceivers are trying to get away with something against the rules: using illegal equipment, skipping a base, or receiving credit for a catch where one has not been made.

How should we judge a catcher framing a pitch? Framing can be understood in two different ways, one acceptable and one not acceptable. It is moral to catch a pitch in a way that gives the umpire a good look. The catcher keeps the mitt from moving out of the strike zone so the pitcher might get a call on a pitch on the corner. This is a skill to be mastered. On the other hand, it is not proper to pull a pitch and attempt to persuade the umpire that a ball was really a strike. Over sixty years ago, Ethan Allen, an old-time major leaguer and later baseball manager for Yale University (where he coached ex-President George Bush, Sr.) wrote a book that explained exactly how a catcher

---

[9] Hal Lebovitz, "Sosa, Spitballs, and Baseball Cheats," *Mansfield News Journal* (June 9th, 2003).

should pull a pitch.[10] Though it's widely practiced, it is still bad sportsmanship. The same thing is true for the first baseman who masters the skill of pulling his foot the moment he catches the ball and one who is taught to pull his foot an instant before catching the throw in order to get the call on a close play.

3. What Is the Context of the Lie?

Many plays of deception should not be classified as lies because of the context. At most, such lies are jocular ones and thus not immoral. Lies told in the context of an artificial game or set-up are not equivalent to any other lie. They should be excused if they are told as part of strategy in a game but not to gain an unfair advantage. Deceiving Manny Ramirez by telling him it is a foul ball and asking Mike Hegan to step off the base are examples of jocular lies. This type of lying is expected and acting is part of the game. The participants, or those duped, have agreed in advance to be a part of a contest which could involve deception. It is excluded from the prohibitions against lying since no harm is intended and it is expected by all wise participants. Baseball is trivial; no one really gets hurt. Players should be taught that opponents should never be completely trusted in the midst of the contest. A joke cannot be a lie.

Of course this cannot be carried beyond the field. There are forms of deception which involve lying but not all forms of deception involve lying. Many of the deceptive plays in baseball are more like keeping a "poker face" in a game of cards than like lying to a girlfriend about going out on her behind her back. Aquinas seems to have it right when he said that there are jocular lies, and Bonhoeffer has it right when he introduced the context of lies.

4. What Is the Age and Skill Level of the Participants?

The age and skill level of those participating must be considered. T-ballers should not be taught to use the hidden ball trick. By high school, players should know the game well enough not

---

[10] Ethan Allen, *Major League Baseball: Techniques and Tactics* (New York: Macmillan, 1938).

to be duped by the various deceptive plays. Also, plays of deception that risk injury to younger players should be banned. It is important to understand, though, that various deceptive plays force coaches to know and teach the fundamentals to athletes at an early age. No runner should be caught by the hidden ball if he learns not to begin his lead until the pitcher is on the mound. When stealing second she should be taught to glimpse over her shoulder toward the plate, and if she does so, she will never be fooled by a catcher throwing a pop up to the infielders who call "mine." Good coaching of fundamentals eliminates the success rate of these plays and can even make the team attempting them look "bush." Only because so few players really know the game, there seems to be an increase in the use of these plays. But age appropriateness must be considered.

5. DO THE DECEPTIVE ACTIONS RESPECT THE GAME AND THE OPPONENTS?

There must be respect for the game--its written and unwritten rules—along with respect for one's opponents. Cheaters do not respect the game. Neither do coaches who spend more time on trick plays than on fundamentals. A third base coach who sprints a couple of steps toward the batter in an attempt to distract the pitcher into committing a balk has no respect for the game or the opponents. Major leaguers know how to retaliate in ways that attempt to keep respect for the game, but the physical means they use cannot be used at lower levels of play. Coaches at lower levels should talk to their players about what it means to respect the game and to respect the other team. As odd as this may sound, respect also must be reinforced by umpires and fans. Someone who has played and really understands the game of baseball should be able to teach which acts of deception are respectful of the game and of one's opponents. If, though, strategic plays of deception can be occasionally used, they should not be used to detract from or replace a team's basic skills. And though young players should be taught to be alert and that the members on the other team should not be believed naively, it is crucial to treat opponents with respect.

So perhaps Diogenes wouldn't be completely satisfied if he wandered into one of our ballparks. He might have to continue on down the road, still hoping to find an honest man, maybe in football stadiums instead. Plays of deception will continue to be a part of baseball, but they should be examined and evaluated. The illegal form of the double squeeze, the Perry puffball, and the corked bat are immoral and should be penalized severely. We must renounce and disallow those deceptive plays that create an unfair advantage or attempt to deceive the umpires. They cannot be morally justified.

Character does matter, and the player who lies to or deceives the umpires is not playing with honesty or integrity; he does not understand the nature of sport, and is diminished in his character. Plays that might injure baseball novices should be banned. However we should watch for and enjoy those trick plays that are good strategy and should be expected by opponents. Baseball players should know and learn at an early age that the opponent is not to be blindly trusted in the context of the contest. The jocose lie should be an expected strategic part of sport. Finally, respect for the opponent and the game should be maintained. This respect should prohibit plays of deception from becoming such an important form of strategy that they replace the real strategic decisions of the game, such as when to bunt or steal, when to replace a pitcher, or how to execute a proper squeeze play.

Fifth Inning:
Baseball and
America

Baseball has always been a distinctly American game. While the rest of the world plays soccer, American children wear baseball caps and spit sunflower seeds in the hopes of making it to the show. While some fans believe the wealthy, bickering New York Yankees of the 1970s personified America at its worst, Eric Bronson argues that such sports page drama is good for democracy. William J. Morgan thinks that fans understandably romanticize baseball, not because Americans are perfect, but because they dream it's possible.

9 | Democracy and Dissent: Why America Needs Reggie Jackson

ERIC BRONSON

If the world were a perfect place, it wouldn't be.

—Yogi Berra, baseball philosopher

Pittsburgh Pirates slugger Willie Stargell was never much of a singer. And yet, there he was in October, 1979, all over the local television and radio shows, leading a host of tone-deaf Pirates in a rousing rendition of Sister Sledge's hit single, "We are Family." Down 3 games to 1 to the formidable Baltimore Orioles, Pittsburgh's adopted anthem never seemed more fitting. The Pirates loved their coaches, their fans, and especially their captain Stargell, affectionately nicknamed "Pops." The soon-to-be comeback World Series champions really *were* a family.

What a difference a year makes.

When the New York Yankees won the World Series in 1978, nobody was singing songs of familial love. Their manager had resigned midway through the season after a nervous breakdown, their solitary captain was barely on speaking terms with the team's superstar, and throughout the year, the press was awash with stories of backstabbing and infighting. The famous words of nineteenth-century novelist Leo Tolstoy rang true: "All happy families are alike; every unhappy family is unhappy in its own way."

Obviously, there are many paths to success. While sports radio is filled with brilliant diatribes on the importance of team

143

chemistry, defining "chemistry" isn't so easy. Sometimes angry dissension is just as important as happy consensus. We find a parallel argument in political philosophy. According to some philosophers, conflicting personalities and spirited discord are often helpful to the larger society. Where egos clash, people are forced to rethink their values, and that sets the stage for personal growth. Without such growth, societies (and baseball teams) can become stagnant.

A foray into political philosophy might be helpful in figuring out how to understand team chemistry. America loves a good argument. If there's anything to learn from the Yankees' success in the late 1970s, it's that dysfunctional relationships can be just as American as apple pie and Sister Sledge.

Long Live Both King Georges

Dissension and disorder are generally thought to be detrimental to a team's success. In Japanese baseball, for example, disrupting a team's "harmony" is one of the worst things a player can do to a team.[1] The 1978 and 1979 Yankees did not have harmony (or team chemistry, as it is more commonly referred to in America). Roger Kahn begins his excellent book on the Yankees by observing, "Whoever first proclaimed the mantra, 'There is no I in team,' was a better speller than a thinker."[2] So how important is getting along with each other?

Political philosophers have long struggled with this question. America's founding fathers, for example, argued frequently (ironically) over the issue of how much dissension should be protected or encouraged in a free society. In seeking to establish a strong union, they had the onerous task of finding the balance between the destructive breakdown of order and the need for free speech in all strong democracies. Ultimately, they decided that democracies, like baseball teams, can thrive with a little friction along the way. In this essay, I have no intention of arguing that baseball teams are democratic. They aren't. But if we look at the political philosophies behind the American experiment and the ideas behind the construction of the

---

[1] See Chapter 14 in this volume.
[2] Roger Kahn, *October Men* (Orlando: Harcourt, 2003).

Yankees in the late 1970s, we find a consistent message: people are selfish, and that can be a very good thing.

First, let's be clear about what we mean by "democracy." The word comes to us by way of the Ancient Greeks, combining the Greek word, *demos*, meaning "people," and *kratia*, meaning "rule by." This gives us our handy definition, "rule by the people." In a time of kings, pharaohs, and gods, rule by the people was a revolutionary concept. Around 430 B.C.E., Pericles, the dynamic leader of Athens, gave his version of the Gettysburg Address, honoring the fallen heroes of the Peloponnesian War. Defining Athenian democracy, Pericles said, "In the settling of private disputes, everyone is equal before the law. Election to public office is made on the basis of ability, not on the basis of membership to a particular class."[3] This was the democratic way of life that Pericles believed was worth fighting for.

Western Europe took another two thousand years to realize that the Greeks might have known a thing or two about government, after all. During the Enlightenment of the seventeenth and eighteenth centuries, philosophically-minded folks like John Locke in England, Jean-Jacque Rousseau in France, and Thomas Jefferson in America finally began to seriously reconsider the Athenian model of free speech and democracy. In 1776, Jefferson's Declaration of Independence made a formal break from the feudal aristocracy of King George III. Thirteen years later, the French followed suit, basing their revolution on Enlightenment ideas that looked to Greek philosophy for inspiration.

Thanks to the Ancient Greeks, and later the Enlightenment thinkers, the belief that everyone is equal before the law and that people should be judged on ability, not birthright, have become almost common sense in the United States.[4] Such faith in the meritocracy was also a hallmark of the 1979 Pirates. Good ol' Pops was famous for handing out gold stars to anyone who made a nice play on the ball field. It didn't matter how much money you made or how influential your parents were. When Stargell gave you a star, you stuck it on the left hand side of your

---

[3] "The Funeral Speech," in Thucydides, *The Speeches of Pericles*, translated by H.G. Edinger (New York: Unger, 1979) pp. 33–34.
[4] For arguments to the contrary, see Chapters 11, 12, and 16 in this volume.

baseball cap and wore it with pride. Richie Hebner, a veteran journeyman infielder, once earned a gold star after hitting a pinch-hit grand slam off feared closer Lee Smith. "I'd been around forever, but it gave me goose bumps," Hebner recalled. "Imagine how a young player felt after getting a star from Pops."[5]

Let's not make the mistake of assuming that the Pirates were all treated equally. Pops was treated differently from Hebner, and as a veteran, Hebner was treated differently than rookies. But there is still a considerable difference between the Pirates and the Yankees of the late 1970s. The swashbuckling Yankees have never handed out stars, nor have they ever been so warm and fuzzy. From Babe Ruth to Reggie Jackson, individual self-interests are a little more pronounced when you wear the pin-stripes. Even Joltin' Joe DiMaggio held out for more money than the stalwart Lou Gehrig was earning in 1938. "I'll stick right here until I get what I want," DiMaggio insisted.[6] Ultimately, he caved in, but the message was clear. On the Yankees, the individual is sometimes more important than the team.

It is therefore no surprise that when George Steinbrenner bought the Yankees in 1973, for the modest price of $10 million, baseball's noisiest aristocracy (rule by the privileged class) would be kept intact. In 1975, Steinbrenner forever changed the face of baseball when he signed pitcher Catfish Hunter to a five-year deal totaling $3,750,000. Two years later, the brash home run hitter Reggie Jackson broke the bank again, signing another mega deal with the Yankees, propelling them to World Series victories in 1977 and 1978. Since Catfish's signing, and the beginning of free agency, baseball salaries have skyrocketed at a mind-numbing clip, and to this day, small market fans still caustically dismiss Steinbrenner's Yankees as "the best team money can buy."

Steinbrenner is a hands-on owner; that isn't exactly a news flash. From 1977 to 1989, he fired managers fifteen times, had players traded or sent to the minor leagues immediately after poor performances, fired one long-time secretary after she took too long to answer a phone call, and generally kept himself

---

[5] http://www.usatoday.com/sports/baseball/comment/bodley/
2001-04-10-bodley.htm.
[6] Quoted in Richard Ben Cramer, *The Hero's Life* (New York: Simon and Schuster, 2000), p. 116.

involved in all aspects of the Yankees' day-to-day operations. On Steinbrenner's Yankees, a belligerent hierarchy is still firmly in place. Frequently spoofed on *Seinfeld* and *Saturday Night Live*, the man America loves to hate covets his power and relishes his apt nickname, "The Boss."

Critics argue that Steinbrenner's bullying style of leadership is bad for baseball and, by extension, bad for America. His aristocratic, even dictatorial, pursuit of profits at the expense of personal relationships and human emotions flies in the face of the simpler Puritanical values that revolutionaries like Benjamin Franklin endorsed. While Boss George's disdain for his employees may be more reminiscent of King George than of George Washington, the Yankees' "evil empire" adds an important component to our world. We rightfully rejoice when affable teams like the 1979 Pirates, the 2002 Anaheim Angels, and the 2003 Florida Marlins win the World Series, but we also need the drama of the old-time cocky, brooding, temperamental Yankees. At least that's what political philosopher Alexis de Tocqueville (1805–1859) might have said, were he alive to see Reggie Jackson hit three home runs at Yankee Stadium in the decisive game six of the 1977 World Series.

A *Philosophe*[7] in America

There was a time, believe it or not, when the French loved America. After the American Revolution, Thomas Jefferson and Benjamin Franklin were international celebrities, living abroad in Paris, where the French were gearing up for their own assault on the long-standing aristocracy. Later, the French would give us the Statue of Liberty as a symbol of the bond of democracy that connected both countries.

The French Revolution didn't end as cleanly as the American war, however. In 1831, Tocqueville, uneasy with France's political instability, left for the New World in the hopes of learning something about democracy. "No novelty in the United States struck me more vividly during my stay there than the equality of

---

[7] *Philosophe* is French for "philosopher." "The *Philosophes*" also refers to a specific group of eighteenth-century French philosophers, artists, and scientists who believed in reason and progress—typical Enlightenment values that influenced Tocqueville.

conditions," Tocqueville wrote on arrival, grandly proclaiming, "A great democratic revolution is taking place in our midst." Thus began the introduction to his monumental work, *Democracy in America*, published in his native French.[8] In search of American democracy, Tocqueville criss-crossed the country, interviewing Americans of all stripes, including the last living signer of the Declaration of Independence, Charles Carroll. Through Tocqueville's eyes, we can learn something about our own democratic way of life, its strengths and limits, and exactly what the George Steinbrenners and Reggie Jacksons of the world can offer us.

There was much in the American life that Tocqueville believed would benefit the French. Individual rights and the distinctive disregard for honorific titles pointed to the true essence of a democratic revolution that was noticeably absent in nineteenth-century France. The administrative stability of the New World was virtually unheard of elsewhere. For sixty years, Tocqueville observed, Americans had been "not only the most prosperous but also the most stable of all the peoples in the world."[9] The remarkable calm in America contrasted starkly with the political tumult that followed the revolution in France. Tocqueville, of course, spoke almost exclusively with white men. Like their Greek counterparts, American voters did not include slaves or women, so words like "equality" and "majority rule" should ring false to the modern ear. Still, Tocqueville observed that in the countryside, rebellions were few and far between. A placid contentment had washed over the citizenry in the first half of the nineteenth century; homespun friendliness was palpable in every town. As Tocqueville humorously observes, "If I contradict every word an American says to show him that his conversation bores me, he will constantly renew his efforts to convince me. . . . Unless I tell him plainly, the man will not understand that he exasperates me. . . ."[10] In the United States, majority rule was enforced in many aspects of American law and culture, and the newly independent Americans were the first ones to talk about it.

---

[8] All further references to Tocqueville are to *Democracy in America*, J.P. Mayer, ed., translated by George Lawrence (New York: Harper and Row, 1969).
[9] Author's Preface to the twelfth edition.
[10] p. 569.

Along with such pathological good humor, however, Tocqueville also discovered some problems with this new democratic experiment. Where everyone is equal, everyone is looked at as the same. One offshoot of equality is that "the democratic citizen sees nothing but people more or less like himself around him."[11] And while it is true that rugged individualism breeds new people, new ideas, and a regular flow of new expressions, the old cliché reminds us that the more things change, the more they remain the same. "American society appears animated because men and things are constantly changing," Tocqueville writes, but "it is monotonous because all these changes are alike."[12] Democratic societies can go through a leveling in which even the most gifted citizens aspire to mediocrity.

What naturally occurs in democratic societies such as ours is what German Philosopher Friedrich Nietzsche (1844–1900) termed "the herd mentality." Given the choice, people generally prefer to go along with the pack rather than risk independent thought. There is comfort and protection when one joins the dominant group. Tocqueville observed this group thinking in his travels. He writes, "The majority in the United States takes over the business of supplying the individual with a quantity of ready-made opinions and so relieves him of the necessity of forming his own."[13] Tocqueville's concern about majority rule still resonates with us today. Consider, for example, the hugely popular *Matrix* movies and their persistent theme of breaking out of the herd in order to think independently.

When the majority rules, people with minority viewpoints are often afraid to speak out or are pressured to stay silent. This democratic leveling can have nefarious consequences for those who do take the red pill and speak against authority. Whereas in feudal Europe the king could not entirely control all opposing viewpoints, the democratic majority has the power and the will to keep dissenters quiet. Tocqueville noticed that one can argue against an unpopular politician, but not against the prevailing majority viewpoints. In our own time we've seen people berated for sailing against the prevailing winds. When comedian

---

[11] p. 439.
[12] p. 614.
[13] p. 435.

Bill Maher and the country music group, Dixie Chicks, spoke out against the wars in Afghanistan and Iraq, they were castigated not by the law, but by public opinion. Maher lost his job altogether as host of the television show *Politically Incorrect*, later claiming he was the first to be "Dixie Chicked."[14]

Tocqueville foresaw this ruthless strain in democratic societies. He saw two potential paths of equal rights: "one turns each man's attention to new thoughts, while the other would induce him freely to give up thinking at all." And if we go the latter route, then how far have we really progressed from the shackles of the old aristocracy? "Men would by no means have found the way to live in independence; they would only have succeeded in the difficult task of giving slavery a new face. There is matter for deep reflection there."[15]

If Tocqueville is to have any relevance today, it is in his prophetic cautions about the dangers of democracy. Whenever everyone thinks alike, no one thinks. If we are serious about our freedom of thought and speech, then we need to safeguard and encourage dissident voices wherever they cause a disturbance. In democratic societies it is healthy and important to have headaches, conflicts, unpopular opinions, outrageous personalities, thoroughly unlikable neighbors. America needs its outcasts and outlaws. In short, America needs the Yankees.

The Bronx Zoo

In the New York press, the "Bronx Zoo" became the fashionable nickname of the championship teams. Even while they were winning, Reggie Jackson and his malcontent teammates routinely broke the rules and consistently tried to break each other. Today, baseball's corporate culture encourages camaraderie and acceptance. But Yankees owner George Steinbrenner had a different take in 1977. "Confrontation is good for a ball club," he said. "Some ball clubs get better in crisis."[16] Tocqueville theo-

---

[14] It's also true that Maher's ratings had already been slipping, but the backlash to his remarks certainly sealed the deal.

[15] p. 436.

[16] Quoted in Maury Allen, *Damn Yankee* (New York: New York Times Books, 1980), p. 207.

rized that confrontation could be good for a democracy. Can we apply his theory to baseball teams?

When Jackson came to the Bronx in 1977, he turned the Yankees upside down. But let's not give Mr. October too much credit. The Bombers had their share of turmoil before Jackson swaggered onto baseball's biggest stage. They weren't exactly forming lasting friendships with each other in the clubhouse.

New York won the pennant against the Kansas City Royals the year before, on Chris Chambliss's dramatic home run in the bottom of the ninth inning. Earlier in the year, pitcher Mel Stottlemyre questioned the trade for Chambliss, innocently asking, "What the hell do we need him for?"[17]

The Yankee captain at the time was all-star catcher Thurman Munson, not exactly your Mister Sunshine. Teammate Sparky Lyle once said of him, "Munson's not moody, he's just mean. When you're moody, you're nice sometimes." Rich Gossage recalls that Munson once handed him the ball and asked him how he intended to blow the game. Not that "Goose" was a clubhouse joy himself. His 1979 season was cut short after he broke his thumb in a vicious fistfight outside the showers with teammate Cliff Johnson (though, to be fair, it was Reggie Jackson who instigated the fight).

While we're on the subject of pitchers, Steinbrenner's free-agent poster child Catfish Hunter came from the Oakland A's, a team with a reputation for less than wholesome behavior. The 1974 A's, featuring Hunter and Jackson, "stopped swinging at each other long enough to play a complicated game brilliantly."[18] Before coming to the Yankees, Catfish's résumé on the A's included instigating a fight that left future Hall of Famer Rollie Fingers with five stitches in his head, fighting his own friend Sal Bando on a fairly regular basis, and, less seriously, calling his boss "a cheap son of a bitch."

In baseball the team often takes on the personality of its manager. In 1976, Steinbrenner hired one of the best minds in

---

[17] There are a number of sources detailing the Yankees' public relations lapses. Rich Gossage writes of the Yankees' travails in *The Goose Is Loose* (New York: Ballantine, 2000), pp. 111–187. I have also relied heavily on *Damn Yankee*, David Falkner's, *The Last Yankee* (New York: Simon and Schuster, 1992), and Kahn's *October Men*.

[18] *Sports Illustrated* (September 6th, 1999), p. 80.

baseball, Billy Martin. Martin's overly aggressive style of play became known as *Billy Ball*, while his overly aggressive barroom decorum became known as *Billy Brawl*. His battles with Steinbrenner soon became a tabloid writer's dream. Martin shared some of Steinbrenner's aristocratic tendencies. "Let him manage," Martin often huffed, "and I'll count his money." The Yankee manager also frequently questioned his players' honesty. When asked his opinion about the perceived Jackson-Steinbrenner alliance, Martin retorted, "One's a born liar and the other's convicted." Steinbrenner, to his credit, fired Martin five different times before offering him a lifetime contract in the late 1980s.

The point is that when the Yankees signed Jackson, they knew he'd make himself right at home. Non-baseball fans were introduced to number 44 in 1988, when he attempted to kill the English Queen in the movie, *Naked Gun*. But on the field, Jackson had already earned a reputation for playing by his own set of rules. In 1969, Jackson, then on the Oakland A's, started a brawl with the Minnesota Twins by charging the mound, after a pitch went four feet over his head. The first-year manager who ordered the bean ball was, of course, Billy Martin. Like Martin, Steinbrenner, Catfish, and nearly every other Yankee, Reggie put himself first, the team second. His autobiography, published by Playboy Press, informatively begins, "My name is Reggie Jackson and I am the best in baseball."[19] It took a dedicated psychiatrist to help the 1973 American League MVP learn "that R-E-G-G-I-E doesn't spell J-E-S-U-S."[20]

Before Jackson even took a swing in pinstripes he graciously put the hard-nosed Yankee captain on notice. "I'm the straw that stirs the drink," he said. "Munson thinks he can be the straw that stirs the drink, but he can only stir it bad."[21] It was obviously only a matter of time before Jackson took on his manager.

The most famous Martin-Jackson dispute played out in Boston's Fenway Park in June of 1977. Martin, believing Jackson loafed getting to a Jim Rice hit (allowing Rice to stretch it into a double), made an unusual move. While going out to change his pitcher, Martin also yanked his right fielder, humiliating Jackson

---

[19] *Reggie: A Season with a Superstar* (Chicago: Playboy Press, 1975).
[20] *Ibid.*, p. 5.
[21] Jackson later denied using those exact words. See *October Men*, p. 137.

on national TV. Jackson calmly loped off the field and then charged Martin in the dugout for all the country to see. As the two prepared for their long awaited fistfight, coaches immediately jumped in to salvage what was left of Yankee pride.

One year later, after they made nice and hugged in the locker room, Martin called for his cleanup hitter to lay down a bunt, another unorthodox baseball move. When the infield moved in, Jackson was instructed to hit away. Gravely insulted, Jackson ignored Martin and bunted two more pitches foul, striking out. Jackson was later suspended by the team, and Martin was forced to resign soon after. Just another bump in the road to a second World Series victory.

Perhaps there is some merit to Steinbrenner's guide to success. Some crises, however brutal, *are* good for us. In 1776, the great Scottish philosopher Adam Smith (1723–1790) published his magnum opus, The *Wealth of Nations*. In it, he argues that if people are encouraged to pursue their self interests, society will benefit as a whole. Today, for better or worse, America's capitalist culture still revolves around Smith's principle.

Even two hundred years ago, Smith's brand of *laissez fare* capitalism was an easy fit with newly-formed democracies like the United States. In the idealized market economy, everyone is on equal footing. Only supply and demand should dictate who lives and dies with the most toys. If everyone has a chance to strike it rich, then there naturally develops a fierce competition to see who can outperform the other. People will trade goods and think up wonderful new inventions just to get an edge up on their neighbors. While it may seem like a dog-eat-dog world on the inside, the community is strengthened by the competition.

The Yankees played hard and well against the other American League teams of the late 1970s, and as we have seen, they also competed against each other. Obviously, the Yankees had good pitching and hitting, which largely explains why they won the World Series two years in a row. But lots of teams are good on paper and never win. That's where the intangibles come in. The Yankees were good in 1976, but were swept by Sparky Anderson's Big Red Machine in the World Series. With the addition of Jackson, New York got more than a topnotch home run hitter. The Yankees added passion and discord, and with those intangibles, they also added two World Series trophies. Careful readers of Adam Smith should not be surprised.

Our Big, Fat, Greek Democracy

The truth is, many famous philosophers besides Smith have argued in favor of personality conflicts. In the time of Pericles, it was Socrates (470–399 B.C.E.) who staked his life on his freedom to irritate the majority. In the *Apology*, Plato writes about his mentor's trial after the masses condemned Socrates to death for crimes against the majority. Socrates believed these crimes amounted to no more than questioning majority viewpoints. "I have never lived an ordinary quiet life," Socrates bemoans. "I did not care for the things that most people care about . . ."[22] He compares himself to a gadfly on a horse, rousing the great city of Athens to question its contented ignorance. Socrates was condemned for his minority viewpoint and put to death. The great democratic experiment self-destructed soon after.

The Athenian democracy ultimately did not encourage the individual to break rules and challenge authority. And, it might be argued that such intolerance marked the beginning of the end for Athens. Tocqueville also has warned us not to allow the majority to silence its rebels so easily. Will we listen?

Even the most astute of America's founding fathers weren't big fans of Plato and Socrates. Jefferson struggled with Plato's political philosophy, finally dismissing it as "foggy-minded." John Adams was kinder to Plato. From his reading of the Greek philosopher, Adams learned "that sneezing is a cure for the Hickups," so one should always carry snuff.[23] It's easy to understand Tocqueville's disgust: "Less attention, I suppose, is paid to philosophy in the United States than in any other country of the civilized world."[24]

Not every American is well versed in Socrates or Tocqueville, and we continue to discourage dissent. In 1963, four years before Reggie Jackson broke into the big leagues, Martin Luther King, Jr. (1929–1968) was arrested for participating in a civil rights demonstration without a legal permit. While in jail, King

---

[22] *The Apology*, in *The Collected Dialogues of Plato*, Edith Hamilton and Huntington Cairns, eds., translated by Hugh Tredennick (Princeton: Princeton University Press, 1989), 36b.

[23] Letter to Thomas Jefferson, dated July 16th, 1814, in *The Adams-Jefferson Letters*, ed. Lester J. Cappon (Chapel Hill: University of North Carolina Press, 1987), p. 437.

[24] *Democracy in America*, p. 429.

received a letter from rabbis and priests imploring him to follow the rules. In an open letter, King responded that following rules oftentimes causes more long-term damage than breaking rules. Tension and conflict, he argued, is healthy for democracy.

> This may sound rather shocking. But I must confess that I am not afraid of the word *tension*. . . . Just as Socrates felt that it was necessary to create a tension in the mind so that individuals could rise from the bondage of myths and half-truths to the unfettered realm of creative analysis and objective appraisal, we must see the need of having nonviolent gadflies.[25]

It is the majority of Americans, quietly following unjust laws, that destroys our country more forcefully than any common criminal can. As King writes in his letter, "Lukewarm acceptance is much more bewildering than outright rejection."[26] King, as we know, was killed for speaking out against the majority. As Tocqueville warned, such people are oftentimes silenced by other citizens when majorities are allowed to rule democracies.

Jackson usually spoke his mind, but of course, he was no Martin Luther King. My point is only that Jackson's brawling 1978 Yankees, and Stargell's brotherly 1979 Pirates are *both* good models for successful leadership. While the Pirates remind us of what good values can accomplish, the Yankees force us to rethink such values.

In a democratic society where, as Bob Dylan sings, "everybody must get stoned," the pressures to conform are too powerful to go unquestioned. But besides this political necessity of building tension, there is something aesthetically appealing about the American "rebel without a cause." It is almost as though we have some dim recognition that democracies can level the field *too* much, and we who follow the rules appreciate all the more those who bust out, trampling upon decorum. Journalist Maury Allen once asked a psychiatrist from New York's Bellevue Medical Center to comment on our seemingly irrational fascination with Billy Martin. The psychiatrist allegedly replied:

---

[25] " Letter from Birmingham City Jail," in *I Have a Dream: Writings and Speeches that Changed the World*, James Melvin Washington, ed. (San Francisco: HarperCollins, 1992), pp. 86–87.

[26] *Ibid.*, p. 91.

He acts out our own anger. The athlete in America is a hero figure because we can sublimate our anger through his action. It wouldn't be socially acceptable to slug someone at a bar. It would be socially acceptable conduct to sit in the stands and egg Billy Martin on against an umpire, an authority figure. He fights our battles for us at no loss of status and with no pain.[27]

So perhaps the Martins, Steinbrenners, and Jacksons help us vicariously experience a more dangerous side of life, left behind in the democratic revolutions of the eighteenth century. Democracies breed order, and we all aspire to a well-ordered life. But an orderly routine quickly becomes an *ordinary* one and then we long for something more. From New York's malcontents we can learn the value of dissent. In democracies, when such dissatisfaction is silenced, life becomes dull. More importantly, as King points out, a contented agreement also breeds injustice and sometimes violence.

Unlike the Pirates, the Yankees acted outrageously, or at the very least, out of the ordinary. They were a happy family only in the way that Archie and Edith Bunker, Gloria and Meathead were happy in the popular TV show, *All in the Family*. In that 1970s comedy, everybody fought with everybody else. And we, laughing along from the comfort of our living rooms, could turn to the Yankees game, still singing along with Archie and Edith: "Those were the daaaaays!"[28]

---

[27] *Damn Yankee*, p. 218. The name of "one of the nation's leading psychiatrists" is not given.

[28] For all their help on this draft, Bill Irwin, Smash'em Bassham, Richard Bronson, Aryn Martin, and Steve Libenson deserve a curtain call.

10 | Baseball and the Search for an American Moral Identity

WILLIAM J. MORGAN

In his fine book, *Achieving Our Country*, Richard Rorty opines that "the only version of national pride encouraged by American popular culture is a simpleminded militaristic chauvinism."[1] I think Rorty is wrong about this, and baseball is my reason for thinking so.

I say baseball because Americans have long claimed baseball as their national game, despite its unmistakable English pedigree, and because their designs on the game were from the very outset moral in character. In the eyes of many, then, baseball conjured up a moral image of America at its best—a nation of strivers moved not so much by greed and crass self-interest as by a larger vision of excellence, one obtained only by arduous effort, social cooperation, and an abiding sense of fair play. Baseball thus gave America a highly visible moral standard by which to measure itself, a standard much in evidence in the daily lives of its citizens as they gathered around the proverbial water cooler to discuss and debate the plays and decisions of yesterday's game.

But while few people question baseball's grip on our national consciousness—it must also be said that few deny that its hold on us has waned of late—some do question its moral

---

[1] Richard Rorty, *Achieving Our Country* (Cambridge, Massachusetts: Harvard University Press, 1998), p. 4.

force. Indeed, the naysayers, or muckrakers, insist that the professed moral credentials of baseball and the other two major sports that make up the holy trinity of American sports (football and basketball) are just a smokescreen meant to divert our attention from what they really are: big businesses fueled by greed and naked self-interest. Moral ideals like fair play, teamwork, playing for the love of the game or the honor of one's country serve here, they argue, only to mask the moral narcissism at work in sports like baseball. What these ideals make it so hard to see is that baseball was never played or watched for moral reasons, that the impulses it inspired were hardly pure or laudable, and that the collective emotions it inflamed were meant to conceal our moral frailties not to correct them.

There is doubtless a grain of truth in their moral indictment. Indeed, there is enough truth in this black and white view of baseball, in the moral failings of those who play and adoringly watch our national pastime, to give moral muckrakers all the ammunition they need to launch their attacks. But there is also something deeply unsatisfying about this cynical picture. What it misses is that our national love affair with baseball is based, at least in part, in what Roger Angell has called the "experience of caring—caring deeply, really caring"[2] It is this caring, this "really caring," that explains why, despite the unceasing commercialization of baseball, people still cling to the ideal of playing the game for something other than monetary reward.

What's going on here is not a triumph of wishful thinking over sober moral analysis, but rather a recognition that because of our all too human moral imperfections we need moral ideals like those projected by baseball to live by. This recognition allows for a different way to approach and analyze baseball as a moral phenomenon, what I call moral reckoning; which, like its muckraking opposite, counsels us not to let our critical guard down, but which, unlike its muckraking opposite, also counsels us that moral criticism cannot survive without something to hang its hat on, namely, without moral ideals.

It's this latter notion of moral reckoning that I want to explore. If America is writ large in baseball, then a primary rea-

---

[2] As quoted in E. Gorn and W. Goldstein, *A Brief History of American Sports* (New York: Hill and Wang, 1993), p. 208.

son why is that the story it tells draws a moral picture of America that is at odds with two prevailing, and morally unflattering sketches of it. I'm referring to the claim that the story of America is nothing more than the story of capitalism, of a country hell-bent on selling itself to the highest bidders, which presently, ironically enough, are mostly foreign bidders, and the not unrelated claim that America is not really a country at all, a commonwealth, but a ragtag collection of a few fortunate folks (the rich and their professional minions) and a not so few unfortunate folks (the working and non-working poor) who have less and less in common with one another.

In opposition to these unflattering portrayals, baseball has always conveyed the idea that America's greatness has nothing essentially to do with making money, but almost everything to do with its collective spirit, with its trying to live up to the standards of a true commonwealth, one devoted to the common good of all rather than the private good of a privileged and moneyed elite.

Don't Show Me the Money!

Walt Whitman, the great chronicler of nineteenth-century America, made the standard case for the first part of this story when he wrote that the charm of baseball derives from the respite it offers from monetary pursuit.[3] Whitman's point is that baseball is anti-capitalistic in character because it is played and watched for the love of the game and not for the love of money, to produce and see excellence and not to see mercenaries exploit baseball for all its worth. This view of baseball as an alternative to money-grubbing business was a constant theme of youth baseball literature of the time, for instance, Gilbert Patten's baseball novels and Frank Merriwell's series (by the end of the nineteenth century these books even surpassed Horatio Alger's rags-to-riches stories in popularity).[4] And despite the unprecedented commercialization of baseball and other sports in recent decades, people still tenaciously cling to the ideal that

---

[3] Walt Whitman, *The Gathering of the Forces* (New York: G.P. Putnam's Sons, 1920), p. 207.

[4] See Bill Brown, "The Meaning of Baseball in 1993," *Public Culture*, Vol. 4, No. 1 (Fall, 1991), p. 54.

sports like baseball are to be valued for something other than
financial gain. In other words, Whitman's story is still in a very
important sense America's story.

But before I consider what makes this part of the tale a moral
one, I must first admit that in echoing Whitman's anti-market
view of baseball, I am already in hot water. Perhaps Whitman is
simply imagining a golden age, when baseball was played and
watched only with the purest motives in mind. Of course, it may
be true that such an innocent time has never really existed.
Again, I defer to Rorty, who writes, "Stories about what a nation
has been and should try to be are not attempts at accurate rep-
resentation," rather they are "better described as . . . argument[s]
about which hopes to allow ourselves and which to forego."[5]
The plain fact is that there isn't any way to tell such stories
because there isn't any way to shed our cultural skins, to transcend our social and historical station, so that we can objectively
evaluate from afar or above, take your pick, what story about
America warrants telling. Also, I'm the first to admit that such
purity of purpose is unknown to baseball and other sports,
which were never immune to the temptations of fortune and
fame, but it is also unknown to any practice human beings have
ever seen fit to take up in a sustained way. It must not be imagined that when Americans stubbornly separate baseball from
business they are guilty of such overreach, of believing that
baseball is played and watched by saints rather than flawed
mortals.

How, then, should we regard these narrative efforts to dis-
entangle baseball from the market? The answer, as suggested
above, is in a moral way, as an attempt to convey that what
makes baseball America's game is its moral import not its ability to attract capital.

My claim that baseball's anti-market laced narrative can be
plausibly read as an attempt to reserve a prominent place for
ethical considerations in our national self-image has something
importantly to do with the morally unfriendly character of the
market itself. For the market is nothing if not a self-regarding
institution in which the private interests and values of the individual reign supreme. That is because the market, by its very
nature, transforms individuals into self-interested actors, and

---

[5] *Achieving Our Country*, p. 13.

their social relations with one another into secondary ones. Whatever value persons, things, and practices enjoy in the market, therefore, is conferred by the subjective desires and preferences of its individual actors. In a word, what I desire is good and what I do not desire is not good. Since I have no reason to care for or value persons, things, and practices save as they affect me personally and practically, there is no room in the market for ethical considerations of these things. Indeed, markets themselves are hostile not only to moral narratives but to narratives of any kind because they are distinctly private forums of expression rather than public ones. For what the market promises to all those who have the desire and capital to enter its inner sanctum is that each of us can pursue our self-interests without having to take into account the reasons, values, and ideals of other market actors.[6]

Viewed in this light, baseball's historically consistent message that it is more than a business, not only invites but mandates moral consideration. For the story it is peddling here is that moral considerations cut to the very heart of baseball and America. That does not mean, to reiterate, that baseball is impervious to market incursions. But it does mean that unlike most of the rest of life, baseball and games like it cannot endure such incursions wholesale without ceasing to be what they are. And what goes for baseball here certainly goes for the self-image of America it projects.

In claiming that baseball is not immune to efforts to commodify it, I am admitting that use value[7] plays some role in sports of this kind. What this concession comes to is that individuals play baseball for much the same reasons they do anything else in everyday life, be it to make money, gain social acceptance and fame, or some combination of these and other features. To the extent it is these subjective reasons that move them to play or watch baseball it is clear that use value is not foreign to baseball or other sports. It's equally clear, however, that use value cannot be given the free reign it is allowed

---

[6] I am indebted here to Elizabeth Anderson's astute analysis of the market. See her *Values in Ethics and Economics* (Cambridge, Massachusetts: Harvard University Press, 1993).

[7] Use value means here treating things, objects, and practices as means to achieve individually conceived and valued ends.

in the market because baseball contains as well goods that are peculiar to it. That is to say, baseball is a social practice that was constructed with certain purposes and goals in mind, and which gave birth to a form of life that otherwise would have been unavailable to us. This form of life is predicated, as are other social practices of its perfectionist kind, on two internal goods.[8] In the case of baseball, these goods include: 1) the good involved in achieving the excellences specific to it, and, 2) the good of a certain kind of life, one devoted to excellence, required by baseball. The social character and special kind of social interchange mandated by these internal goods of baseball explains why use value must be subordinated to them. Indeed, it is only when this social background is left out of account, that the notion that baseball is just another business gets its purchase.

Baseball's Got the Goods

There are, then, two features of the internal goods of baseball that are relevant to my argument: their special social constitution, and their irreducible social character. With regard to the first feature, my argument is that baseball has centrally to do with the pursuit of bodily excellence. This pursuit and the internal goods it puts in play are peculiar to baseball in the sense that they can only be conceived, realized, and appreciated by being a member of the practice itself. So the thrill of turning a double-play, making a clutch hit, pitching a stellar game are unknown to those not initiated in the game. So too is what it means to live one's life devoted to such excellences, for example, the discipline, hard work, concentration, and commitment such a life entails. And while many features of these excellences and the form of life they embody involve non-moral values (aesthetic values, for example), they also most assuredly involve moral values.

This is most evident in the virtues a game like baseball summons up. Consider virtues like honesty about one's failings and shortcomings, justice in giving others their proper due, the

---

[8] This notion of internal goods was introduced by Alasdair MacIntyre in *After Virtue* (South Bend: University of Notre Dame Press, 1984), p. 188.

courage to play through fatigue and pain, and countless others. It is virtues like these which are crucial to the realization of the internal goods of baseball, and which distinguish baseball from other wholly technical engagements. To be a baseball player or fan, then, is to be a part of a way of life in which moral concerns play a central role.

The second feature of the internal goods of baseball, their social character, further explains why baseball's effort to cordon itself off from the market adds a moral dimension to its narrative. Goods specific to the practice of baseball are social ones, through and through. The goods internal to baseball are "out there" not in the sense in which lumps of coal are out there in the world independent of and indifferent to our human existence. The goods have been put out there by us, literally constructed by us, to serve some collective purpose, about which we care deeply or else we would have not gone to the trouble of putting them out there in the first place. And what we put out there in the world socially we put out there morally as well. For social construction is also moral construction since pursuing excellence in baseball carries with it certain moral implications, such as teamwork and fair play.

In an important sense, then, the moral compass of baseball is set by its particular cultural context, where that context itself is what makes the actions that occur in them morally praiseworthy or blameworthy. So stealing home in baseball is a good if performed in a certain way and at a certain point in the game. And what makes it a good is precisely the setting in which it occurs. Whereas, a pitcher who deliberately throws at a batter's head deserves our moral reproach because the game context makes it possible to distinguish between "beaning" a batter and "pitching" to a batter. In addition, the moral compass of baseball is further set by the fact that its goods, as noted, are shared ones, that they embody a common understanding and appreciation of their value. What is unique about sports like baseball, then, and what makes them uniquely suited for the narrative role they play in American life, is the public register in which they are expressed, the fact that their internal goods matter and are valued not just by me or by you, but collectively, by us. And it is precisely their being-for-us that is constitutive of their goodness. In this sense, the goods of baseball are very much like those of friendship, in which an important part of what is valued is the very fact that they are shared. Philosopher Charles Taylor reminds us that becoming someone's friend requires us to transform our own desires for the sake of the mutual good of the relationship.[9] Similarly, becoming a member of the baseball fraternity also requires us to transform our own desires for the sake of the common good of the game.

Baseball's portrayal of itself as something significantly more than a business makes it a moral force to be reckoned with, and one that serves well its narrative account of America as a nation distinguished not so much by its market share as its moral mettle. But that is only half of the story since it does not yet speak to the idea of America as a moral commonwealth, as a community that sees and judges itself in terms of its commitment to the common good of all rather that the private good of a select few.

America's Game

This second part of the story builds on our understanding of baseball as a social practice whose goods are distinguished at least in part by their irreducible social character. But I want to ratchet up this account of baseball as a pre-eminently social affair so that it now encompasses the idea of America itself. And this points my inquiry in a direction that I have thus far only alluded to in passing: the wide following baseball has long enjoyed in American culture. The basis of that attraction, I suggest, is owed in part to a top-down initiative by America's elite to chasten an unruly mass of immigrants, and a bottom-up gesture by these same immigrants to establish some larger American identity that they might rally around and claim as their own. Baseball, as we now know so well, fit the bill perfectly, and soon became an integral part of the conversational "process by which America strives to see itself coherently," what Brown so aptly labeled the "American Imaginary."[10]

What exactly, it might be asked, does this have to do with morality, with living a moral life? Gorn and Goldstein supply a helpful clue. They suggest that in baseball "the identification of a 'home team' moves the private conception of home, as in the

---

[9] Charles Taylor, *Philosophical Arguments* (Cambridge, Massachusetts: Harvard University Press, 1995), p. 139.
[10] "The Meaning of Baseball in 1993," p. 52.

Victorian family circle, . . . into the public realm." The significance of this, they continue, is that it provided a "bridge by which Americans connected their family lives to the larger social world," such that by establishing a "relationship to a home team . . . millions of uprooted Americans" were able to connect "to a sentimental language and cluster of values . . . for which they hungered."[11] Now, this enlargement of the conception of a "home" effected by baseball says at least two important things about what it means to live a moral life. The first can be traced to the moral philosopher Annette Baier's important point that a child's trust in her mother is where all our moral ladders begin. The second can be traced to Rorty's significant insight that to live a moral life requires a moral community of shared values and lives.

Let's begin with Baier's moral take on familial trust. Her main argument here is that notions like good and bad and right and wrong derive their moral force from our solidarity with others, rather than from abstract, general moral principles. The specific kind of solidarity she has in mind is best exemplified in healthy familial relationships, in which our trust in one another is well placed, secure, and binding. It is just this sort of trust, she argues, that sets the gold standard for our moral relationships with others beyond our immediate family circle. For without such trust, our moral relationships with others would quickly fray no matter how sure we are of our private moral code.[12]

The British moral philosopher Bernard Williams provides a beautiful illustration of Baier's claim. He asks us to picture a man who, at no great risk to himself, can save one or two people caught up in some perilous situation. It turns out that one of the people he ends up saving is his wife. Now, a moral theorist for whom only general moral principles matter might reason that in cases like this one ought to save one's wife. But Williams thinks that our hypothetical moral philosopher is guilty here of one thought too many, because he argues the man's first thought—*that's my wife*—is moral justification enough for trying to save her. The moral Williams wants to draw from this story is not just that our solidarity with others might, and often does,

---

[11] *A Brief History of American Sports*, p. 188.
[12] Anette Baier, *Moral Prejudices* (Cambridge, Massachusetts: Harvard University Press, 1995).

come into conflict with abstract moral precepts, but that were it not for such deep attachments to others there would not be enough moral substance in a person's life to make life worth living. As he so succinctly puts it, "life has to have substance if anything is to have sense, including adherence to an impartial [moral] system; but if it has substance, then it cannot grant supreme importance to the impartial system, and that system's hold on it will be, at the limit, insecure."[13]

This is where the wide narrative grip of baseball on the American Imaginary comes squarely into the moral picture. For the connections to larger America it forged gave many Americans, especially the downtrodden, a substantive moral idea of America to cling to, a real sense of solidarity and belonging. Here was a home away from home that inspired, though, alas, not infrequently disappointed, a moral vision of life beyond the cramped quarters of the economic self so carefully crafted and polished by the world of business. In short, baseball gave many Americans a reason to trust one another, which, as Baier astutely observes, means more than depending on the habits or fears of others not to do us harm, but on the genuine goodwill of others to treat us well.

Thus, what the French existentialist writer Camus once said of his favorite sport soccer—that he had learned most of life's important moral lessons from his involvement in the game[14]— could just as easily be said of Americans' involvement in baseball. And as I have tried to show, an important part of that lesson was to underscore the important role trust plays in a moral life. But one of the things that makes this kind of trust so vital to an ethical life is that it provides the glue needed to patch a moral community together. And it is this notion of a moral community that takes me to the second point I mentioned above, baseball's transformation of the idea of "home" from a private to a decidedly public concern.

Baseball's inflation of the conception of home to fit the notion of a community based on trust,[15] and so a distinctly moral

---

[13] Bernard Williams, *Moral Luck* (Cambridge: Cambridge University Press, 1981), p. 18.

[14] ""The Wager of Our Generation,"" in *Resistance, Rebellion, and Death*, translated by Justin O"Brien (New York: Vantage, 1960), p. 242.

[15] See Chapter 1 in this volume.

community, offers an important answer to two perennial questions that cut to the heart of moral philosophy: 1) Why be moral? and, 2) How can we justify our moral beliefs and actions? One useful way to think about these questions is suggested by Rorty's exhortation to stop thinking of morality "as the voice of the divine part of ourselves and instead think of it as the voice of ourselves as members of a community, speakers of a common language."[16]

Moral philosophers like MacIntyre, Taylor, and Rorty think that it is answerability to our peers rather than an unadulterated self or world that is crucial to moral inquiry. They think that moral reflection is pre-eminently a conversational affair, a matter of persuading our peers (those we trust and identify with) that certain beliefs and actions are morally exemplary and others morally reprehensible. The normative force of moral judgment here is entirely intersubjective in character—that is, entirely based on our success in convincing the members of our community that what we call morally good or bad is what they would call good or bad.

Our moral responsibilities and obligations are wrapped up in our practical identities (those descriptions under which our life takes on meaning), and our practical identities are wrapped up in the communities to which we belong. Thus, to lead a moral life is to live in a manner that is faithful to the moral self-image of one's community. Herein lies the answers to the two questions posed above: Why be moral? Because as Scanlon puts it, "we have a basic desire to be able to justify our actions to others on grounds that they could not reasonably reject.[17] How do we justify our moral beliefs and actions? We persuade our peers that our reasons for thinking a certain belief or action is right or wrong carry weight.

This alternative, communicative view of ethics is able, then, to explain baseball's pervasive hold on the American imagination precisely because of the moral community it inspires. Here baseball's wide appeal to Americans near and far is to be understood as a moral appeal, as an important answer to the ques-

---

[16] Rorty, *Contingency, Irony, and Solidarity* (Cambridge: University of Cambridge Press, 1989), p. 59.
[17] T.M. Scanlon, *What We Owe to Each Other* (Cambridge, Massachusetts: Harvard University Press, 1998), p. 5.

tion, "Who are we?" This is why scandals in baseball often excite the sharp-edged moral outrage that they do in America.

The famous 1919 Black Sox bribery scandal is a case in point. Anguished fans demanded to know what had happened to their game, more specifically, how had their beloved sport been hijacked by common criminals who dared to turn America's game into their own private con game. The force of that moral outrage was immortalized in the plea of a little boy who confronted the famous and now disgraced Black Sox player Shoeless Joe Jackson on the street outside the courtroom. The boy's plaintive cry, "Say it isn't so Joe," is nothing if not a powerful moral demand to justify his actions, to square morally his actions with the American public, to reinstate his moral identity as one of us. And to those critics who insist such moral cries no longer figure in baseball or, for that matter, anywhere else in the world of sports today, I offer as reproof the recent Sammy Sosa corked bat incident.[18] As I logged on to the internet to learn more about this story, my eyes quickly spied the headline which introduced it: "Say It Ain't So Sammy Sosa." It's in moments like these, despite the tawdry backdrops, that the idea of America as a moral beacon is most luminous.

---

[18] The great attention focused on Sosa's use of a corked bat has also to do with his great moral stature in the game and in larger America as well. This was made clear in the *New York Times* survey of contemporary American moral beliefs, which served as the empirical backdrop for Alan Wolfe's important book, *Moral Freedom* (New York: Norton, 2001). When asked to identify modern-day saints, Americans unsurprisingly mentioned moral luminaries like Mother Teresa and Albert Schweitzer, but they also mentioned in the same breath, surprisingly, at least to Wolfe, Sammy Sosa (p. 190).

Sixth Inning:
Where Have
You Gone, Jackie
Robinson?

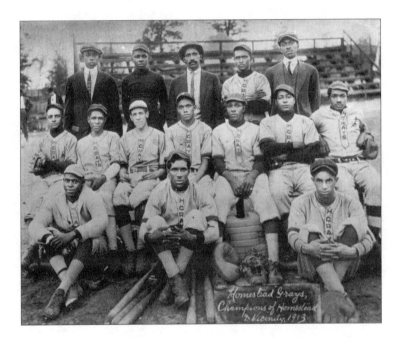

Baseball, like America, also has its crueler side. When Major League Baseball rejected black athletes in the nineteenth and twentieth centuries, it damaged itself almost as much as its excluded players. Alex and Rob Ruck look to destructive strains of Social Darwinism to explain the philosophical reasoning behind the injustice. Pellom McDaniels III points out that philosophies of resistance can help us understand why black players persevered, continuing to play the game they loved.

11 | The Negro Leagues and the Contradictions of Social Darwinism

ALEX RUCK AND ROB RUCK

In 1920, Andrew 'Rube' Foster brought together a number of men who operated black baseball teams in the Midwest to form the Negro National League (NNL). This meeting was a turning point for black sport. One of the first national black institutions to emerge since slavery's end, the eight clubs were located in northern cities whose black populations had swelled with southern migrants. These locales allowed for a degree of black attainment that might have been crushed in the South. Overall, the league was a bold effort to establish black sport on a more professional basis. If unable to join the major leagues, black America would form one of its own.

Sports and Race

American sport, it is often said, should be above politics, free of troubling cultural and social realities. But that goal has rarely been attained, especially where sport intersects race. For over a century, sport in America has been indelibly stamped by the dimensions of race—by color lines, the quest for a white hope, the struggles of black athletes, and philosophies of racial superiority. How the nation thought about race shaped its sporting life. That was true in the late nineteenth century and remains so today.

Pose the question whether African Americans are inherently superior athletes. The chances are that many of those respond-

173

ing will assert that they are, arguing that African Americans are naturally more gifted for sport, primarily as a result of their genetic make-up. To defend this position, some will point to the exceedingly high percentages of black athletes in professional basketball and football, others to their domination of track and boxing, and a few to sport's reigning triumvirate of commercial endorsers, Michael Jordan, Tiger Woods, and George Foreman. "After all," someone is bound to joke, "white men can't jump."[1]

Others, of course, dispute this theory of an inherent athletic edge. They question the very nature of racial categories, asking why individuals who by appearances are more Caucasian than African are considered black, not white. Tiger Woods, for example, is a blend of racial backgrounds whose identity transcends simple categorization. They argue that environmental factors are more influential than anything else in creating sub-cultures of sporting excellence. That would explain why San Pedro de Macoris has become the City of Shortstops in the Caribbean and the Rift Valley in Kenya is the home of the best marathoners on the planet. Both locales cultivate large crops of spectacularly trained athletes. Their success has not been due to race but the ability to build an athletic infrastructure in a rugged environment where poverty and a sporting tradition motivate many to aspire to become the best at what they do.

A century ago, the prevailing wisdom regarding blacks and sport was just the opposite. Most whites contended that African Americans were genetically inferior at sport, lacking the emotional equilibrium, endurance, and psychological make-up necessary for athletic achievement. Many believed that black boxers were plagued by weak stomach muscles, unable to absorb a blow. Nor did they think that African Americans had the stamina to run long distances or perform well late in a game.

Such beliefs were used to justify the near-total exclusion of blacks from the mainstream of sport. By the 1890s, many of the gains won during Reconstruction had eroded as segregation and sharecropping replaced slavery in the South. The black athletes who worked as jockeys, boxed professionally, and played baseball found it harder and harder to pursue their trades. Soon,

---

[1] In 1988, Jimmy "The Greek" Snyder lost his job as a CBS football analyst over his argument that the genetic breeding of slaves was cause for the disproportionately high number of African Americans in sports.

black jockeys no longer rode mounts in the Kentucky Derby, a color line blocked blacks from boxing for the heavyweight title, and African Americans playing in baseball's major leagues were chased off the field.

During these years, African Americans were also forced off the voting rolls throughout the South and lynched with mind-numbing frequency, so exclusion from sport was hardly their most pressing grievance. But exclusion from a visible and mesmerizing American institution affected how the country viewed African American citizens. Their absence reinforced assumptions of black inferiority. Segregation also meant that black athletes had little chance to disrupt philosophies of white superiority. They could not win if they could not compete, at least in the short run.

Ironically, sport was widely touted as a meritocracy, where ability—not class, religion, or nationality—mattered the most. Baseball, which dominated the sporting landscape at the time, was held up as the sport that would Americanize successive waves of immigrants. It had the power to teach them American values and habits. The exclusion of African Americans, therefore, suggested they were not up to attaining American ideals. Some rationale was necessary to justify sport's segregation.

Social Darwinism

In the 1890s, the capacity of sport to pave the way to democracy was trumped by a potent social philosophy known as Social Darwinism. Its ideas about race, society, and power took an undemocratic stance and built part of the ideological foundation of segregation in American sport.

Social Darwinism traces its origins to 1859, when Charles Darwin (1809–1882) introduced the theory that organisms developing favorable adaptations would have an increased chance of survival. Such organisms, in turn, passed these traits on to their offspring, who became more adept at survival. Darwin observed that organisms enjoying genetic advantages, such as giraffes with longer necks, were so endowed on a totally random basis. Hence, natural selection and evolution seemed to be a sort of "guess and check work" on the part of Mother Nature. Darwin noted that evolution was more creative than it was destructive. Natural selection was not meant simply to weed out the weak.

Instead, animals that were better able to survive would pass along certain advantages to their offspring. Those species that could not find nourishment and protect themselves would eventually become extinct.

Darwin's theories radicalized notions of natural history. No one had yet covered as much of the Earth with such scientific care as Darwin in his travels to virtually every type of ecosystem while aboard *H.M.S. Beagle.* Darwin's revolutionary theory of evolutionary development not only sparked controversy by challenging the creation myth of Adam and Eve and questioning whether or not people were the special creations of an all-knowing god. It also led to the late nineteenth-century philosophy of Social Darwinism, which adapted Darwin's theories to race and nationality. Darwin would have been appalled at the abuse of his research in the hands of the Social Darwinists, but he could do little about them.

Social Darwinists claimed that some people sank to the bottom of society as a result of natural law. The philosophy asserted that genetic make-up made certain races and nationalities better than others. "Scientific studies" conducted in the late 1800s attempted to classify races biologically along an evolutionary continuum. According to Social Darwinists, Caucasians, especially Western and Nordic Europeans, ranked above all others. Virtually every other race, they argued, was biologically inferior to the white race. Thus, Caucasians dominated the world, with other races "rightfully" situated below them because of the white race's genetic superiority, not because they were fortunate or had improperly used force to get there. Conveniently enough, European nations were carving Africa and South East Asia into colonies at the time, while segregation and white supremacy reigned in the United States.

British philosopher Herbert Spencer (1820–1903) was the father of Social Darwinism. He argued that human social interaction was exactly the same as the interaction of animals in nature. Spencer coined the phrase "survival of the fittest." In a famous passage of his book, *Social Statics*, he writes:

> It seems hard that a laborer, incapacitated by sickness from competing with his stronger fellows should have to bear the resulting privations. It seems hard that widows and orphans should be left to struggle for life or death. Nevertheless, when regarded not sep-

arately but in connection with the interests of universal humanity, these harsh fatalities seem to be full of beneficence.[2]

In other words, life is a jungle and the strong will survive. Do not try to protect the weak or inferior from the inevitable. Government should do no more than protect property and preserve order. Social reforms were shunned as soft-headed sentimentalism. They would inevitably fail to achieve their desired ends.

There was, however, a paternalistic cast to Social Darwinism which softened its harsh "society is a jungle" mentality. According to thinkers like Spencer, the white race had a duty to civilize the lesser, and as some said, "childlike" races of the world. They believed that "colored" people did not belong in high society and that whites had benevolently erected a system of segregation to keep them in their place. Rudyard Kipling, for example, saw Social Darwinism through the prism of Britain's colonization of India. In his poem about imperialism entitled "White Man's Burden," Kipling argued that imperialist powers owed a duty to those under their sway.

Spencer himself was a staunch anti-imperialist and not especially anti-black in his views. But others distorted his beliefs and cast Social Darwinism as a rabidly racist and nationalistic social philosophy.

The term "Social Darwinism" is misleading because Darwin's theories actually undermine the exact basis upon which Social Darwinism was founded. In his 1871 book, *The Descent of Man*, Darwin concluded that mammals had all descended from one similar organism. Humans, therefore, had evolved out of animals, most recently from highly advanced primates. However, Darwin said that once humans evolved, natural selection played far less of a role in their development. Cultural evolution—such as the development of institutions, the creation of religion, and a stable family unit—overshadowed natural selection. Darwin believed that once humans took on a form similar to the way they appear today, they began evolving culturally instead of physically.

But Social Darwinists paid Darwin's actual writings little mind. Instead, they justified segregation by pointing to how poorly African Americans fared when compared with whites in

---

[2] Quoted in Jackson J. Spielvogel, *Western Civilization* (Minneaopolis: West, 1997), p. 852.

most endeavors. This subordinate position, Social Darwinists said, was a result of their racial inferiority. When it came to sport, they argued that African Americans were less able in all aspects of baseball and thus had no business being a part of the major leagues. There was some truth in what they said. On the surface, black baseball then was not competitive with white baseball. Sport was far less developed in the African American community and black ball players were, by and large, not as skilled as their white counterparts.

When a few black athletes proved capable of competing with whites, popular wisdom concluded that these exceptions were better able to harness their more 'animalistic' natures. U.S. Olympic track coach Dean Cromwell saw black athletes' success at sprinting and jumping as a function of how much closer they were to the primitive. "It was not so long ago that his ability to sprint and jump was a life-and-death matter to him in the jungle."[3] Others conjectured that African Americans possessed some skeletal or muscular quirk such as longer heel bones or exceptional Achilles tendons.

But did African Americans lag behind in baseball because of a genetic unsuitability for the game or were other historic forces at work? Social institutions, not genes, provide the answer. During slavery's grip on the South, African Americans had little time to engage in athletics. Since sport and play were equated with freedom and work with slavery, African Americans were left off the team. In the North, with its longer tradition of freedom, black communities formed ballclubs soon after the Civil War. But African Americans were latecomers to the fields of play. It was more difficult for them to devote the time needed to gain expertise at the game and to acquire the muscular memory that baseball requires. It was harder to develop the infrastructure of teams, coaches, leagues, role models, and rivalries necessary to improve the level of play.

But forced out of baseball's mainstream, African Americans fell back on their own resources. They formed a score of ballclubs and a few leagues, trained a cadre of coaches and instructors, and began to create a sporting world of their own. The sporting life they built on the other side of America's racial boundary would eventually put the lie to Social

---

[3] Dean Cromwell, *Championship Techniques in Track and Field* (New York: Whittlesey House, 1949), p. 6.

Darwinism and the other racial ideologies that were in vogue during segregation.

Challenging Philosophies of Race

Black Americans thoroughly rejected Social Darwinism but could not ignore its impact. During the early twentieth century, however, a range of new social philosophies took hold in black circles. They stressed self-reliance, "negritude," and black nationalism. These intellectual currents helped sustain a separate but more assertive black culture and a range of black businesses and social institutions. Among the latter was a black-run baseball league. An eclectic mix of intellectuals and activists boosted these developments. Franz Boas, a German anthropologist, argued as early as 1887 that scientific racism was invalid. A few decades later, Marcus Garvey, a charismatic Jamaican black nationalist, worked to help blacks overcome the mindset that they were in any way inferior.

Franz Boas (1858–1942), challenged the accepted scientific racism of the day. In 1894, he publicly charged that modern anthropology was dominated by racist assumptions. Boas stated, contrary to the beliefs of Social Darwinism, that no evidence existed that could prove that any given race was unable to reach higher civilization. He stressed the critical role of environment in shaping evolution. A racist environment, not genetics, explained why blacks lagged behind whites. History, Boas argued, should teach us not to "interpret as racial character what is only an effect of social surroundings."[4]

In his attack on prevailing "scientific" assumptions, Boas worked on a 1912 federal study on immigrants. This five-hundred-page report invalidated the popular belief in the genetic inferiority of the Eastern Europeans then flooding American shores. Boas was initially dismissed by a public and a scientific establishment that had internalized Social Darwinism, but his work did not go unnoticed. His arguments undermined the very foundation of Social Darwinist thought and allowed intellectuals

---

[4] Franz Boas, "Human Faculty as Determined by Race," *Proceedings of the American Association for the Advancement of Science*, no. 43 (1895), p. 308, quoted in Lee D. Baker, *From Savage to Negro: Anthropology and the Construction of Race, 1896–1954* (Berkeley: University of California Press, 1998), pp. 100–08.

like W.E.B. Du Bois to advance arguments about race and
equality that would eventually capture the day.

While Franz Boas addressed a small, academic circle, Marcus
Garvey (1887–1940) reached millions. Garvey, born in Jamaica
in 1887, grew up amidst the exploitation of blacks by the British
colony's often arrogant white elite. Garvey believed that black
people, oppressed for so long, had accepted a sense of inferiority. His answer was to build a black nationalist movement to
overcome that self-defeating assumption. By 1919, he had organized Universal Negro Improvement Association branches
across the United States, the Caribbean, and Latin America. They
spread Garvey's philosophies of self-pride and black equality.
Garvey set up the Black Star steamship line, corps of black
nurses and aviators, and an influential newspaper, *The New
Negro.*

Garvey stressed a Pan-Negro Nationalism that advocated the
creation of a separate black nation. Different races, he argued,
needed to develop their societies in different ways. With a new
nation, blacks could not only escape oppression, but constitute
the majority. Garvey's 'Back to Africa' movement urged all members of the African diaspora—the descendants of Africans who
had spread throughout the world—to return to the motherland.
There, he said, they would create a powerful black republic,
"free to work out their own salvation. Free to create their own
destinies. Free to build up themselves for the upbringing and
rearing of a culture and civilization of their own." Garvey's 'Back
to Africa' movement was unrealistic, but the ideals of black independence and self-reliance took hold of black imagination.[5]

The social philosophies advanced by Boas and Garvey took
root in a black America undergoing fundamental change. At the
turn of the century, about ninety percent of all African
Americans resided in the South. But when World War I created
greater job opportunities in the North, a wholesale exodus
began. Black migrants streamed into northern cities and took
advantage of their greater workplace, educational, and cultural
options. These cities were fertile soil for newer, more positive
ways of looking at blackness to take root.

---

[5] A.J. Garvey, *Philosophy and Opinions,* Vol. 2, p. 118, quoted in John T. McCartney,
Black Power Ideologies (Philadelphia: Temple University Press, 1992), p. 83.

On the Other Side of the Racial Divide

With the economy soaring to historic heights, a shorter work week allowing for more leisure time, and radio revolutionizing popular culture, the 1920s were the golden age of American sport. Rube Foster's Negro National League thrived. But Foster, the man called the father of black baseball, had health problems in 1926 and was soon on the sidelines. The league, meanwhile, struggled after the stock market collapse in 1929 ushered in a deep depression that hammered black Americans the hardest. The NNL collapsed a few years later.

But black baseball revived. The NNL reformed in 1933 and was based in Pittsburgh. During the 1930s, Pittsburgh became to black baseball what Harlem had been to black art and literature in the 1920s, the center of its renaissance. There is a certain irony that the league's second coming took place in the city that industrialist Andrew Carnegie had helped make into a symbol of Social Darwinism in practice. Carnegie was an avowed Social Darwinist and devotee of Herbert Spencer. "Before Spencer," Carnegie proclaimed, "all for me had been darkness, after him, all had become light—and right."[6]

Carnegie found ample justification in Social Darwinism for the brutal treatment of the men who labored in his company's mills and mines. Eager to show off Social Darwinism in action, he persuaded Spencer to come from England to America in 1882. For Carnegie, the highlight of Spencer's tour would be his visit to Pittsburgh, where the elites justified their power by a sense of inherent superiority over the working classes. Carnegie, however, was crushed when Spencer was overwhelmed by a visit to one of the steel magnate's smoldering mills along the Monongahela River. The British philosopher told his host that "Six months' residence here would justify suicide."[7]

Pittsburgh offered a microcosm of the nation's contradictory and uneven racial patterns. On the streets of its Hill District and other racially mixed communities, black and white boys played with and against each other. As some who grew up in the Hill recalled, they'd get a "whuppin' from their white mama and their black mama" when they got in trouble. As these youths

---

[6] Joseph Frazier Wall, *Andrew Carnegie* (Pittsburgh: University of Pittsburgh Press, 1989), p. 381.
[7] *Ibid.*, p. 386.

joined more organized teams, they were segregated by race. But they still played against each other on the city's sandlots where fair competition showed them who was best.

Both of Pittsburgh's NNL clubs came from these sandlots. Black steelworkers at Carnegie Steel's Homestead Works formed a baseball team in 1900; they took the name of the Homestead Grays in 1912. Homestead native Cumberland Posey, Jr. joined the club as an outfielder and later became their manager and owner. Posey, one of the nation's top basketball stars, made the Grays the best black club in the region. He soon began attracting black players from throughout the United States and the Caribbean and made the Grays one of baseball's premier squads. Posey exemplified the leadership qualities that Social Darwinists found lacking in black Americans. He made the Grays a winner, on the field and at the gate. "We didn't just play and think we were inferior," infielder Clarence Bruce pointed out. "We thought we were great ballplayers and I think we walked with that air. When we walked into a town, we held our heads high."[8]

Soon a challenger to the Grays emerged on the sandlots of the city's Hill District. In 1925, black youth formed a team they named after their sponsor, the Crawford Bath House. The Bath House helped European immigrants and Southern migrants adjust to urban and industrial life. It also sponsored sport. A few years later, the Crawfords were joined by several players from a ballclub at the Edgar Thomson Steel Works.

When the Crawfords added Josh Gibson, they were ready to challenge the Grays. After Gus Greenlee became their owner in 1930, the Crawfords became a key franchise in the second Negro National League. Greenlee, a flamboyant nightclub owner who ran the numbers—an illegal but popular lottery game in Pittsburgh—turned the Crawfords into the champions of black baseball. With Cool Papa Bell flying around the base paths, Josh Gibson drawing accolades as the black Babe Ruth, and Satchel Paige intentionally walking the bases loaded, telling his fielders to sit down, and striking out the side, the Crawfords' fame spread across the country and into the Caribbean. They might have been baseball's best team ever.

---

[4] Rob Ruck, *Sandlot Seasons: Sport in Black Pittsburgh* (Champaign: University of Illinois Press, 1993), p. xiii.

While Pittsburgh's two Negro League teams were unable to book games against the major league Pittsburgh Pirates, they were much sought after as opponents by other white teams in the region. When the Grays or Crawfords came to an all-white mining town in western Pennsylvania, the game was the most anticipated sporting event of the year. White ballplayers relished the challenge of facing Cool Papa Bell or Buck Leonard. Decades later many of these white players would boast of having been struck out by Satchel Paige or surrendering a home run to Josh Gibson. It was their badge of honor simply to have been on the same field as these future Hall of Famers.

Pittsburgh became the crossroads of black baseball. The two franchises won over a dozen Negro League championships, including the Grays' nine consecutive Negro National League titles (1937–1945), and sent seven of the first eleven Negro Leaguers selected to the Hall of Fame. "The Pittsburgh Crawfords and the Homestead Grays," Hall-of-Famer Monte Irvin remembers with a smile, "dominated baseball at that time."[9]

The Crawfords, like the Grays, became a vital local institution. "Gus," his brother Dr. Charles Greenlee explained, "was a race man." He consciously advanced efforts by African Americans to create their own institutions and assert their equality. Greenlee built the finest black-owned ballpark in the country, Greenlee Field, atop the Hill. The Crawfords and the Grays played benefits for black causes. And fans, both white and black, watched clubs owned and managed by African Americans, where not only the players and managers, but the umpires and vendors, were black.[10]

The Negro Leagues were not the equal of the major leagues in terms of salaries and profits. Teams suffered from greater financial instability and often had a harder time making it through the season. But when they played white major leaguers, black ballplayers more often than not triumphed. Some of these barnstorming games involved intact Negro League and major league clubs; others were made up of *ad hoc* teams recruited by stars like Satchel Paige and Dizzy Dean. In the Caribbean, baseball's first truly inter-racial and international venue for the game, black, Latin, and white ballplayers played

---

[9] *Ibid.*, p. xii.
[10] Interview with Dr. Charles Greenlee, Pittsburgh, June 18th, 1980.

with and against each other. White ballplayers often lauded the abilities of their black opponents. Joe DiMaggio once said that Satchel Paige was the toughest pitcher he ever faced. The Yankee great recognized what the Social Darwinists did not see, that race did not limit ability.

These leagues did more than develop the capacity of African Americans to play baseball. They displayed organizational capacity on a broader scale. Black baseball showed that African Americans could own teams and run them effectively, even with limited resources. It showed that their managers, from Rube Foster and Cum Posey, to Candy Jim Taylor and Vic Harris, were as astute as white skippers. Most of all, the Negro Leagues disproved that African Americans could not successfully compete against whites. They were proof of what Boas and Garvey had been arguing all along.

Because sport afforded African Americans a chance to display grace and competence in ways they could not elsewhere in society, baseball was critical to black collective self-identity. It was a force for cohesion in a black community troubled by divisions over social class, skin color, and splits between Southern migrants and Northern-born. And though the major leagues were segregated, baseball on the sandlots and games between Negro League and white clubs fostered substantial racial interaction.

Crossing the Color Line

In the wake of World War II, American society began to integrate. The process was painfully slow and revealed how difficult it was for a nation to come to terms with a legacy of slavery.

During World War II, African Americans mobilized to fight and work. The war energized the push for civil rights and in its wake, sentiment for integration grew. Major League Baseball had long denied that it had ever imposed, much less maintained, a ban on blacks. But in October 1945, the Brooklyn Dodgers announced that they had signed Kansas City Monarch shortstop Jackie Robinson to a contract with their Montreal Royals farmclub. The signing electrified black America. Robinson, the *Pittsburgh Courier* wrote, carried "the hopes, aspirations and ambitions of thirteen million black Americans

---

[11] *Pittsburgh Courier* (October 29th, 1945).

heaped on his broad, sturdy, shoulders."[11] All eyes turned toward Robinson.

The impact of integration on baseball was astonishing. Robinson, rookie of the year in 1947, was only the first to cross the color line. Robinson begat Larry Doby, Monte Irvin, and a score of other stars. Some were the Negro Leagues' best young players, such as Willie Mays, Ernie Banks, and Henry Aaron. Others were veterans like Luke Easter and Willard Brown. Even Satchel Paige, at least 42 years old, crossed the color line. Debuting with Cleveland in 1948, he won six games against only one loss as he helped the Indians win the World Series that year. Josh Gibson never got the chance. He died suddenly in 1947 at the age of 35. His death drew little attention as black players entered the majors. During the 1950s, black ballplayers won a hugely disproportionate number of Rookie of the Year and Most Valuable Player awards in the National League. Roy Campanella won an astonishing three MVP awards in a five-year-stretch.

Black players became the best fresh source of talent in the game's history. They also changed its rhythms and dynamics. The Negro Leagues had emphasized speed, going from first to third on a single, bunting, and stealing bases, while the majors had relied more on power. Integrated baseball became an amalgam of both speed and power. Integration also opened the door for Latin Americans. Soon, fans could watch Felipe Alou, Juan Marichal, and Roberto Clemente.

Clemente, a Puerto Rican who became the first Latin star in the majors, received scant attention outside Pittsburgh and the Caribbean until late in his career. Maligned as an undisciplined hothead who lacked toughness, the Pirate rightfielder eventually won over critics with his fearless and graceful play. After his death on a relief mission to help earthquake victims in Nicaragua on New Year's Eve 1972, Clemente's nobility was lauded as much as his athletic ability. He became the role model for countless Latin youth.

The emergence of Latin players illustrates what can happen when a culture of sporting excellence takes hold. By the twenty-first century, Latin Americans outnumbered African Americans in the game and made up over a quarter of all major leaguers. Latin players, who come from African, Indian, and Caucasian backgrounds, or some mix thereof, have not succeeded due to race but because they grew up in an environment in which baseball was stressed. They grew up emulating men who made it to the majors, received excellent instruction and training, played hard against other good athletes, and saw the tangible rewards of making it. Baseball offered more than cutting cane or working in the tourist trade.

By the 1950s, the Negro Leagues had withered, unable to withstand the better capitalized major leagues that took their best young players and paying fans. Autonomous, black-controlled sport disappeared and black owners and managers were soon a relic of the past. Meanwhile, black participation in baseball declined and the integration of colleges and universities encouraged many to seek athletic scholarships to play football and basketball instead. Soon, the percentages of African Americans in these sports soared. That rapid growth ironically led to the new racist perception regarding sport—that blacks were genetically favored in athletic pursuits.

This new line of thought regarding genetics and athletic excellence reproduces some of the same illogical conclusions about race and sport that plagued the nation during the heyday of Social Darwinism. It, too, seeks a simple racial explanation for a far more complex reality. These discussions of genetics are not based in genetics but in social attitudes. Sport has yet to transcend the politics and philosophies of race. It remains inextricably linked to its social context and will for the foreseeable future.

12 | We're American Too: The Negro Leagues and the Philosophy of Resistance

PELLOM McDANIELS III

They'll see how beautiful I am
And be ashamed—

I too, am America

—LANGSTON HUGHES

Since the Emancipation Proclamation, African Americans have asked the question, "What does it mean to be American?" Is being American a right inherited by birth, a position appropriated by hard work and sacrifice, or a notion of freedom that is defined by the very Constitution of the United States? How does one become American? Who decides?

Hoping to answer these questions, African Americans migrated by the hundreds of thousands to northern industrial cities to escape the brutal racism of the south, and to take advantage of financial opportunities that they thought being American entitled them to in the early 1900s. By moving to cities such as Chicago, Detroit, and Kansas City, African Americans challenged and created their own conceptions and definitions of what it meant to be American. Most ethnic groups (immigrant, native, or displaced) have had the opportunity to assimilate and take advantage of the freedoms that achieving full status allows. The same cannot be said for a majority of African Americans who, under slavery, had directly contributed (although reluctantly) to the development, wealth, and prosperity of the country that they called home. By 1919, many African Americans had moved into urban centers filled with European immigrants who had come to the United States eagerly seeking the American dream. Excluded from enjoying the benefits of being American, most African Americans were denied jobs that were systematically given to European immigrants. In no other place was this exclusion more evident than in America's pastime: baseball.

The aim of this chapter is to examine the Negro Leagues through philosophical lenses provided by Friedrich Nietzsche and Cornel West. Recognizing the presence of resentment as a motivating factor in the performances of black baseball players in the segregated leagues, I will explain the individual and collective fight against hegemony, through the African American tradition of resistance. Additionally, because of their genuine love for the game and what they sacrificed to play during their respective times, Negro League players sought and found a freedom in their performances that could never be taken from them. Baseball became a ritual that elevated not only the players, but raised the collective sense of community, humanity, and patriotism that the black masses felt whenever a black baseball team took to the playing field. Even though they were excluded from participating in America's pastime as full-citizens with all the privileges that being American entailed, those men who participated in the Negro Leagues shouted clearly with every pitch, every swing, and every steal, "I am a man."

The black baseball players of the Negro Leagues developed a philosophical approach to athletic performance, leadership, and community that can be linked to the African American tradition of resistance. The Negro Leagues 1) provided access to opportunities both financially and socially; 2) granted the opportunity to display their talent as a way to refute theories of racial inferiority; and 3) encouraged the development of sport as a vehicle for new meanings of black masculinity to be accessed, evaluated, and recreated.

The Birth of the Negro Leagues

Prior to the turn of the twentieth century, African Americans participated and played baseball on the plantations and streets of the South and in the fields of the cities of the North. Many participated to take advantage of the economic, social, and political benefits associated with the game, forming teams and associations to manage the way in which the game was played and who was allowed to participate. Although limited in numbers, African Americans by the 1870s participated in league play with white organizations. Succeeding on the field with their white counterparts were African American players like John "Bud" Fowler, who in 1872 played second base for a professional white team in New Castle, Pennsylvania (when he was only fourteen), Moses Fleetwood Walker, a catcher who played for the Toledo Blue Stockings in 1884 (along with his brother, Welday), George Washington Stovey, a pitcher who played for Newark in the International League in 1885–86, and Frank Grant, a second baseman who played in the Eastern League in 1886.

In 1887, Stovey became the object of racial contention when one of the game's most popular white players, Cap Anson, refused to play in an exhibition game against any team with a black player on its roster. Newark, Stovey's team, initiated a meeting that would begin the exclusion of blacks from the major leagues (until Jackie Robinson in 1947). In response to this unofficial exile, blacks formed their own competitive teams to play against one another. Local organizations like churches, haberdasheries, grocery stores, and newspapers had teams. Not until 1920, was there an organized league in place to regulate play. New rules were developed for a playoff system modeled after the major leagues.

On February 13th, 1920, Rube Foster of the Chicago American Giants and other willing owners of the top black Midwestern teams met at the YMCA in Kansas City, Missouri, to discuss the formation of the Negro National League. Agreeing that there was a need for such a league, they established the first all-black baseball league, which comprised eight teams: the American Giants, the Kansas City Monarchs, the St. Louis Stars, the Detroit Stars, the Indianapolis ABCs, the Chicago Giants, the Cuban Stars, and the Dayton Marcos. Except for J.L. Wilkinson, owner of the Kansas City Monarchs, the other seven owners were black. As long as segregation persisted, there was black baseball to generate streams of revenue for African American communities where the teams played regularly, as well as the frequent barnstorming teams that brought excitement to the local black masses. A majority of those who played did so under the mantle of the democratic ideal: using one's ability to be one's own man while achieving a sustainable degree of wealth and success through hard work and sacrifice. Most athletes earned more money than other black men of the time.

Some athletes sought to define and defend their sense of masculinity, humanity, and individual identity through their athletic performances, by combining their physical gifts and talents with showboating and clowning. The goal was clearly to play baseball in front of a paying crowd, thereby gaining access to economic opportunities. As I will discuss later, these athletes bodied forth, through their performances, a black masculine type of resistance that redirected feelings of resentment resulting from slavery, Reconstruction, and the banishment from the white majors, into an impressive and progressive display of "black power." Under the direction of Rube Foster, baseball became an institution in African American communities across the United States during the first quarter of the twentieth century. Even as segregation limited the movement of African Americans into mainstream society, the ability of African American men to perform at the same level (or higher) as their white counterparts endeared them to their communities. As we shall see, their performances were counter-narratives to notions of racial inferiority.

Resentment, Resistance, and the Blues

The creation of rituals, symbols, and sensibilities is the result of certain social, cultural, economic, or political structures that dominate society as a whole. Individuals on the margins of society are excluded from participating in institutionally endorsed activities, which are defined by the dominant group as important to their group identity. In other words, if you don't meet the requirements, you don't get to play. Black feminist scholar and cultural critic bell hooks suggests that this *absence of presence*, or the *presence of absence*, represents a struggle for the oppressed "against not forgetting" who they are within the context of a racist society. Furthermore, the "effort to remember [the past] . . . is expressive of the need to create spaces where one is able to redeem and reclaim the ever present legacies of pain, suffering, and triumph . . . that transform present reality," clarifying hegemonic definitions of race, class and gender.[1] This act of remembering one's history creates a shared understanding which is the foundation of a community. Without this shared understanding, there can be only defeated, isolated individuals.

According to German philosopher Friedrich Nietzsche, the denial of one's economic, social, and political opportunities in general, and the negotiation of one's morality in particular creates the desire to resist and revolt against those who dictate the rules and limitations.[2] Nietzsche introduces us to his notion of resentment as a type of revolt against dominant institutions. The oppressed react against the limitations placed on their morality and rights by oppressive circumstances and situations. These individuals, as a result of their oppression, are deprived of the opportunity to properly respond to external events, and are coerced to negotiate their convictions and morality as a means of survival. Forced to make compromises, they lie to protect themselves, their families and their communities. Marginalized people devise creative ways to compensate, be it as individuals or through collective forms of agency based on traditions. These traditions speak through simple, non-threatening gestures, which become layered with complex meanings. For those who seek justice, resentment can be manifested in covert deception, as well as overt revolution. Nietzsche recognizes the necessity of such rituals.

> For every sufferer instinctively looks for a cause of his distress; more exactly, for a culprit, even more precisely for a guilty culprit who is receptive to distress—in short, for a living being upon whom he can release his emotions, actually or in effigy, on some pretext or other:

---

[1] bell hooks, "Choosing the Margin As a Space of Radical Openness," in Jane Rendell, Barbara Penner, and Iain Borden, eds., *Gender Space Architecture: An Interdisciplinary Introduction* (New York: Routledge, 2000), pp. 204-05.

[2] Friedrich Nietzsche's philosophical musings and seminal works have been at times unfairly recognized as an inspiration or justification for the world's nihilists, doomsayers, and even the creation of the Third Reich in Nazi Germany. This chapter does not explore Nietzsche's political ramifications. Reference to Nietzsche throughout this chapter will be to one of his concepts that I have taken the liberty to contextualize within the hegemonic structures of slavery, segregation, and the pursuit of the American Dream through baseball.

because the release of emotions is the greatest attempt of relief, or should I say, at anaesthetizing on the part of the sufferer, his involuntary longed-for narcotic against pain of any kind.[3]

According to Nietzsche, men of power will rebel against the slavish morality of the slave masters. And while he never endorses moral compromises, he does understand the need of the sufferer to release the pent-up rage. This expression of frustration, caused by being marginalized for so long, is central to understanding African American forms of resistance. On the plantation, African Americans would often dance outrageously (some would say grotesquely) when they were requested to entertain whites, marginalizing their own morality and humanity. Yet their performances were often crude imitations of the whites themselves performing the same dance steps, which were encoded within the performance. In utilizing dance as a form of ritual release, blacks on the plantation were able to let go and facilitate a response to the oppressive circumstances of plantation life.

Contemporary American philosopher Cornel West suggests that the human struggle "is a form of tragic thought in that it confronts candidly individual and collective experiences of evil in individuals and institutions, with little expectations of ridding the world of all *evil*."[4] Through art and political uprisings, we can wage our little battles, fully recognizing that in the long run, death defeats even the just. This tragic understanding of our existential plight is what separates the philosopher West from other sociologists and economists in African American studies today. Moreover, as West suggests, the relationship between "tragedy" and "revolution (or resistance)" is interconnected with that of "tradition" and "progress," in that all human struggles are guided by democratic ideals that have been shaped by the tenets of integrity, fairness, compassion, and morality. To struggle against oppressive forces, calls upon those traditions of resistance from which "[t]his oppositional consciousness draws its sustenance."

---

[3] Nietzsche, *On the Genealogy of Morality* (Cambridge: Cambridge University Press, 1994), Keith Ansell-Pearson and Carol Diethe, eds., p. 99.
[4] Cornel West, *The Cornel West Reader* (New York: Basic Books, 1994), pp. 166–68.

Playing baseball in the Negro Leagues came to represent cherished qualities of African American life, while simultaneously carrying forth the shared traditions. These traditions were able to resist pervasive forms of white supremacy, which were responsible for the deterioration of both family and community life amongst the black masses. According to West, African Americans experience a "tragicomic sense of life" that propels them towards "suicide or madness." Without the doggedness of "ritual, cushioned by community or sustained by art" the tragicomic sense of life would lead to the psychic demise of the "folk."[5]

Novelist Ralph Ellison (1914–1994) identifies similar qualities of black resistance to oppressive circumstances, traditions, and circumstances in the blues idiom.

> The blues speak to us simultaneously of the tragic and the comic aspects of the human condition and they express a profound sense of life shared by many Negro Americans precisely because their lives have combined these models. This has been the heritage of a people who for hundreds of years could not celebrate birth or dignify death and whose need to live despite the dehumanizing pressures of slavery developed an endless capacity for laughing at their painful experiences. This is a group experience shared by many Negroes, and any effective study of the blues would treat them first as poetry and as ritual.[6]

The blues represent a ritual that buffers and insulates African Americans from the maddening affects of the "unrelenting assault on black humanity."[7] For Ellison, the traditions of resistance exist within the realm of a larger society that West identifies as "towering examples of soul making and spiritual wrestling that crystallize the most powerful interpretation of the human condition in black life."[8]

The blues, according to Ellison, recognize the horrors of slavery and the survivors who were created through the experience. These survivors recognized that their ability to function in the world was both limiting and limitless, depending on their

---

[5] *Ibid.*, pp. 89–90.
[6] Ralph Ellison, *Shadow and Act* (New York: Random House, 1964), pp. 254–56.
[7] *The Cornel West Reader*, p. 101.
[8] *Ibid.*, p. 100)

ability to express themselves in other realms of human contact and emotion. Of these various realms, musical expression and storytelling were the most important means of contesting racial inferiority, political injustice, and moral degradation. Within this context, baseball, like the blues, could be used as a social, cultural, and political tool to communicate the intense feelings that the black masses systematically concealed from the white majority. Through performance, African Americans could celebrate the joys of life, while protesting the frustrations of second-class citizenship.

Both Nietzsche and West argue convincingly that the past is the key factor in the development of new forms of resistance for the future. These new forms often resemble an enhanced and expanded version of the old traditions, but most importantly, these new renderings maintain the essential qualities of the old customs, providing continuity through hidden signs, metaphors, and stories. West, in particular seeks to understand those historically significant moments and their "webs of significance" as having influenced the "choices, sufferings, anxieties and efforts" of those who have been constrained both physically and spiritually. As West poignantly states, "We are all born into and build on circumstances, traditions and situations not of our own choosing."[9] It is the creative response to historical circumstances that interests such disparate philosophers as Nietzsche and West.

Those who have studied American history in general, and African American history in particular, recognize the importance of West's philosophical statement as a prelude to understanding the importance of the black baseball players who dared to play what was designated as a white man's sport. Within the ritual space of the baseball stadium, black baseball players confronted issues of race, masculinity, and identity every time they stepped onto the playing field. These black men were heroes in the communities from which they hailed and where they played. Their individual and collective exploits brought them considerable fame and prestige. But they did not become wealthy playing the grueling schedules and traveling under inferior, often dehumanizing conditions. As "Double Duty" Radcliff makes clear:

---

[9] *Ibid.*, p. 9.

Sometimes you'd be in a town down south in Alabama or Mississippi, they'd want you to go to the back of the restaurant and sit on a box and eat, and some of the boys had too much pride, they wouldn't do it. And if you pick up the hose to drink some water, they say put them hose down nigger, white folks get you a Coca-Cola bottle. It was awful. We took a beating. But if we don't keep playing, they wouldn't be playing today.[10]

Their ability as baseball players was sufficient to endear them to generations of black men, both young and old throughout the United States and Latin America. Young black men observed the players, those archetypes of success, privilege, and influence, and modeled themselves after them. Like the blues man who signifies through his "double voiced" medium of song the tensions that exist in society, the black baseball player personified survival despite the tensions between desire, ability, and access. Individuals such as Satchel Paige, Buck O'Neil, and Josh Gibson played baseball with a passion, because it proved that they could perform just as well as, if not better than, the white players in the major leagues.

Performance and the Bingo Long All-Stars

Although a fictitious celebration of black baseball of the 1930s, the movie, *The Bingo Long Traveling All-Stars & Motor Kings* (1976) offers a fascinating glimpse of several interconnected aspects of the segregated league, relating to racism, sexism, masculinity, and violence. In the movie, several telling scenarios reflect the importance of baseball to the identity of the men playing the game, and to the spectators watching from the stands. Bingo Long (played by Billy Dee Williams) and Leon Carter (played by James Earl Jones) represent the "amazing athletes" of the Negro Leagues who often "showboated and clowned, but never failed to play great baseball."[11] Long and Carter's characters provide us with the opportunity to ask some philosophical questions about the role of performance in expressing resistance.

---

[10]*The Journey of the African American Athlete*, HBO Sports, produced by Ross Greenburg, 1996.
[11] *The Bingo Long Traveling All-Stars and Motor Kings,* Produced by Michael Chinich and Rob Cohen, Universal Studios, 1976.

"Invite pitch, invite pitch, invite pitch," the crowd yells harmoniously as the star pitcher of the St. Louis Ebony Aces, Bingo Long, makes his way to the mound. As the mantra takes over the stands, Long listens as the crowd begins to resemble a congregation of hand clapping, foot stomping churchgoers, whose minister has climbed into the pulpit and is preparing to lead his faithful flock on a spiritual journey. From the home team's dugout, the rest of the Ebony Aces run to the first base line and stand at attention, as if forming a receiving line for the divine one, waiting for him to command them to action. In dramatic fashion, Long climbs to the top of the mound and turns to the crowd. As he raises his hands, a calm comes over the masses in attendance. They listen as Long answers their cries. With his arms uplifted and a smile on his face, Long breaks the silence and the crowd responds in a cadence familiar to the black church: the African American tradition of call and response. Calling for those sinners present to repent and be saved, Long begins his sermon on the mound:

Long: *"Who's"*
Crowd: *"Who's "*

Long: *"gonna hit"*
Crowd: *"gonna hit"*

Long: *"my"*
Crowd: *"my"*

Long: *"invite pitch?"*
Crowd: *"invite pitch?"*

His answer comes swiftly from the visitor's dugout, as we hear and see footsteps moving towards the steps leading up to the field. Leon Carter of the Baltimore Elite Giants has waited patiently, anticipating the calling before his participation in the spectacle that has begun to unfold within the context of a black baseball game. Carter is a big man who, with his large, strong, and nimble hands, reaches down and picks up four wooden bats. He swings the bats to and fro, discarding three as he strides to home plate to meet the man on his challenge.

"You put the ball over the plate, I'll put it over the fence," Carter shouts to Long on the mound. As Carter readies himself at the plate, Long knuckles the ball in his glove, winds up and throws the ball. "Strike one," the umpire yells, as Carter looks down at the ball, still hot in the catcher's glove. As Long motions for the rest of his team to join him on the field, Carter calls out to him:

Carter: *"Hey Bingo, I do believe you be slowin down."*
Long: *"It ain't nice to be throwin hard to old men."*

Carter: *"Don't make any excuses for your arthritis now."*
Long: *"Ah, okay Monkey Face, just for that you're going to get a taste of my vanish ball."*

Playing along, the catcher replies, "Go on and show it to him, he can't see it—I can't see it." Long knuckles the ball once again in his glove as Carter digs in for the second pitch. The wind up, the pitch—"Strike two!" the umpire yells from behind the plate as Carter begins to unfurl his twisted body. Embarrassed by his showing, and needing to gain the edge over Long in some way, Carter decides to try distracting him by humiliating him front of his teammates, fans, and friends:

Carter: *"Bingo, I heard that you done taken up with a hot number named of Violet."*
Long: *"Well, you heard right. Wait till you lay eyes on her."*
Carter: *"Well, if that's Violet Granite you talking about, I done laid more than eyes on her already."*

In an instant Carter has gained Long's attention, distracting him from his previous concerted efforts. As Long winds up for the third pitch, he chides Carter saying, "Ah, Leon, you trying to get my dander up, but I-is-un-ruffable." Carter, however, connects with the pitch, hitting the ball long and straight over the centerfield wall, out of the ballpark. As Carter struts around the bases, smiling and tipping his "ball hat" to the ladies in the stands, and the gents on the field, Long quietly tries to save face like an adolescent appearing indifferent to his peers. "I's getting tired of Violet anyhow," he says. Crossing home plate, Carter makes sure that Long sees him strut like the top cock on the block as he makes his way to his waiting teammates in the visitors' dugout.

Some would say that the showboating and clowning displayed by some of the Negro League players was an active form of Nietzsche's resentment within the context of traditional African American forms of resistance to white supremacy. This is a tradition going back to the gallows humor of slaves in the nineteenth century. Such humor was used as an act of resentment against otherwise unbearable conditions. As Joseph Boskin writes of the slaves, "The laughter of resistance . . . was invariably enlarged by the ongoing challenge to survive." It was a "means of disarming the adversary."[12] Similarly, clowning around on the ball field can be seen as a means for fighting the unjust exclusion from Major League Baseball. Others contend that black baseball players exemplified hyper-masculine attributes by parading their abilities. I say that these African American ballplayers were continuing a tradition of resistance that had been engrained in their psyches since slavery. They used the game and its devices to act out differing aspects of the "black condition."

The Gift of Baseball

My grandfather wanted me to play baseball when I was a child, and not until my adult years did I understand why. His heroes were great baseball players such as Jackie Robinson, Hank Aaron, Willie Mays, and Satchel Paige, to name but a few. These men were the role models and the celebrities of my grandfather's youth. While their efforts belonged to American history, these black baseball stars were the culmination of generations of African Americans who sought full citizenship, who were often denied the right to pursue the American dream. Individual athletes, such as Robinson, became lionized examples of courage and dignity, possessing wholesome morals and values that all could admire and emulate. Like most African American men of his generation, my grandfather imagined himself, I'm sure, stealing home plate like Robinson, hitting a home run like Aaron, making a magnificent over the shoulder catch like Mays, and throwing blinding fast balls (or a "vanish pitch" or two) like

---

[12] Joseph Boskin, "African-American Humor: Resistance and Retaliation," in Felton Best, ed., *Black Resistance Movements in the United States and Africa, 1800–1993: Oppression and Retaliation* (Lewiston: Edwin Mellen, 1995).

Paige. These men, through their efforts on the playing field, proved to be valuable beacons of hope for African Americans living in a racist society that did not value their presence.

My grandfather, whom I have admired since I was old enough to understand what it meant to be raced and labeled as different, provided me with a clear example of what it meant to be a man at a time when I was unsure myself. Only now can I understand and recognize his selfless acts and quiet ways, as the result of his modeling himself after those brave individuals—those athletes who took it upon themselves to represent the whole of the black masses. Those black baseball stars, through the pursuit of professional sports in general and baseball in particular, could transcend the brutality of the America that my grandfather knew, and the America that I have come to face.

The story of the Negro Leagues is the story of how black players transcended institutional racism in American society. Cornel West believes that "[w]e are all born into and build on circumstances, traditions and situations not of our own choosing; yet we do make certain choices that constitute who we are and how we live in light of these fluid circumstances, traditions and situations."[13] Segregation, and its separate but equal policies, denied African Americans the same opportunities allotted to other ethnic groups. It was within this context that the Negro Leagues flourished and prospered, and where black baseball players carried forth the traditions of resistance that African Americans had long incorporated into their daily routines.

For my grandfather, the opportunity to watch Robinson, Aaron, Mays, and Paige succeed helped him discover his own humanity, masculinity, and pride in being black. Moreover, they represented his birthright to pursue and achieve the American dream: to have the right to work and live as he chose, to raise, care for, and protect his family, and to be counted as a man.

Masculinity, like femininity, is an extremely difficult concept to pin down. *Black* masculinity is even more complex. Hazel Carby has written an excellent book detailing the changing conceptions of black masculinity by examining men from W.E.B. Du

---

[13] *The Cornel West Reader*, p. 3.

Bois to Tiger Woods.[14] West believes black masculinity is "the elephant in the room no one dares mention."[15] He argues that "black self-hatred and self-contempt has to do with the refusal of many black Americans to love their own black bodies . . ."[16] For West, the love of one's body is an essential component to both masculinity and femininity. And for men like my grandfather, the athletes of the Negro Leagues helped awaken this newfound love of the black body.

Harlem Renaissance poet Sterling A. Brown (1901–1989) writes about the experience of slavery and the reactions that black men had to the institution:

> You sang:
> > Keep a-inchin' along
> > Lak a po' inch worm. . . .
>
> You sang:
> > Bye and bye
> > I'm gonna lay down dis heaby load. . . .
>
> You sang:
> > Walk togedder, chillen,
> > Dontcha git weary. . . .
> > > The strong men keep a comin' on
> > > The strong men git stronger.[17]

Brown's poem speaks for the generations of African American men, women, and children who have been the victim of racism in America. Players in the Negro Leagues also spoke for the generations of the disenfranchised. For African Americans the notion of a collective memory is a reality. The black ball players were able to create meaning out of turmoil, while shouting loudly, "We're American too."

---

[14] *Race Men* (Cambridge, Massachusetts: Harvard University Press, 1998).
[15] *The Cornel West Reader*, p. 514.
[16] *Ibid.*, p. 516.
[17] "Strong Men," in Michael Harper, ed. *The Collected Poems of Sterling Brown*, (Evanston: Northwestern University Press, 1980), p. 56.

Seventh Inning: The Japanese National Pastime?

Hitting a baseball is one of the most difficult things to do in any sport. With such a high failure rate, professional ball players have to train their minds almost as much as their bodies. Gregory Bassham believes that borrowing some basic concepts from Japanese Zen Buddhist philosophy can help prepare a hitter for the back door curve. Michael Brannigan attributes the recent influx of Japanese stars like Ichiro Suzuki to a training regime that is steeped in ancient philosophy.

13 | The Zen of Hitting

GREGORY BASSHAM

> There is a force in the universe that makes things happen.
> And all you have to do is get in touch with it. Stop thinking.
> Let things happen. And *be the ball*.
>
> —TY WEBB (CHEVY CHASE), in *Caddyshack*

Since Eugen Herrigel's classic *Zen in the Art of Archery* (1953), a host of writers have applied Zen Buddhist principles to a variety of sports and activities, ranging (plausibly) from martial arts and golf to (lamely) falling in love, casino gambling, and proposal writing. Among the Zen principles invoked by these writers are patience, relaxation, self-knowledge, visualization, practice, *kime* ("tightening the mind"), and *mushin* (overcoming subject-object dualism—Chase's "being the ball"). Many of these principles, I shall show, are echoed in the advice of great hitting instructors such as Ted Williams and Charley Lau. Thus, there is indeed a Zen of the art of hitting.

Zen Basics

Zen Buddhism is the Japanese branch of the Meditation School of Buddhism. Like all forms of Buddhism, Zen is rooted in the central teachings of Buddha (Siddartha Gautama, died ca. 480 B.C.E.): the impermanence of all things, the pervasiveness of suffering, the unreality of any enduring ego or self, rebirth,

205

universal compassion, and the pursuit of inner peace and enlightenment through the extinction of all egocentric and grasping desires. Zen, however, isn't your garden-variety Buddhism; it's a fusion of Indian Buddhism and Chinese Taoism; and this gives Zen its own unique and iconoclastic spirit. The uniqueness of Zen is captured in the ancient formula attributed to Bodhidharma, the Indian monk who reputedly introduced Zen to China ca. A.D. 520:

> A special transmission outside the scriptures;
> No dependence upon words and letters;
> Direct pointing at the soul of man;
> Seeing into one's nature and the attainment of Buddhahood.[1]

Four distinctive features are highlighted in this passage. First, Zen sees little value in religious dogmas or creeds; its emphasis is on direct experiential learning under the guidance of an acknowledged Zen Master, not reliance upon sacred texts or verbal doctrines. Second, Zen teaches that the deepest truths about reality cannot be grasped by the intellect or expressed in language; indeed, concepts and words are seen as obstacles to enlightened understanding. Third, Zen holds that Ultimate Reality ("Buddha reality") is absolutely unitary and distinctionless; that all ordinary objects of experience are *sunya* (empty, void); and that one's true self, one's "Buddha nature," can only be grasped by a "pure seeing" into one's innermost essence. Finally, Zen teaches that salvation (*nirvana*) cannot be achieved through good works or pious devotion, but only by a kind of immediate insight or enlightenment (*satori*) into the Oneness of reality. To achieve such enlightenment may take years of dedicated training, or it can occur in a flash in the midst of one's daily activities. In this way, Zen sees itself as faithful to the original spirit of Buddhism as a path—open to all—to inner peace and enlightenment.

In Japan, China, and other countries strongly influenced by Buddhism, arts such as painting and the martial arts are not intended merely for practical or aesthetic purposes. They are spiritual disciplines, ways of training the mind that can help their practitioners get in touch with their spontaneous, intuitive

---

[1] William Barrett, ed., *Zen Buddhism: Selected Writings of D.T. Suzuki* (New York: Doubleday, 1956), p. 61. In China, Zen Buddhism is known as Ch'an Buddhism.

natures. Let's see how Zen can be applied to the supremely difficult art of hitting a baseball.

Patience

Patience, the essential quality of a man.

—Kwai-Koo-Tsu[2]

Zen, like all forms of Buddhism, stresses the importance of patience. While Zen recognizes that enlightenment is open to all, and can occur at any time in a sudden, spontaneous revelation, it also teaches that enlightenment usually requires years of disciplined meditation and diligent effort. In all Zen-inspired arts one of the most persistent lessons students learn is the need to "conquer haste."[3]

Patience is also, of course, a cardinal virtue in hitting. The first rule in the book, says Ted Williams, is "get a good ball to hit."[4] Hitters need to know the strike zone, lay off pitches they have trouble hitting, and recognize that in most situations "a walk is as good as a hit."

Patience is important, as well, in the mechanics of good hitting. Hitting a baseball with authority is largely a function of timing, weight shift, hip torque, and bat speed. That's why you often hear coaches reminding hitters to "stay back." Hitters lose power when they overstride, "drift" (shift their weight too far forward before they swing), open their hips too soon, or pull their shoulder out too early. Occasionally you'll find great hitters like Yogi Berra and Kirby Puckett who will swing at and hit almost anything that's pitched to them. But the odds favor the patient, disciplined hitter.

Relaxation

Tension is the enemy.

—Charley Lau[5]

---

[2] Quoted in Joe Hyams, *Zen in the Martial Arts* (New York: Bantam, 1979), p. 26.

[3] *Ibid.*, p. 23. See also Eugen Herrigel, *Zen in the Art of Archery*, translated by R.F.C. Hull (New York: Vintage, 1953), p. 35 (discussing the importance of patience in archery).

[4] Ted Williams and John Underwood, *The Science of Hitting*, second edition (New York: Simon and Schuster, 1986), p. 24.

[5] Quoted in Mark Gola and John Monteleone, *The Louisville Slugger Complete Book of Hitting Faults and Fixes* (Chicago: Contemporary Books, 2001), p. 28.

Zen monks typically spend many hours a day in the practice of *zazen* (sitting meditation), seeking to calm and purify the mind. Zen-inspired arts such as archery and calligraphy also stress the importance of being "centered" and relaxed. In traditional Japanese archery, for example, students typically spend many months simply learning how to breathe and draw the bow "spiritually," that is, in a relaxed, tension-free manner.[6]

Tension can be a big problem for hitters. One common mistake many youngsters make is gripping the bat too tightly—what hitting guru Charley Lau calls the "white-knuckle syndrome."[7] A death grip on the bat causes tension in the arms and shoulders, which results in slower reaction time and less control. Usually an overly tight grip is related to another common hitting fault: holding the bat in the hands rather than in the fingers. Holding the bat in the hands slows your swing, limits bat control, and makes it harder to roll the top hand over and snap the wrists. In hitting, just as in golf or tennis, control is the name of the game, and control lies in the fingers, not in the hands.

Mental tension can be an even greater enemy to hitters than physical tension.[8] As Mickey Mantle points out, this is particularly true when a hitter is struggling:

> When you get into any kind of slump, you start to press, and the more you press, the worse you hit, so it becomes a catch-22. You slump, so you press, and when you press, you slump some more. The only way to get out of a slump is to relax and do things naturally.[9]

Good hitters know that slumps are part of the game.[10] The important thing is not to make things worse by beating up on yourself or over-intellectualizing. Relax, check your mechanics,

---

[6] *Zen in the Art of Archery*, pp. 19–27.

[7] Charley Lau and Alfred Glossbrenner, *The Art of Hitting .300* (New York: Hawthorne, 1980), p. 40.

[8] Recall Yogi Berra's sage remark: "Baseball is ninety percent mental; the other half is physical."

[9] Mickey Mantle and Phil Pepe, *My Favorite Summer, 1956* (New York: Dell, 1991), p. 174.

[10] As Hall of Famer Catfish Hunter once philosophically observed, "The sun don't shine on the same dog's ass all the time." Quoted in George F. Will, *Men at Work: The Craft of Baseball* (New York: Harper, 1990), p. 218.

and if these are sound, just concentrate on seeing the ball and "doing things naturally," or in other words, relying on muscle memory rather than conscious analysis. Soon you'll be making good contact again, and the hits will fall.

Self-Knowledge

Hitter, know thyself.

—TED WILLIAMS and JOHN UNDERWOOD[11]

Like all great religious and spiritual traditions, Zen sees itself as a pathway to self-realization and self-discovery. The first rule of Buddha's Eightfold Path is "right understanding." This involves not only a correct understanding of central Buddhist teachings about the nature of reality (rebirth, karma, and so forth), but also a grasp of fundamental truths about the self—how negative thoughts and emotions are rooted in egocentric attachments, how one's innermost essence (one's "Buddha nature") differs from one's conscious ego, and, at least for Zen, how enlightenment is possible only by learning to quiet the mind and draw upon a source of wisdom that lies deeper than the conscious, rational intellect.

"Know thyself" is also one of the cardinal rules of good hitting. All hitters have their strengths and weaknesses, and good hitters are aware of their own. If they're built like little Freddie Patek (5'5", 148 lbs.), they don't try to jack the ball out of the park like a Mark McGwire or a Barry Bonds. They know which pitches they can drive and which to lay off. Keen students of the game, they know the fundamentals of hitting, study pitchers closely, are open to constructive criticism, and work tirelessly to improve.

Visualization

See your future. Be your future.

—TY WEBB (CHEVY CHASE), in *Caddyshack*

Visualization—the process of vividly imagining one's own successful performance—is something almost all great athletes do.

---

[11] *The Science of Hitting*, p. 14.

Basketball players picture their shot swishing through the net. Gymnasts imagine themselves sticking the perfect landing. Great hitters also visualize their own success. Reggie Jackson used to envision himself putting the sweet spot of the bat on the ball and hitting a line drive to center field.[12] When Willie Stargell was slumping, he wouldn't analyze the problem; he would "see, feel and hear myself getting the result"[13] he wanted. Jason Giambi visualizes a "hitting box" in front of him that represents his strike zone.[14] Barry Bonds pictures himself at the plate, swinging hard and hammering the ball high and deep over fences that are deeper than they actually are.[15] And fans of Mark McGwire will remember televised images of him during his assault on Roger Maris's single-season home run record, standing in the on-deck circle, eyes closed, bat resting on his shoulders, envisioning his next at-bat.

How does visualization work? In two ways. First, it sharpens mental focus. Muscles are like three-year-olds: they're easily distracted, love picture books, and aren't very good with words. By visualizing, a hitter's brain sends a precise mental picture to his muscles saying, "See this; this is what I want you to do."

Second, visualization enhances self-confidence and the power of positive thinking. Martial arts film star Bruce Lee, who was a keen student of Zen, explains the power of positive thinking this way:

> The mind is like a fertile garden. It will grow anything you will plant—beautiful flowers or weeds. And so it is with successful, healthy thoughts or with negative ones that will, like weeds, strangle and crowd the others. Do not allow negative thoughts to enter your mind for they are the weeds that strangle confidence.[16]

A hitter always faces two contests, one with the pitcher and one with himself. The first contest is won when the hitter gets on

---

[12] *The Louisville Slugger Complete Book of Hitting Faults and Fixes*, p. 173.
[13] H.A. Dorfman and Karl Kuehl, *The Mental Game of Baseball: A Guide to Peak Performance*, third edition (Lanham: Diamond Communications, 2002), p. 113.
[14] Jack Curry, "Giambi Envisions Perfect Pitch," *New York Times* (March 10th, 2002).
[15] Stephanie L. Smith, "Learn from the Pro: Hit a Home Run Like Barry Bonds!" ChannelOne.com, October 8, 2001. Online at http://www.channelone.com/sports/articles/2001/10/08/learn.from.pro.
[16] Quoted in *Zen in the Martial Arts*, p. 108.

base or advances a runner, the second when he performs to the maximum of his ability. Nothing a batter does can guarantee success in the first sense; even the best hitter fails, on average, six or seven times out of ten. But there are things smart hitters can do to maximize personal performance. Visualization is a proven technique for boosting self-confidence and harnessing the power of positive thinking.

Practice

> Between the stages of apprenticeship and mastership there lie long and eventful years of untiring practice.
>
> —EUGEN HERRIGEL[17]

According to tradition, Buddha's dying words to his disciples were to "work out your salvation with diligence."[18] Without question, Buddhism is an arduous path for those who would tread its cloud-hidden upper reaches. To root out all selfish passions and attachments, to fill one's heart with compassion for all sentient beings, to know in one's bones (not merely in one's head) the unity of one's innermost essence with the Buddha-nature—these are not the work of a day or a month or a year. This is why, as Buddhist scholar Thich Thien-An explains, Zen requires dedication, commitment, and practice:

> Learning Zen is . . . like learning how to swim. When a person goes to a swimming class, the instructor will show him some basic methods and techniques, and then the rest is up to him. . . . If he practices hard enough, he may become a good swimmer. In Zen Buddhism it is the same way. If we want to become enlightened, we must go to a teacher and receive instructions. But once we receive instructions, the most important thing is to put them into practice. Only through practice can we hope to achieve enlightenment.[19]

Practice for a Zen Buddhist means many long hours of highly disciplined meditation. For a hitter it means wearing out an awful lot of batting gloves in batting cages or neighborhood sandlots.

---

[17] *Zen in the Art of Archery*, pp. 85–86.

[18] John B. Noss, *Man's Religions*, fifth edition (New York: Macmillan, 1974), p. 127.

[19] Thich Thien-An, *Zen Philosophy, Zen Practice* (Berkeley: Dharma, 1975), pp. 24–25.

Charles Garfield, a clinical psychologist at the University of California School of Medicine, interviewed approximately 1,500 high achievers. He found that "the single most powerful predictor of success in the long run [is] commitment."[20] Nowhere is this more true than in baseball.

Young hitters often fall into the trap of thinking that hitting is a natural gift, like good foot speed. It isn't. As Rogers Hornsby once remarked, "A great hitter isn't born, he's made."[21] Baseball, in fact, is a lot more like tennis than it is like track. It takes years of dedicated practice and repetition to develop the speed, power, and fine motor skills of a great tennis player. The same is true of hitting.

As a little leaguer, I was always one of the top hitters in the league, usually hitting over .500. As I got older, however, my average started to dip, and by my senior year in high school I was hitting under .300. At the time, I had a thousand excuses: I was too small, my eyes were going bad, I couldn't hit a curve ball. Ten years later, however, when I was in grad school, I began going to batting cages regularly, and I noticed a dramatic improvement. In three seasons of grad-league baseball, I hit over .400 against better-quality pitching than I had ever faced in high school.

Only then did I realize how important practice is in hitting. As a little leaguer, I was constantly swinging the bat in pick-up games with my friends. By high school, I was down to maybe thirty or forty swings a week in batting practice and games. That isn't enough swings to stay sharp. Hitting a baseball may or may not be the single most difficult thing to do in sport, as Ted Williams liked to argue.[22] But without question it is *one* of the most difficult, and no one can be really good at it without dedicated, persistent practice.

Kime (Tightening the Mind)

Although he was only five feet eight inches tall and weighed less than 150 pounds, Bruce Lee could hit like a ton of bricks. Once, in a practice session, Lee was challenged by a brawny

---

[20] Quoted in *The Mental Game of Baseball*, p. 45.
[21] Quoted in *The Science of Hitting*, p. 24.
[22] *Ibid.*, pp. 7–9.

weightlifter and decided that a gentle demonstration was in order. He asked the weightlifter to take a position about five feet from a swimming pool, placed his hand, fingers outstretched, on his chest, and asked him to brace himself. Lee suddenly closed his hand into a fist—a movement of perhaps a quarter of an inch—and the weightlifter went flying backward into the pool. Later, Lee was asked how he did it. "I relaxed until the moment I brought every muscle of my body into play, and then concentrated all the force in my fist," he replied. "To generate great power you must first totally relax and gather your strength, and then concentrate your mind and all your strength on hitting the target."[23]

What Lee was demonstrating was the power of *kime*, a martial arts technique for concentrating all of one's mental and physical energy on a single striking point. The secret of *kime*, Lee explains,

> is to exclude all extraneous thoughts, thoughts that are not concerned with achieving your immediate goal. . . . A good martial artist puts his mind on one thing at a time. . . . Like a Zen master, he is not concerned with the past or the future, only with what he is doing at that moment. Because his mind is tight, he is calm and able to maintain strength in reserve. And then there will be room for only one thought, which will fill his entire being as water fills a pitcher.[24]

In baseball, of course, coaches constantly stress the importance of concentration and focus. Hitting requires both perfect timing and split-second adjustment, and neither is possible without a laser-like concentration of mind. As former Dodger great, Steve Garvey, observes, once a hitter reaches the plate and takes his stance, all preparation and planning is past, and everything "now depends on concentration on the ball, body control, and reaction to the pitch."[25] In hitting, the margin of error is so small that the slightest distraction, the slightest wandering of attention,

---

[23] *Zen in the Martial Arts*, p. 114.
[24] *Ibid.*, p. 78.
[25] Quoted in *The Louisville Slugger Complete Book of Hitting Faults and Fixes*, p. 171. Similarly, Dale Murphy once remarked, "When you don't hit good, it's usually because you're thinking too much about everything else except the ball. And when you're hitting good, you're not really thinking about anything" (*The Mental Game of Baseball*, p. 154).

will almost always mean that the bat is not going to be at the right place at the right time. From the moment a pitcher's arm reaches the release point, a batter needs to be locked on to the ball with every ounce of energy and purpose, ready to uncoil and explode at the point of contact.

Mushin (No Mind)

Full head, empty bat.
—Hall of Fame General Manager BRANCH ("THE MAHATMA") RICKEY[26]

At the heart of Zen is the conviction that the center of human existence lies not in the rational intellect or personal ego, but in the unconscious. For it is in the unconscious, Zen teaches, that one finds an intuitive wisdom that lies deeper than all thought or emotion.

According to Zen, the highest state of human awareness—the "total consciousness" *Caddyshack*'s Bill Murray expects to achieve on his deathbed—is a state of complete egolessness in which all distinction between subject and object vanishes. This mystical or unitive state of consciousness is also the ultimate goal of Zen-inspired disciplines such as archery and the martial arts. In Zen archery, for example, mastery is achieved only when the art becomes an "artless art"[27] in which the archer becomes attuned to the Unconscious and acts simply on instinct, rather than from any conscious thought or calculation.[28]

The Japanese word for this state of egoless, unselfconscious attunement is *mushin* ("no thought"). According to Zen, conscious thoughts and emotions cause "psychical stoppages"[29] that interfere with the perfect fluidity of an artist or athlete's performance. Training and technique are essential, but ultimately—to use Wittgenstein's famous metaphor—these are rungs in a ladder that must be pulled up once one has climbed to the top.[30]

---

[26] Quoted in *Men at Work*, p. 210.

[27] D.T. Suzuki, "Introduction," in *Zen in the Art of Archery*, p. vi.

[28] In the iconography of Western pop culture, the best-known depiction of this Eastern concept is the scene from "Star Wars" in which Obi-Wan tells Luke, "Don't trust your eyes; they can deceive you. Trust your feelings."

[29] Daisetz T. Suzuki, *Zen and Japanese Culture* (Princeton: Princeton University Press, 1970), p. 144.

[30] Ludwig Wittgenstein, *Tractatus Logico-Philosophicus*, translated by D.F. Pears and B.F. McGuiness (New York: Humanities Press, 1974), sec. 6.54.

In baseball, too, it is a commonplace that too much thinking can result in "analysis paralysis" and interfere with peak performance. As Tony Gwynn remarks, "When you're going good, you don't worry about anything mechanical at the plate. You just go up there and see the ball and react to it."[31] Mickey Mantle recalls a conversation he had with Ted Williams once at an All-Star game. According to Mantle, Williams

> started talking about hitting. And he was wanting to know if I use my bottom hand when I'm hitting left-handed, do I pull the bat with this hand and guide it with this one, . . . which is your strong hand? And he was telling me all this stuff about hitting, and after I left the All-Star game I went like 0 for 30 . . . because I was trying to think of things that he told me to do."[32]

Hearing Mantle's story, readers of Alan Watts's classic *The Way of Zen*[33] are apt to recall the charming poem by Sir Edwin Ray Lankester that Watts quotes to illustrate the Zen doctrine of *mushin*:

> *The centipede was happy, quite*
> *Until a toad in fun*
> *Said, "Pray, which leg goes after which?"*
> *This worked his mind to such a pitch,*
> *He lay distracted in a ditch,*
> *Considering how to run.*[34]

The point, of course, is that nature has wisely left some things to instinct, reflex, and autonomic functioning. Some things, like blinking, breathing, and hitting a baseball, are just too important to be left to the vagaries of the conscious mind.

This isn't to say that a hitter's mind should be an absolute blank. The point, as Watts notes, "is not to reduce the mind to a moronic vacuity, but to bring into play its innate and spontaneous intelligence by using it without forcing it."[35] It is good for

---

[31] Quoted in *Men at Work*, p. 218. Compare George Brett: "When I'm good, I'm simply unconscious." Quoted in *The Mental Game of Baseball*, p. 153.
[32] Interview in Ken Burns, *Baseball: A Film*, PBS Home Video, 1994 (7th Inning).
[33] New York: Pantheon, 1957.
[34] *Ibid.*, p. 27.
[35] *Ibid.*, p. 21.

a hitter to visualize and to have a confidence-boosting thought ("I can hit this pitcher") or a simple reminder ("Stay back") running through his head. But a hitter worrying about his stance or his grip is asking for a quick trip back to the dugout. A ninety-mile-an-hour fastball reaches the plate in less than half a second. Most people I know take at least eight times that long to figure out the tip on a seven-dollar lunch tab. Only muscle memory—the fruit of long hours in the batting cage—gives a hitter the bat-speed, fine-motor adjustment, and smooth mechanics needed to hit with consistency and authority.

Ballparks, Dojos, and Other Places of Enlightenment

Big hitter, the Lama

—CARL SPACKLER (BILL MURRAY), in *Caddyshack*

Kendo, the ancient Japanese art of swordsmanship, is practiced in a dojo, a Japanese word that means "place of enlightenment." If the thesis of this chapter is correct, couldn't ballparks and batting cages also be seen as places of enlightenment, Bally's Gyms for the soul? Of course, many great hitters like Cobb, Ruth, Hornsby, Williams, and Mantle don't immediately leap to mind as models of egoless humility and mystical wisdom, so perhaps such comparisons shouldn't be pushed too far. But it is certainly true, as George F. Will notes, that "for an athlete to fulfill his or her potential, particularly in a sport as demanding as baseball, a remarkable degree of mental and moral discipline is required."[36] Many Zen principles clearly do apply to the art of hitting. Indeed, I would go further and suggest that hitters would benefit if these principles were more explicitly taught and more deeply appropriated and practiced. Perhaps it is true, as Zen teaches, that Enlightenment can occur anywhere—even on one's neighborhood sandlot.[37]

---

[36] *Men at Work*, p. 226.
[37] Thanks to Shoeless Joe Bronson and OH Ichiro Brannigan for helpful comments on an earlier draft of this chapter.

14 | Japanese Baseball and Its Warrior Ways?

MICHAEL BRANNIGAN

Riding the boat to fame and exorbitant salaries, a surge of young Japanese stars are following in the wake of pitcher Hideo Nomo, the first major leaguer from Japan since 1965. Nomo won the National League Rookie of the Year award the year he joined the Los Angeles Dodgers in 1995. The Dodgers then signed another ace hurler Kazuhisa Ishii for a four-year $12.3 million contract. And there is Kazuhiro Sasaki, the All-Star relief pitcher for the Seattle Mariners. The Mariners also acquired Ichiro Suzuki for a three-year $14 million contract. In winning the 2001 American League MVP award, lead-off hitter Suzuki became the second rookie to ever win the MVP. In that same year, he took the league's batting title with a .350 average and tallied 242 hits, the most hits in one season in the major leagues since 1930. Then there is the All-Star left fielder for the Yankees, Hideki "Godzilla" Matsui, who signed on in 2002 for a three-year $21 million contract.

Why this sudden surge in salaries for new Japanese talent? It's not surprising when one understands "Japanese" baseball and the philosophy that informs it.

New Sport, Old Roots

The Meiji Restoration in 1868 imported the American sport of baseball (*besuboru*), often referred to as *yakyu*, or "fieldball." Soon after two American teachers, Horace Wilson and Albert

Bates, introduced baseball to the Japanese in 1873, there was an opening volley of criticism from purists who believed that anything foreign would pollute the "true" Japanese spirit. Nevertheless, baseball caught on especially because it was American. As American, it embodied Western modernism, which the Japanese were all too eager to adopt after centuries of seclusion from the rest of the world.

Throughout their self-imposed quarantine, the Japanese had not thought of sports as a form of entertainment. Instead, playing sports was a serious and strict discipline primarily between individual competitors as in sumo, karate, and kendo. It thus made perfect sense for the Japanese to shape this foreign import along the lines of Spartan-like, martial arts training, the training embodied by the samurai warrior, or *bushi*. Japanese baseball has thus often been compared to the traditional Code of the Warrior known as Bushido, with its emphasis on relentless training and austere tests of body and will. Baseball also ushered in a new feature—the team. The Japanese carved out its team approach quite literally so that baseball acquired a significantly cautious and deliberate character, with walks far exceeding the number of strikeouts, unending squeeze plays and sacrifice bunts, and numerous consultations during the game. Redefined as a paradigm in moral training, Japan's new sport built on its cultural roots.

The Way of the Warrior

Bushido originated at the end of the Heian period, ca.1200, and then flourished for well over six centuries. When I first started training in the fluid-style Japanese karate known as Wado Ryu (Way of Peace), I was painfully introduced to its rigorous philosophy of struggle and sweat. As part of our sessions, we were taught to lie supine and pull ourselves across the hardwood gym floor solely by our knuckles. Within months, our knuckles went from being bloodied to scarred to calloused. Sure, we learned the art of evasion and counterstrike. But my hands paid a high price. And well over ten years of daily training and seven years of teaching later, they've become stiffer, more arthritic. But, that was the founder Hironori Ohtsuka Sensei's way. It was the Japanese way—pain, blood, and guts.

In Bushido, there is first the emphasis on self-denial. The good of the team always trumps individual achievement. Furthermore, each player must exhibit strict self-control. Despite grueling workouts, players must not complain. Next, just as Bushido underscores undying loyalty to one's lord, or *daimyo*, the Japanese ballplayer commits himself totally to the team, especially to his coaches and manager, with the manager having the last word. Yomiuri Giant Tetsuharu Kawakami's philosophy of "managed baseball" stressed absolute loyalty so that he would have the final say in just about every part of his players' lives. Not all coaches shared his philosophy. But neither did they share his remarkable success of piloting the Giants to eleven league titles and nine championships.

The Way of the Warrior also demanded austere and endless training. In like manner, players would field balls until exhaustion and pitchers would throw over a hundred pitches a day (occasionally incurring long-term injuries). Suisha Tobita, manager of Waseda University's team and one of the most famous figures in Japanese baseball, charged his young players to practice until they literally dropped from fatigue. His philosophy of baseball was known as *shi no renshu* ("training of death").[1]

Japanese now play the same 162-game schedule as Americans, but differences abound. The Japanese balls are slightly smaller. The Japanese strike zone is slightly wider. Most Japanese ballpark dimensions are slightly smaller than in the U.S. with 298 feet on the sides and 394 feet to center field.

More notable differences appear to reflect cultural values. For instance, after either four hours of play or else a set amount of innings (fifteen in the Central League and twelve in the Pacific League) the Japanese allow tie games. Ties count in the official standings. Ties are viewed as a respectable conclusion to a game since no team "loses face," that is, loses honor. From our American perspective, nobody wins in ties. From the Japanese perspective, nobody loses. Winning not only means outscoring your opponent; it can also mean not losing to your opponent. This difference helps explain Japan's more cautious approach to baseball. For instance, because the strike zone is wider by one

---

[1] Robert Whiting, *You Gotta Have Wa* (New York: Vintage, 1989), p. 38.

baseball on each side of the plate, the pitching style and strategy is somewhat different. There are numerous sacrifice strategies, especially bunts, even in the opening innings. Let us now look more closely at certain features of the game that are of particular interest to Japanese.

Resolve and Training

Japanese baseball takes resolve (*kesshin*, meaning "will power" and "determination") and training to new heights. It applies the martial arts principle that there are virtually no limits to physical ability and that resolve can perfect the body. It's the mind that imposes the limits. As for training, whereas American players begin their spring training in March, the Japanese start in the dead of winter, in mid-January. Japanese players spend all day on the field, hours of strategy meetings, hours of indoor training, and running five to ten miles a day. Even during the regular season, hours are spent on the field in intensive two-hour pre-game workouts followed by a game that usually lasts four hours, followed by a strategy and review meeting. The pre-game drill is just as critical as the game for it allows the teams to publicly display their resolve and fighting spirit, or *konjo*. No game is played without this pre-game show. If a pre-game practice is suspended due to rain, there is no game, even if it stops raining by game time!

Training is mental as well as physical. Mind and body work together so that proper mental attitude reveals itself in proper behavior. Many clubs do not allow their players to grow beards and long hair, and they prohibit drinking, smoking, and appearing on advertisements during the season. The Yomiuri Giants are especially strict. Not only do they forbid facial hair, but they require their players to wear ties in public. Late night carousing is absolutely prohibited, and players are not allowed to speak with reporters.

Proper behavior is required on the field. Displays of temper are anathema. Japanese pitchers throw their fair share of beanball pitches, aimed deliberately at the batter to throw him off balance. Yet the batter must train himself to get out of the way quickly enough. A pitch aimed at the batter does not erupt in a shouting match or a bench-clearing brawl. If a batter gets hit, it's his own fault. Indeed, Japanese fans heavily scorn any form of violence on the field. Not only is it improper behavior, but it disrupts the team's harmony, or *wa*. As Robert Whiting illustrates, American ball players in Japan have difficulty in this respect and often lose the respect of both their team and the fans by acting out their anger and frustrations on the field. The key is proper character, and character shows itself in the player's decorum. Players who violate team rules face stiff penalties such as heavy fines and even expulsion from the team.

The underlying philosophical premise behind resolve and training is that perfection can *only* come through ongoing, unqualified commitment, resolve, and practice. Stars are fashioned, not born. Effort (*doryoku*) is everything, for effort demonstrates resolve. Indeed, effort means more than the outcome. What ultimately matters is resolve.

The Self as Relational

What would Japanese baseball be without its numerous group meetings? The manager will even call spontaneous, *ad hoc* huddles with all of his players during a game. Much of this has to do with the virtual absence in Japanese thought of the notion of an individual, private self. Instead, the "self" is primarily relational. The term for individual, *ningen*, contains the character, *aidagara*, which literally means "in-betweenness" (a key idea in the writings of philosopher Tetsuro Watsuji, 1889–1960). This relationality, or "in-betweenness," is evident in the emphasis upon group wellbeing and in the all-important relationship among manager, coach, and player. The philosophy behind the martial arts reinforces this vital bond between teacher (*sensei*) and student (*senshu*). And though this bond is hierarchical, there is a working-together to hone discipline, technique, and resolve in a cooperative effort to abandon ego. Indeed, the genuine *sensei*, the true martial artist (there are many counterfeits), is egoless. The student, or player, in turn seeks to emulate this egolessness by throwing himself totally into his discipline and entrusting himself to his *sensei*, or manager.

Japanese thought traditionally discourages the notion of independence and individualism (*kojinshugi*). This has deep cultural roots particularly in the teachings of Buddhism and Confucianism. Buddhism, having its origins in India, rejects the claim of Hindus that there is a personal soul or self, an *atman*.

For Buddhists, there are no grounds to assert the existence of an independent self. Buddhists claim that each one of us is intimately connected with all other life forms in a complex web of cause-and-effect. There is no independent, private, autonomous self. The Japanese school of Zen Buddhism goes on to apply this teaching in radical ways; Zen is the fundamental spirit behind the martial arts, which in essence is the art of the sword—to slice away at the illusion of ego.

Combine this Zen insight with the core teaching in Confucianism—that a person's genuine identity is formed by the relationships that person engages in, and identity is, again, relational. I am my father's son, my mother's son, my wife's husband, my brother's brother, my sisters' brother, my friends' friend, my student's teacher, and so forth. Confucianism was readily assimilated in Japan since it underscored the Japanese emphasis upon special human relationships, the most important being the family. By extension, the baseball team is also a family so that the identity of ballplayers rests upon their belonging to the team. Link these two traditions—Buddhism and Confucianism—and we see the philosophical basis for group wellbeing and harmony, known as *wa*.

Got *Wa?*

Robert Whiting and many other observers claim that *wa* is the pervasive principle throughout Japanese culture. This makes perfect sense in a culture that views the self as relational, where the good of the team far exceeds that of individual players. For instance, there are free agents. But team loyalty still assumes a powerful priority over individual salaries, wages that are less than half that of American major leaguers. A Japanese sports newspaper printed the headline, "Egawa! You Greedy S.O.B.!" after the Giants' star pitcher Suguru Egawa requested a ten-percent salary raise.[2] And even though there are players' unions, strikes are rare.

This emphasis on *wa* affects views concerning the relationship between rights and duties. Although in principle rights and duties coexist on an equal level, in an American culture that stresses individualism and independence, rights are emphasized

---

[2] *Ibid.*, p. 71.

more so than duties. We feel violated when our natural or legal rights have been infringed upon. However, in Japan, where group harmony and wellbeing are all-important, duties are emphasized more than rights. Note the following ten rules that the Yomiuri Giants issue to their players. Though they are meant for all players, the Japanese press occasionally refers to them as the "Gaijin Ten Commandments" (*gaijin*, "outside person," meaning foreigners, in this case, American ball players).

1. Obey all orders issued by the manager.
2. Do not criticize the strategy of the manager.
3. Take good care of your uniform.
4. Do not scream and yell in the dugout or destroy objects in the clubhouse.
5. Do not reveal team secrets to other foreign players.
6. Do not severely tease your teammates.
7. In the event of injury, follow the treatment prescribed by the team.
8. Be on time.
9. Do not return home during the season.
10. *Do not disturb the harmony of the team.*[3]

Sadaharu Oh—Paragon of Bushido?

Given all of this, can we now maintain that there is a distinct "Japanese" baseball? Are the above traits—Bushido, resolve, fighting spirit, self as relational, harmony—genuinely universal traits in the way baseball is played in Japan? We must address one of the most controversial issues in the study of Japanese culture, the issue of so-called "Japaneseness." There is a literary genre called *Nihonjinron* that highlights a Japanese character and identity quite distinct from other national identities. It explains a litany of Japanese qualities like group harmony and interdependence as opposed to individualism and independence. Yet we need to be cautious. Presenting absolute differences between Japan and the rest of the world is tricky and dangerous. It is tricky because it oversimplifies the complex web of similarities and differences among cultures. It is dangerous because it can spawn a hyper-nationalism that encompasses attitudes of hubris and superiority.

---

[3] *Ibid.*, pp. 84–85. Italics mine.

We thus need to avoid casting Japanese baseball solely in terms of contrasts to American baseball. This is what William Kelly, a Yale University anthropologist who has written extensively about Japanese baseball and culture, dubs the "Whiting problem," the tendency to polarize Japanese baseball and American baseball as "finesse vs. power, manager-centered vs. player-centered, conservative play vs. imaginative tactics, harmony vs. individual pride, *ad nauseum*."[4]

To illustrate, let's look at Sadaharu Oh, generally believed to be the archetype of Japanese baseball. Japanese baseball has its share of heroes like Shigeo Nagashima of the Yomiuri Giants with six batting titles, and Sachio Kinugasa, the Hiroshima Carp third baseman who held the longest playing streak in baseball history, 2,215 consecutive games (Cal Ripken, Jr. later surpassed him, setting the world record at 2,632 consecutive games). And there is the "new breed" of superstars now playing in the American major leagues. Yet the top icon is still Sadaharu Oh, the Yomiuri Giants first baseman and later manager, with his home run record of 868 in 22 years (1958–80), far outpacing Hank Aaron's 755 and Babe Ruth's 714.

The left-handed slugger had a hallmark swing known as the "flamingo" style, with his right foot poised in the air just as the pitcher released the ball and before stepping into the swing. In his autobiography, *A Zen Way of Baseball*, Oh attributes his swing and his ensuing success to his batting coach and spiritual mentor Hiroshi Arakawa. Arakawa introduced Oh to the martial art forms of kendo and aikido, forms that clearly embody the spirit of Zen Buddhism.

Under Arakawa's tutelage, Oh had difficulty linking the philosophical basis of both aikido and kendo to the pragmatics of hitting. Nevertheless, Arakawa encouraged Oh to consider their connections more seriously. Whether Oh was able to recognize and appreciate the way of Zen is debatable. What is certain is that his hitting drastically improved. He won all sorts of batting titles including back-to-back Triple Crowns (leading the league in home runs, batting average, and runs-batted-in in one

---

[4] William W. Kelly, "Caught in the Spin Cycle: An Anthropological Observer at the Sites of Japanese Professional Baseball," in Susan O. Long, ed., *Moving Targets: Ethnographies of Self and Community in Japan* (Ithaca: Cornell University Press, East Asia Papers, 2000), p. 144.

season) and hit the single season record for home runs in 1964 with 55, a record that has not been broken (though the American player for the Kintetsu Buffaloes, Tuffy Rhodes, tied his record in 2001).

However, according to Kelly, it is a mistake to think of the relationship between Arakawa and Oh as representative of the *sensei-senshu* (master-student) relationship in the martial arts. In this traditional relationship, the *sensei* performs and acts out the forms and techniques and assumes center stage while the student learns by watching and imitating. Yet in the case of Arakawa and Oh, Arakawa was more or less on the sidelines guiding Oh, while Oh played center stage.[5] We can thus infer that, on the one hand, Oh was certainly a paragon of Bushido in his absolute commitment and loyalty to his *sensei* and martial arts mentor, Arakawa. On the other hand, it is questionable whether Oh genuinely understood and appreciated the philosophy behind his batting style.

Bushido Resolve?

As noted earlier, resolve necessarily entails *konjo*, or "fighting spirit," similar to the martial arts term *gambatte*, which means to do *more* than your best, to exceed your limits. Are resolve and *konjo* ubiquitous features of baseball in Japan? Whiting claims that *konjo* captures the essence of Japanese baseball. Kelly disagrees. He argues that *konjo* has no doubt expressed itself during certain times in the history of the sport, but is not in itself a universal trait. He singles out three historical moments. First, during the Meiji restoration, *konjo* was stressed in baseball as a way to prove to critics the moral and physical fiber of the newly adopted sport. Second, as professional baseball became increasingly commercialized and profit-oriented, Suishu Tobita forged his "training of death" philosophy. Yet this did not curb commercialization nor did it deter players from engaging in all sorts of scandals and deals on the side. Third, by applying the philosophy of *konjo*, the Yomiuri Giants earned the pride of the

---

[5] William W. Kelly, "Learning to Swing: Oh Sadaharu and the Pedagogy and Practice of Japanese Baseball" in John Singleton, ed., *Learning in Likely Places: Varieties of Apprenticeship in Japan* (New York: Cambridge University Press, 1998), p. 279.

nation, and many Japanese identified with their success and their fighting spirit.

Dominating the world of baseball with their record nine consecutive championships, the Giants were the quintessential Japanese team. Indeed, when Tetsuharu Kawakami became the manager of the Giants and demanded absolute loyalty and rigorous training, he also insisted upon having a team without *gaijin* in order to sculpt a team that was all-Japanese. And the fact that two of the greatest players in the history of Japanese baseball, Sadaharu Oh (ironically not pure-blooded Japanese, with a Chinese father) and Shigeo Nagashima piloted the Giants to their remarkable success lent a special aura to the Giants.[6] For many Japanese, the Giants embodied the spirit of Japan, or at least the Japan they wished to see restored. Yet, as Kelly reminds us, the Giants' resolve and *konjo* was not shared by all other Japanese teams.

Who Needs *Wa*?

Did the resounding success of the Giants really rest upon the philosophy of team harmony, *wa*? According to Kelly, the team's success was due essentially to the individual talents of star players like Oh and Nagashima. In Oh's case, his coach Arakawa's focus on aspects of martial arts training to help him with his batting swing might lead us to think of Oh as symbolizing the Japanese spirit that is antithetical to strict individualism. But this anti-individualist picture isn't entirely accurate. Oh admits as much in his autobiography:

> Of course Mr. Kawakami stressed harmony among us . . . But it was his approach to the game that distinguished him most. Play with greed for victory, he taught, and this he most peculiarly emphasized as an individual thing. One strove for the highest individual goal possible and did so relentlessly . . . We had an obligation to the team, but this obligation was best fulfilled by learning to use ourselves individually to the limit.[7]

---

[6] William W. Kelly, "Blood and Guts in Japanese Professional Baseball," in Sepp Linhart and Sabine Frühstück, eds., *The Culture of Japan As Seen Through Its Leisure* (Albany: SUNY Press, 1998), pp. 104–06.
[7] Cited in "Learning to Swing," p. 281.

Nonetheless, the *image* of team spirit was skillfully presented to the public. It was an image that the Japanese wanted to believe in, especially after the banner year 1964: the year that Oh hit his 55 home runs, and the year of the stunning gold medal victory of the women's volleyball team over the Russians as Japan hosted the Olympics.

What's Wrong with Generalization?

Does *yakyu* mean the same for Japanese as it does for Americans? Can we refer to baseball in Japan as "Japanese" baseball distinct from "American" baseball?

Adding the qualifier "Japanese" to baseball has three strikes against it. Strike one: It conveys the false notion that there is a completely separate and unique entity known as Japanese baseball. Strike two: It conveys the equally false idea that all Japanese think alike when it comes to baseball and approach the game in the same way. Strike three: It inflates the differences among cultures so that there is "American" baseball, "Taiwanese" baseball, "Cuban" baseball, and so on.

We naturally generalize, seeking to understand. Generalizations underscore what appear to be prevailing patterns of behavior and thought. For this reason, generalizations necessarily allow for exceptions. The danger creeps in, however, when we assume that they do not, when we think of generalizations more as monolithic nets that we can cast upon an entire culture. This is especially risky when the culture is both complex and seemingly alien.

There is now in Japan the "new breed" of baseball players, players who candidly disdain the older traditional ways of playing ball by exuding individuality and independence. For instance, Hiromitsu Ochiai, third baseman for the Lotte Orions who won the Triple Crown an unprecedented three times (1983, 1985, 1986), has openly criticized teams' excessive drills. While admired by younger Japanese, many still think of him as embodying pure individualism. And there is "You Greedy S.O.B." Suguru Egawa who refuses to put in the same practice regimen as his teammates. Fans and media alike have faulted him for lacking both duty (*giri*) and kindness to his team. Yet these remain exceptions. Surely, younger Japanese players continue to tout their freedom from the old ways and claim their new independence, but are they truly becoming more individualized? Only the test of time will tell. In summary, one thing is clear. While exercising prudence in generalizing, it is apparent that a nation's sport can be a reliable mirror of that nation's character and beliefs. Likewise, the way baseball in Japan is viewed and played speaks volumes about the Japanese, their culture, philosophies, and values.

When the Bad News Bears went to Japan in 1979, Hollywood's favorite little league team learned that the young stars across the Pacific Ocean were formidable foes. Now that Japanese ball players are making their way to the major leagues, fans everywhere are treated to a whole new generation of stars. Ichiro's MVP year was no Hollywood ending. In fact, it's only the beginning.

Eighth Inning:
Behind in the Count

*Who deserved the MVP award last year?
Is Barry Bonds better than Babe Ruth?
In debating and answering questions like
these we inevitably turn to statistics.
Jay Bennett and Aryn Martin explore the
nature of numbers and the people who
trust them. There is one thing all great
major league players have had in
common: they've all been men. Leslie
Heaphy draws on some fundamental
themes in feminist philosophy as she
questions the prejudice against
women in "America's" game.*

15 | The Numbers Game: What Fans Should Know about the Stats They Love

JAY BENNETT AND ARYN MARTIN

There's an old *Peanuts* cartoon in which Charlie Brown, the unluckiest player-manager in baseball, gives up a walk-off home run in the last game of the season. His hapless team ends the year with 0 wins and 20 losses. Some time later, Schroeder, the team's statistician, consoles his sad-sack pitcher.

> I've worked up some interesting statistics here about our baseball team Charlie Brown . . .
>
> I think you'll find that they say something to us . . .
>
> Last year our opponents scored three thousand and forty runs to our six! They made forty-nine hundred hits to our eleven and they made nineteen errors to our three hundred . . .

Charlie Brown, disheartened, finally shouts, "Tell your statistics to shut up!!"[1]

Playing the Numbers Game

Baseball fans (with the possible exception of Charlie Brown) love statistics. More than in any other sport, fans of America's pastime pore over tables to venerate and vilify players, teams,

---

[1] Charles M. Schulz, *Slide, Charlie Brown! Slide!* (Greenwich, Connecticut: Fawcett 1962).

233

and managers. Numbers seem to transcend time and place as they allow fans to compare events and players that are miles and years apart. Why are baseball fans so fond of stats? Is it simply because the numbers tell the story about streaks and slumps? Is it because fans are drawn into the game as participants and amateur mathematicians? Is it because, during a slow game, scribbling on the scorecard passes the time between trips to the hot dog stand? "Baseball fans are junkies, and their heroin is the statistic."[2] You can miss a game and still get a quick fix of ERAs, RBIs, and HRs to prevent withdrawal symptoms. In the stands, our expectations rise and fall with the array of statistics on the digital scoreboard, as though they tell us something very tangible and important about a player's past, present, and future.

Baseball fans have some things in common with another community of avid counters and enumerators. All manner of scientists are daily involved in the generation of numerical constants to describe or predict properties of nature. However, as the philosopher and historian of science Thomas Kuhn (1922–1996) suggests, this has not always been the case.[3] He describes a second scientific revolution (the first having occurred in the seventeenth century with Bacon, Galileo, Newton *et al.*), in which quantification was a central feature. During the mid-1800s, Kuhn argues, physical scientists became newly concerned with generating an "avalanche of numbers." Philosopher of science Ian Hacking summarizes Kuhn's argument: "The world was now conceived in a more quantitative way than ever before. The world is seen as constituted by numerical magnitudes."[4] As an example, Hacking cites a pamphlet published in 1835 by Charles Babbage, the father of computing. In it, Babbage urged the publication of tables of all the numerical constants known in the sciences and the arts, from specific gravities and atomic weights to the amount of oak a man can saw in an hour. The everyday practice of science in the mid to late 1800s—and arguably today—was aimed at devising precise and ingenious instruments and methods for "obtaining very accurate numbers that don't matter much."[5]

----

[2] Robert S. Weider, quoted on http://www.baseball-almanac.com/quotes/stats5.shtml.
[3] Thomas S. Kuhn, "The Function of Measurement in Modern Physical Science," *Isis,* Vol. 52, Issue 2 (1961), pp. 161—193.
[4] Ian Hacking, *Representing and Intervening: Introductory Topics in the Philosophy of Natural Science* (Cambridge: Cambridge University Press, 1983), p. 242.
[5] *Ibid.*, p. 236.

Perhaps it's not coincidental that baseball, a sport afloat in statistics, originated in the mid-1800s, when the scientific world was engaged in a proliferation of measurement. If the urge to enumerate in baseball is similar to what Hacking describes as "the fetish for measuring precise numbers" in the sciences, maybe the motivations are also analogous. Kuhn suggests that with the explosion of statistics in physics came a decrease in the length of controversies about scientific theories, and an increase in consensus that emerged from such controversies. Imagine a debate about the best hitter in baseball without numbers. On what would one base an argument but personal proclivities and scattered observations? Bringing batting averages into the debate shortens controversy and promotes consensus. For example, to answer the question *who was the best hitter in the National League in 2002?*, all we have to do is consult 2002's voluminous statistics and we find that Barry Bonds won the batting championship with the highest batting average of .370. It's all very simple. Just sorting a set of numbers.

What could be complex about statistics, and in particular, baseball statistics? After all, statistics are just numbers and numbers are a definitive means of answering a question. But for statisticians and philosophers, these numbers are complex elements in themselves. They are a synthesis and view of the complex process that created them, an intricate sequence of balls, strikes, line shots, groundballs, running catches, and sprints to the next base on the path home. Vast compilations of batting and pitching statistics in encyclopedias and Internet websites give false comfort in the precision of how well we understand player and team abilities. One of the ironies of statistical analysis is that it often reveals the limitations of our knowledge.

At the end of each season, Major League Baseball (MLB) recognizes the player with the highest batting average in each league as the league's batting champion. The batting average (BA) is simply the number of hits (H) divided by the number of at bats (AB). Over the course of MLB history, there have been many tight races for this championship. In 2003 the NL saw the tightest contest for the batting championship in over 50 years and the AL contest was almost as close. In the last half-century, seven out of the 100 batting championships have been decided by the result of one at bat. That is, if the challenger had just one more hit, he would have displaced the winner as batting champion. The table below lists these seven close races.

Year	League	Player	Team	AB	H	BA	Difference
2003	National	Albert Pujols	St. Louis	591	212	0.3587	0.0002
		Todd Helton	Colorado	583	209	0.3585	
1970	American	Alex Johnson	California	614	202	0.3290	0.0004
		Carl Yastrzemski	Boston	566	186	0.3286	
1982	American	Willie Wilson	Kansas City	585	194	0.3316	0.0009
		Robin Yount	Milwaukee	635	210	0.3307	
1991	National	Terry Pendleton	Atlanta	586	187	0.3191	0.0011
		Hal Morris	Cincinnati	478	152	0.3180	
2003	American	Bill Mueller	Boston	524	171	0.3263	0.0012
		Manny Ramirez	Boston	569	185	0.3251	
1976	American	George Brett	Kansas City	645	215	0.3333	0.0013
		Hal McRae	Kansas City	527	175	0.3321	
1960	National	Dick Groat	Pittsburgh	573	186	0.3246	0.0019
		Norm Larker	Los Angeles	440	142	0.3227	

For example, in 2003, if Manny Ramirez had one more hit in his 569 at bats, he would have finished with a .327 BA, ahead of Bill Mueller. When you consider the number of close plays that could occur over the course of a season, isn't it possible that one of his 384 outs could easily have been a hit? A bang-bang play at first that didn't go his way? Or a line shot barely speared by a leaping infielder? Perhaps it was pure chance that Ramirez did not get that extra hit to win the batting championship. On the other hand, maybe Mueller could have had one less hit which would have given him a .324 BA. Perhaps he was fortunate in a ruling that gave him a hit where an error would have been in order.

Ramirez was not Mueller's only serious challenger for the 2003 AL batting championship. Yankees shortstop Derek Jeter finished with a .324 BA. Two additional hits in his 482 at bats would have given him the title. Maybe he actually was a better hitter than Mueller but luck was not in his favor. From a statistician's perspective, there's an element of chance in any measurement (such as batting average) resulting from a process (such as a baseball season). For a statistician, luck or chance (the terms will be used synonymously) is what is left over after the elements that are controlled or understood are eliminated.

The Luck of the Average

It's not difficult to imagine that luck or chance may have been the final arbiter in determining which of these three players won the 2003 AL batting championship. The same goes for the other six closely contested races. But statistical theory indicates that the set of potential contenders may be much larger.

The theory is based on the premise that each batter has an ability to obtain a hit in each at bat. This *ability* has an unknown constant numerical value. The outcome of each at bat is a random event—that is, one determined by chance subject to constraints from the batter's ability and other possible factors (such as the ability of the opposing pitcher, characteristics of the ballpark, and the vagaries of the weather). For simplicity, we will focus on the batter's ability by assuming that these other factors are either not significant or folded into the chance element.

Under this theory, if a batter's ability is marked at .300, he has a 30 percent chance to get a hit and a 70 percent chance of making an out in each at bat. This is the easy part of the theory. The difficult part of the theory arises from the "unknown" aspect of the definition of ability. The standard assumption is that if a batter gets 30 hits in 100 at bats, then his ability is .300. However, based on statistical theory, in 100 at bats, a batter with .250 ability has a 5 percent chance of getting 30 hits, a 3 percent chance of getting 31 hits, and even a very small chance of getting 100 hits. If we consider all possibilities of getting 30 to 100 hits, he has a 15 percent chance of getting 30 hits or more. So, if we observe a batter with 30 hits in 100 at bats, it is very likely that his ability is close to .300 but there is still a substantial possibility that it could be .250 or even lower.

Of course, over an entire season, regular position players have many more than 100 at bats. According to the *Official Rules of Major League Baseball*, a player in a 162-game season must have at least 502 plate appearances to qualify for the batting championship. Plate appearances include official at bats, along with walks, hit by pitches, sacrifice flies, sacrifice hits, and catcher's interference. (Barry Bonds only had 403 official at bats in 2002, but his 198 walks elevated his plate appearances to qualify for the National League batting championship.) This greatly increased sample size might be expected to have a powerful effect in reducing the significance of chance in batting averages of regular players.

Continuing with our 2002 Bonds example, we observed that Bonds had 149 hits in 403 at bats for a .370 BA. However, according to statistical theory, while .370 is our best estimate of his batting ability, there is a 16 percent chance that his ability was actually lower than .346 and only good luck gave him a .370 BA. It works both ways so that there is also a 16 percent chance that his ability was higher than .394 and bad luck reduced his BA to .370. It's important to distinguish between his ability (which is fixed but unknown) with his BA (which is known from observation but is at least partly the result of chance). Generally, the two are treated as being identical, but they are not. The observed BA is only a clue (albeit an important one) to finding his true ability.

Larry Walker was runner-up to Bonds in the 2002 NL batting championship. With a .338 BA, Walker finished a distant 32 points behind Bonds. Could luck have accounted for such a large difference in BA? Actually, statistical theory indicates that there is about a 16 percent chance that Walker was the better hitter in 2002 and only Barry's good luck and Larry's bad luck made the difference. (Recall that we are using a simple model here that does not account for park effects which could be substantial in any comparison with Walker who played for Colorado.) If luck could have been significant, imagine what that implies about the seven close races discussed earlier. In effect, those six races were decided by luck; the first and second place batters had virtually the same batting abilities.

How powerful is the influence of luck in baseball? Is it possible that *all* Major League hitters have the same ability and only chance determines their final positions in the race for the batting championship? In 2002, 146 players in the American and National Leagues qualified for the batting championship with 502 plate appearances. Their BAs ranged from .215 (Jeromy Burnitz, Mets) to .370 (Bonds) with .278 being the average value. Since we are only considering hitters with a substantial number of plate appearances, marginal players are not included. Therefore, the hypothesis that all have the same ability is not as preposterous as it might seem. Theoretically, if all 146 batters had the same ability (.278 BA), we would expect about 18 hitters to bat higher than .300 and about 10 to bat less than .250 in a season by chance alone.[6] In 2002, 32 hitters had a BA greater than .300 and 25 had a BA less than .250. Since many more batters were observed in the extreme ends of BAs than expected from chance alone, the distribution of observed BAs has greater spread than can be accounted for by chance. It is reasonable to conclude that differences in batting ability play a major role in determining the batting champion as well as chance.

We can actually get a rough idea of the degree to which ability and luck play a role in determining a player's batting average. The variation in observed BAs from .215 to .370 is the result of two sources of variation: ability and chance. We calculated the variation due to chance so whatever is leftover is due to ability. This is a reverse application of Branch Rickey's oft-quoted axiom that "Luck is the residue of design."[7] We are removing the luck factor and assuming that what is left is variation in ability from player to player. Since the variation of BAs due to chance is about half that observed in the 146 player BAs, we conclude that chance and ability played equal parts in determining player BAs observed in 2002. Eliminating chance from the observed BAs, we can estimate that the true abilities of the 146 players are most likely in the range from .230 to .331, rather than .215 to .370.

Batting average is the oldest and most familiar measure of batting performance in baseball. However, many studies have demonstrated that BA is perhaps the weakest of all batting measures in estimating run production.[8] The on-base percentage (number of times reaching base divided by the number of plate appearances) and the slugging percentage (total bases from hits divided by at bats) improve on BA in this respect. Summing these two values together to obtain on-base plus slugging

---

[6] This calculation was performed using a simulation of 1,000 batters all with the same ability in getting hits. In this simulation the number of at bats was randomized from the set of at bats for the 146 players considered. This simulation indicated that if all 146 players had the same ability the mean batting average would be .278 and the standard deviation of batting averages would be .01909. Based on a gamma distribution with this mean and standard deviation, 18 of the 146 players would have observed batting averages greater than .300 and 10 players would have observed batting averages less than .250.

[7] Paul Dickson, *Baseball's Greatest Quotations* (New York: HarperCollins, 1991), p. 356.

[8] See for example John Thorn and Pete Palmer, *The Hidden Game of Baseball* (Garden City: Doubleday, 1985) and Jim Albert and Jay Bennett, *Curve Ball: Baseball, Statistics, and the Role of Chance in the Game* (New York: Springer-Verlag, 2001).

(OPS) is better than either separately. Does luck have the same influence over other batting measures?

If we perform a similar analysis on on-base percentage, slugging percentage, and OPS as we did for BA using the 146 qualifiers for the batting championships in 2002, we find that ability played a much larger role in determining their observed values, about three to four times that of chance. This evidence provides further support for their use instead of BA. Not only are they better measures of run production, but they are also better in discriminating ability from chance.

Great Teams or Just Plain Lucky?

Individual player performances are of great interest to fans, but the heart of any sport lies in team performance, particularly in its quest for a championship. How much does chance affect baseball championships?

Throughout its history, baseball has had its share of miracle teams who surprised everyone, fans and sportswriters alike, in their great achievements beyond all expectations. Perhaps the most famous such team in recent history is the 1969 New York Mets, who won 100 games (most in the National League), swept the Atlanta Braves in the League Championship Series, and won the World Series from the heavily favored Baltimore Orioles in five games. From their record, the Mets sound like an indomitable team. But it didn't appear that way when the 1969 season opened. The 1968 Mets finished one game out of the cellar in a ten-team National League; their .451 winning percentage was their best finish to date in their brief seven-year history. In 1970, they returned to mediocrity with an 83–79 record. Were the Mets truly the best team in baseball in 1969, or were they just lucky?

For the book *Curve Ball*, Jim Albert developed a statistical model of team performance based on historical distributions of team talent. He designed an experiment in which 1,000 baseball seasons were replayed using the current structure of 162-game seasons, followed by a playoff tournament involving six divisional champions and two wild card teams. In each experimental season, each team is randomly assigned a talent within the constraints of historical distributions of team talent. In each game, a victor is determined by comparing the talents of the two teams subject to an element of chance. Unlike the historical MLB record where only the performance is known, both performance and talent are known for the results of these 1,000 virtual seasons. So, we can see how well a team with a certain level of talent can be expected to perform. A team with average talent should only win about half of its games. And yet Albert's experiment indicates that such a team still has a 19 percent chance of getting into the playoffs, a 3 percent chance of winning the pennant, and a 1 percent chance of winning the World Series. Even more startling is that the team with the best talent of all 30 teams has an 11 percent chance of missing the playoffs and only a 21 percent chance of winning the World Series. According to Albert's simulation, about four of every five World Series under the current season and playoff structure are not won by the most talented team!

We can also see the converse: how much performance can tell us about a team's talent. If a team wins the World Series, how good was the team apart from its luck? Almost half of World Series champions are among the top three talent-laden teams in a MLB season. Surprisingly though, more than one out of eight World Series champions has only average talent or worse. ESPN columnist Rob Neyer observed that "winning the World Series isn't about being the best, it's about being the luckiest."[9]

Much of this is a result of the playoff structure. The existence of a wild card team was introduced as a safety net allowing a strong team less favored by its divisional placement to have an opportunity in the playoffs. Albert's results indicate that this system rescues the team with the best talent once every eight seasons. On the other hand, for every such great team given a second chance, almost five teams with average or worse talent are given an opportunity that they may not deserve. Even without the inclusion of a wild card team, the divisional structure gives less talented teams greater opportunity to enter the playoffs where the limited number of games allows chance a greater role. The distribution of talent across divisions is just another way that chance is introduced into the determination of a World Series champion.

Thus, the current MLB structure may not be optimal for determining which team is best. One might ask if the purpose

---

[9] http//www.espn.com (April 2nd, 2003).

of playing MLB games is to find the best team or is it to entertain the MLB fan base? Clearly, the games are played as entertainment. The divisional organization and playoff structure do
provide a greater opportunity for less talented teams to overcome more talented ones. Whether this makes baseball more
entertaining is open to conjecture and may depend on personal
preference. The current structure of playoffs guarantees a cli-
matic series of games at the conclusion of the season at the
expense of never having the season-long suspense of a pennant race for all the marbles in a league. We will have great
championship series like the 1980 NLCS in which the Phillies
topped the Astros in five games, four of which went into extra
innings including the finale. But we will never again have the
1951 NL pennant race in which the New York Giants overcame
a mid-August $13\frac{1}{2}$-game deficit to tie the Brooklyn Dodgers at
the end of the regular season and won a three-game playoff
with Bobby Thompson's "shot heard around the world" on the
final at bat.

In general, the element of chance, the unexpected, does
appear to add to the entertainment value of baseball. However,
too much chance, the appearance that the "best" team does not
win often enough devalues the games. Some compromise
between the two is best. The point at which that compromise
lies is still an open issue.

Numbers and Players

Perhaps players have an intuitive understanding that the luck of
the numbers plays such a big part in their professional accom-
plishments. Baseball players are noted for being the most superstitious of professional athletes. This perceived lack of ability to
control their destiny may be at the root of the many superstitions
that permeate baseball. Mets and Phillies outfielder Lenny
Dykstra was noted for throwing out his batting gloves and
changing his wad of chewing tobacco if he made an out.[10] This
perception may well be influenced by the limited control they
feel in the outcome of a play. They have confidence in their abil-

---

[10] Robert Gordon and Tom Burgoyne, *More Than Beards, Bellies, and Biceps: The Story
of the 1993 Phillies (And the Phillie Phanatic Too)* (Champaign: Sports Publishing, 2002),
p. 62.

ities, but they recognize that their skills may take them only so far. Hall of Fame pitcher Lefty Gomez claimed he would rather be lucky than good.[11] Statistics show that while Gomez may be guilty of hyperbole, there is a solid rationale for his conviction.

Continuing in this vein, managers have less control over game outcomes than players, and as a group are reputed to be even more superstitious. Sparky Anderson never stepped on a foul line when visiting the mound. Gene Mauch never had his uniform cleaned when his team won.[12] (At least the 1964 Phillies, losers of the National League pennant when they dropped 10 of their last 12 games, sank with a skipper in a clean uniform.) In 1911, Charles Victory Faust told John McGraw that a fortune-teller had guaranteed the New York Giants would win the pennant if he pitched for them. Although Faust had no skill whatever as a pitcher, McGraw kept him on the Giants payroll from 1911 through 1913 as a good luck charm. Faust warmed up for every game (though he never started) and the Giants did win the pennant in each of those years.[13]

McGraw, who was nicknamed Little Napoleon, may have been inspired by Bonaparte himself who was reputed to have implored "Give me generals who are lucky!" So, the notion that luck potentially plays a major role in success cuts across all strata and professions. What makes baseball so interesting is that the records kept of performance and the situations in which they occur are more extensive and thorough than in any other profession. They allow us to truly get a quantitative sense of the extent to which baseball player careers (and our own lives) are affected by chance.

Numbers as Players

Numbers, it is oftentimes supposed, strip away subjective opinion in favor of cold hard facts. They turn a chaotic world into orderly tables expressed in a universal and crisp language. They lend an air of irrefutable authority to any claim. As Lord Kelvin famously remarked, "When you measure what you are speaking about and express it in numbers, you know something about it;

---

[11] Bob Chieger, *Voices of Baseball* (New York: New American Library, 1983), p. 153.
[12] http://www.oaklandchamber.com/html/2000_04_As_superstition.html.
[13] Lawrence S. Ritter, *The Glory of Their Times* (New York: Macmillan, 1966), pp. 93–97.

but when you cannot measure it in numbers, your knowledge is of a meager and unsatisfactory kind."[14] Numbers, then, are appealing to baseball fans and scientists alike because they seem to crystallize information so that it can be readily communicated, compared and exchanged.

But it's easy to forget that numbers are wily. Philosophers of science can also be instructive in helping us to ponder some less than obvious characteristics of letting the numbers tell the story. At first glance, baseball statistics, like specific gravities and atomic weights, seem to be purely descriptive: they describe elements of the world in bland and no-nonsense ways. If numbers are descriptive—if statistics reflect what happened in a baseball game—they are at best partially so. Porter reminds us that:

> Mathematical and quantitative reasoning . . . provide no panacea. Mapping the mathematics onto the world is always difficult and problematical. Critics of quantification . . . have often felt that reliance on numbers simply evades the deep and important issues.[15]

Numbers embody all manner of contingencies and subjective moments that lie buried in their making. In particular, the role of chance in producing these numbers (as demonstrated with batting averages) is neglected. The size of the ball park and the particular pitchers faced will impact a hitter's average. Also, factors such as the wind and shadows are not in the hitter's control (though a seasoned hitter will make an effort to adjust). Even human decisions, such as error scorings, can affect the way a hit is recorded and thus become part of the batting average process. As we saw earlier, when statistics are calculated differently—on-base plus slugging instead of batting average, for example—they subtly change how events are described and understood. As Hacking asks, "Do measurements measure anything real in nature, or are they chiefly an artifact of the way in which we theorize?" Statistics don't lie, but they are subject to misinterpretation. A statistical description of a baseball game may be like "a travel book that ignored a charming landscape

---

[14] Quoted in Theodore Porter, *Trust in Numbers* (Princeton: Princeton University Press, 1995), p. 72.
[15] *Ibid.*, p. 5.
[16] *Representing and Intervening*, p. 233.

and its inhabitants in favor of recording precisely the times of arrival and departure of trains."[17]

Some philosophers would propose that numbers are not descriptive but prescriptive: they shape the world they are meant to describe. An anthropologist can change an environment simply by observation. Even in physics, as Niels Bohr (1885–1962) famously observed, measurement itself becomes a part of the phenomenon being measured.[18] Similarly, Theodore Porter suggests that "measures succeed by giving direction to the very activities that are being measured."[19] In other words, numbers have agency in the world. Porter draws on the work of French philosopher Michel Foucault (1926–1984) to assert that "numbers have often been an agency for acting on people, exercising power over them. . . . Numbers turn people into objects to be manipulated. Where power is not exercised blatantly, it acts instead secretly, insidiously."[20] We can see this in baseball where statistics determine decisions such as player drafting and trading, salaries, the hiring and firing of managers, not to mention Las Vegas odds. Milestone numbers are particularly important in shaping the game; among other things, they strongly influence (not without controversy) entrance into the Hall of Fame. Ticket sales soared when Roger Clemens pitched for his 300th victory, although the game itself may have been no better than his 299th or 301st. Consider also the magical 500 home run mark for admittance into the Hall of Fame. Statistics have the capability to illuminate the mysteries of the game and act as a force for improvement in the sport. But, despite their seeming descriptive innocence, their misuse can obscure our understanding and orchestrate elements to the detriment of the game.

So, Charlie Brown you would be wise to heed Schroeder's statistical analysis. But take heart in the success of the 1914 Braves, the 1969 Mets, and the 2002 Angels. Wait 'til next year and don't step on the foul lines!

---

[17] *Trust in Numbers*, p. 18. Porter refers to this comparison made in the 1830s by the Hegelian natural philosopher Georg Friedrich Pohl to describe Georg Simon Ohm's mathematical treatment of the electrical circuit.

[18] In his elaboration of the Heisenberg Uncertainty Principle, Niels Bohr observes that "measurement has an essential influence on the conditions on which the very definition of the physical quantities in question rests." See his "Quantum Mechanics and Physical Reality," in *Nature*, Vol. 136 (1935), p. 1025.

[19] *Trust in Numbers*, p. 45.

[20] *Ibid.*, p. 77.

16 | Women Playing Hardball

LESLIE HEAPHY

Does softball limit women's potential to be equals on the baseball diamond? To address this question we'll look at contemporary American feminist philosophy, and the history of women's participation in our national pastime since the mid-nineteenth century. Though there have been quite a few women who have played the game, they have always struggled for acceptance, and struggled to get past the stereotype that baseball is for men and softball is for women.

Given the physical differences, can women compete with men in sports? Men are typically stronger and may be more physically fit than women, but in baseball that may not matter. Baseball requires timing, co-ordination, knowledge of the game, control, competitiveness, and desire, assets that are not exclusively male. In baseball the smart ball player or the one with more hustle often outplays the big slugger. A 1982 study involving 87 men and 115 women, "Baseball and Softball: Should Girls and Women have to Choose?", concluded that "the impact of gender is rather small when one considers strength differences after allowing for body size and composition."[1] So, perhaps the more pertinent question is, will America accept women's participation in a sport considered to be men's domain?

---

[1] "Baseball and Softball: Should Girls and Women have to Choose?"
http://www.womenssportsfoundation.org.

Softball Stereotypes

In her article, "Woman Is an Island," philosopher Judith Williamson investigates how women are seen in mass culture. Because baseball has been viewed historically as a male sport, women who play are considered too masculine and in danger of losing their femininity. Newspaper stories and photographs suggest that the athletes are women first and ball players second, or they highlight their sexuality rather than their athleticism.[2]

These images of female ball players are important for what they show and what they do not. Williamson argues that women are often associated with home, love, and sex, and not work, class, or politics. Baseball, as a professional sport, is work. Baseball is part of the public world and therefore not proper for women to play. Women should be happy playing softball and other leisure activities designed for them.

The framework of feminist philosophy, confirms much of what Williamson argues. Masculinity and femininity are culturally defined. Masculinity has come to mean power, strength, and muscle; femininity tends to mean weakness, passivity, and grace. In Western culture, women with "too much" muscle are often considered less feminine.[3]

It's ironic that softball is considered to be a sport for women, given that many of the early players were professional baseball players who wanted to stay in shape during the off-season. Softball had a much later start than baseball, invented in 1887 by George Hancock a Chicago reporter. It began as an indoor game and did not even get called softball until the name was suggested in 1926 by Walter Hakanson, a Denver YMCA official. Before 1926, the game was most often called indoor baseball, or simply indoor-outdoor. It did not become a popular sport for women until the 1930s when the Amateur Softball Association was created and tournaments and leagues began to spring up around the country. Girls came to be, and still are, steered toward softball because of the bigger ball, the shorter dimensions of the field, and the perception that it is a game relying less on brute strength and more on agility and thinking.

---

[2] Judith Williamson, "Woman Is an Island: Femininity and Colonization." In Anne Herrmann and Abigail Stewart, eds., *Theorizing Feminism* (Westview, 1994), p. 385.
[3] Susan L. Greendorfer, "Title IX, Gender Equity, Backlash, and Ideology," *Women in Sport and Physical Activity Journal* 7 (1998), pp. 77–78.

Baseball began as a men's sport at a time in the nineteenth century when women were not encouraged to be physically active. According to the experts of that time (doctors and ministers), women were physically inferior to men and therefore needed to be taken care of in the home. Strenuous activity would be bad for women, particularly during child-bearing years. This general view was held by much of American society throughout the nineteenth and early twentieth centuries, though some women challenged it. Many assumed that any woman playing baseball must be a lesbian; after all, she is playing a man's sport. This stereotyping is still rampant on the softball field, though in this sense, softball and baseball are no different from any other sport involving women. Female soccer players in the United Kingdom, for example, defensively claim that they are tomboys, but not "butches" or lesbians.[4]

Baseball teams developed at women's colleges, such as Vassar, shortly after the Civil War. Women were allowed to play so long as they were not participating in mixed company, and not playing in view of others. The women enjoyed the game, but the colleges worried about accidents and parents' complaints. In fact, games were nearly done away with at Vassar after one young lady broke a window at the school. Since some parents even thought baseball was corrupting their sons, explaining to parents that their young daughters were not being morally corrupted by the game of baseball was particularly difficult.

In the late 1800s advertisements appeared in the newspapers inviting young ladies to tryout for a ball club, but there were not many responses. Owners and managers had to assure parents that their daughters would be taken care of and that no moral harm would come to them. Even with those kinds of assurances, newspaper writers wondered about the moral quality of the young ladies who played for the early bloomer teams or worse yet, those who played with men's ball clubs. Descriptions of early women's games focused more on who the young ladies were than on the actual action of the game,

---

[4] Jayne Caudwell, "Football in the U.K.: Women, Tomboys, Butches, and Lesbians," in Sheila Scraton and Beccy Watson, eds., *Sport, Leisure Identities, and Gendered Spaces* (Leisure Studies Association, 2000), pp. 95–110.

often covering what the uniforms looked like before giving the score.

Even the names of many of the early women's teams reflected the difficulty the players had getting people to take them seriously. Today's female players often have had a hand in choosing their team's name. Thus we have clubs such as the San Jose Spitfires and the Detroit Danger, as opposed to the earlier Dolly Vardens, New York Bloomer Girls, and Fort Wayne Daisies. Those early names reinforced the belief that aggressive, competitive games are not for women. Today's names seem to overcompensate for the deficiencies of the past.

At various times throughout the history of baseball, the women who did get an opportunity to play were seen as a curiosity, something to bring in the fans, not serious ball players. After Major League Baseball had begun integration in 1947, three women played in the Negro Leagues in the 1950s with the Kansas City Monarchs and Indianapolis Clowns—Toni Stone, Connie Morgan, and Mamie "Peanut" Johnson. With integration, the Negro Leagues began to suffer in attendance, and perhaps that is why these women were signed, to bolster sagging attendance. It's convenient to overlook the fact that the three ladies had played in their hometown areas before entering the Negro Leagues where they more than held their own. Toni Stone even played in one Negro League East-West Classic.

Baseball is America's national pastime, and consequently, it represents our public world, the world of men. Historically women were expected to remain in the private world, the world of the home where they could take care of the family and raise children without being corrupted by the outside world. The moral purity of women had been considered essential for the development of this country as a virtuous republic since its inception. Women were expected to raise their children and provide a safe haven for their husbands, a retreat from the corrupt and greedy public world. Ball players like Toni Stone or Mamie Johnson broke the stereotype and society did not quite know how to deal with them seriously.

So why were they seen as novelties rather than as serious ball players? And why are women still encouraged to play "soft"ball, rather than baseball?

Body Matters

The roots of softball and baseball discrimination are embedded in the story of Western philosophy. In Ancient Greece, philosophers such as Pythagoras and Plato argued that the body was a weak, temporary vessel for the immortal soul. During the Middle Ages, the Jewish, Christian, and Muslim theologians of Europe argued that the human body was made of earthly stuff, while the soul was made in the image of God. Still later, during Europe's Enlightenment of the seventeenth and eighteenth centuries, philosophers such as René Descartes and Immanuel Kant returned to the idea that the body must be set aside if one is to discover and participate in higher callings. It is no surprise, then, that Western culture has tended to view the body with skepticism. While later philosophers such as Nietzsche and Foucault reminded us that the body also matters, it is contemporary feminist philosophers who have done the most important work in "rehabilitating" our view of the body.

Early feminists such as Simone de Beauvoir (1908–1986) argued that the woman's body in particular had been routinely left out of philosophical discussion. As philosophical ideas filtered down through mainstream culture, this notable absence of the opposite sex—the invisible, silent "other,"—was tolerated, if not outright encouraged. Today, a new wave of feminist philosophers questions whether the "body" has any inherent meaning at all. Obviously, a man's body is different from a woman's body, but interpretations of the differences depend on who observes them. "The human body is always a signified body," philosopher Moira Gatens observes.[5] Understanding the differences between men and women "does not have to do with biological 'facts' so much as with the manner in which culture marks bodies and creates specific conditions in which they live and recreate themselves."[6] Or, as Denise Riley succinctly explains, "The body becomes visible as a female body, only under some particular gaze—including that of politics."[7] So the way the female body is viewed from without and experienced from within contributes to the obstacles women have faced in playing baseball.

---

[5] "Power, Bodies, and Difference," in Janet Price and Margrit Shildrick, eds., *Feminist Theory and the Body: A Reader* (Edinburgh: Edinburgh University Press, 1999), p. 230.
[6] *Ibid.*, pp. 230–31.
[7] "Bodies, Identities, Feminisms," in *op. cit.*, p. 224.

Throwing Like a Girl

Philosopher Iris Marion Young argues that the way men and women understand their bodies and the space around them may affect the way some approach a game like baseball. Recent feminists have argued that the issue is not what the body *is*, but how it is understood. For example, women and men often throw a baseball differently. Hence the derogatory phrase, "throwing like a girl." Why do the sexes often throw so differently? Citing earlier studies, Young rules out common beliefs that breast size, shoulder width, or muscle size is any impediment to throwing a baseball. Instead, Young argues that many women "throw like a girl" because they are not as free as men in their body movements and do not put their whole body into an action. Young writes:

> Not only is there a typical style of throwing like a girl, but there is a more or less typical style or running like a girl, climbing like a girl, swinging like a girl, hitting like a girl. They have in common first that the whole body is not put into fluid and directed motion, but rather, in swinging and hitting, for example, the motion is concentrated into one body part . . . [8]

This lack of fluidity may have a variety of different causes, including lack of confidence, fear of injury, or self-consciousness. Many women perceive their bodies to be a burden, and act accordingly. Instead of believing fully that they can accomplish a physical task such as throwing a baseball correctly, some women believe they are at a disadvantage, and set up a negative self-fulfilling prophecy. Too often others simply reinforce this negative belief.

Women who think they will not be good at baseball have to work harder. Women who already view physical activities as something they cannot do, become more self-conscious and shy away from any activity that draws attention to their lack of physical coordination. When a woman is unsure of what her body can do, she cannot properly control its movements and actions. Her body becomes the focus of attention, distracting her from

---

[8] Iris Marion Young, "A Phenomenology of Feminine Body Comportment, Motility, and Spatiality" in *Throwing Like a Girl and Other Essays in Feminist Philosophy and Social Theory* (Bloomington: Indiana University Press, 1990), p. 146.

the sport itself.[9] Women often limit their participation not because of true physical differences, but because society has not encouraged them to be comfortable in their own skin.

Throwing Like an Athlete

Philip Wrigley proposed the idea for the All-American Girls Professional Baseball League (AAGPBL) during the Second World War because he was worried about baseball being cancelled. As a temporary way to fill the void, he suggested a women's baseball league that started out with softball rules and gradually developed into baseball. The key here was that the league was to be temporary and there was no question that these would be women who played baseball—women first and ball players second. This understanding was reflected in the team names and in the style of uniforms chosen. The ladies played in short skirts, even though this was completely impractical for sliding into bases and resulted in many unnecessary injuries. Image won out over practicality. In addition, each team had a chaperone who was responsible for keeping the girls' behavior in line—no drinking, no overnight guests, no breaking curfew, and so forth. The league even hosted a charm school to teach the girls how to dress, apply their make-up, walk like ladies, and deal with the press. Such reassurances helped many reluctant parents finally give in to daughters hoping to play in the league.

Propriety was especially important. In 1943, the Rockford Peaches had a souvenir booklet explaining that players stayed in only the best hotels on the road and at home they lived in private residences. The same brochure claimed the girls paid regular visits to beauty salons. There could be no question about their femininity. No tomboys in this league. Clearly, the most important issue for the success of the league was image. There was to be no doubt in anyone's mind that baseball would not turn these nice girls into masculine "Amazons." They would learn proper etiquette and behave like ladies, or else be punished accordingly. Newspapers helped reinforce the proper image of these young ladies with headlines such as "World's

---

[9] For a good discussion of the perils of thinking, see Chapter 13 in this volume.

Prettiest Ballplayers," or "Belles of the Ball Game." Articles highlighted the girls' charitable and patriotic work during the war.
When a young lady left a team to get married, she always made
the headlines.

Girls playing baseball made headlines in the 1970s when the
issue became a heated one for little league teams across the
country. Actually this was not a new issue, since Margaret
Gisolo had played American Legion Junior Baseball in 1928.
The following year the American Legion banned women from
playing. Girls were increasingly discouraged from playing all
organized baseball even though they loved the game. Many
gave up fighting to play; it became too difficult to fight the
players, coaches, and fans just to get a chance to get out on the
field and play. When Jackie Mitchell struck out Babe Ruth and
Lou Gehrig in a game, it quickly became just a publicity stunt
and not a serious effort on the part of these professional athletes who were bested by a female pitcher. Justine Warren,
President of the Women's Baseball League (WBL), explained
that she learned her pitching was an attack on the masculinity
of the batter she faced. It called into question the accepted
roles of men and women in society.[10]

The Colorado Silver Bullets enjoyed a bit of history as a traveling female baseball team in the 1990s, sponsored by Coors
Brewing Company and coached by men. There were no chap-
erones, though, and the Silver Bullets wore proper baseball uniforms. Does this mean the image of women as ball players had
finally become accepted? Were all the issues and questions of
the past behind us? Of course not. Newspaper articles still
focused too often on the players' lives rather than their athletic
performance. The Silver Bullets folded after four seasons
because they could not generate enough money for the club's
sponsor. While the uniforms changed, the problematic perceptions remained. People did not see the women as serious baseball players even though they played primarily men's teams and
won their fair share of the games. When the women won, their
success was minimized as that of a professional team playing
amateur and semi-pro men's clubs, taking away from their

---

[10] Justine Warren, "Baseball to Me" (June 17th, 2001), http://www.baseballglory.com/
baseballmeans.html.

success and talent. Why? And, what values are being reinforced each time we portray a woman ball player as a bully, a curiosity, or an oddity?

Today there are a number of women's teams and leagues across the country, and overseas. In 2001 there was a women's World Series played at Skydome in Toronto. The U.S.A. sent a national team of twenty-five female players who earned their spots based on their athletic ability, not their looks or charm. How many people are aware of today's women's teams? How much news coverage do they get? What kind of coverage do they get? A 2001 article from the *St. Petersburg Times* covering Christine Dennis and her experience playing in Toronto focused on why Dennis played baseball when it would be easier to find support to play softball. Dennis's response was typical of many women who play baseball: she plays because it is more of a challenge; it is more fun to push herself.[11]

Wanting to play baseball, women have often found that men's teams were their only option. They were often an unwelcome addition to the team, sometimes accused of taking a boy's spot or simply trying to push an agenda. Before women's baseball can become a respected professional sport, "there are prejudices to overcome, opinions to change, perceptions to shatter and rumors to put to rest."[12] Veronica Geyer, who plays for the New Jersey Nemesis, says there is a long way to go but sees no reason why women's baseball cannot stand alongside softball. Aptly, their team name, Nemesis, recalls the Greek goddess of justice.

The Courageous Ila Borders

After seeing her first major league game Ila Borders decided that she wanted to play baseball. She made the junior high school and varsity teams at Whittier Christian as a pitcher and with the success she enjoyed at the high-school level got a chance to pitch before college scouts. Ila was signed by Southern California College in 1994 and in her first game against Claremont made history, becoming the first female player to pitch a complete game on a men's college team. Encountering

---

[11]Greg Auman, "Dennis Goes to Bat for Women's Baseball," *St. Petersburg Times* (July 3rd, 2001).
[12] Michael Gasparino, "Playing Hardball," http://www.nysol.com/baseball_women.html.

much resistance at SCC, Borders was forced to transfer to Whittier College for her senior year.

With a 4–5 record at Whittier, Borders got a chance to tryout for the minor league St. Paul Saints in 1996 and made the team. Within a month the team traded her to the Duluth Dukes where she pitched in relief for the next two seasons. Though most of her appearances came when the outcome of the game was no longer in doubt, Borders made history again on July 9th, 1998 when she became the first female starting pitcher in a regular season minor league game. The Dukes lost 8–3 but through four innings Borders was in command of a 2–1 lead. Borders followed that first start with another history making appearance, winning her first game on July 24th. Against the Canaries of Sioux Falls, Borders pitched six strong innings and came away with a 3–1 victory.

In 1999 Borders was traded to the Madison Black Wolf where she got a chance to start and pitch the first three innings of all her games. Leading the team in ERA, she helped the Black Wolfs turn around their season, finishing just one win away from the playoffs. Even though Borders enjoyed some success on the field with her male teammates, she never gained full acceptance and remained an oddity. From Borders's view she never set out to prove anything about women's abilities to play baseball with men. She just loved the game and wanted the chance to play.

Softball: The Good Is the Enemy of the Best

A persistent thorn in the side of women trying to play baseball is softball, which provides a seemingly viable alternative, making it seem unnecessary for women to play baseball. This alternative is unlike basketball or volleyball—sports where men and women play the same game.[13] When a woman wants to play baseball, she is asked why. It is not understood that baseball and softball are different games. Individuals and companies do not want to risk their money sponsoring a team or league that has controversial issues to work through when there are plenty of other sports teams, both male and female, succeeding.

---

[13] While women's basketball uses a smaller ball, the size of the court and the height of the basket are not different from the men's game.

The softball alternative thereby became a convenient means for American society to postpone answering some hard questions about perceived gender differences. Women playing baseball instead of softball are still seen as anomalies even though from the beginning of the game women have played hard ball. They started their own teams and leagues when men did not welcome them or society questioned their presence on the diamond. In the nineteenth century, the concern over the moral degradation of women playing this public sport led many parents to discourage or prohibit their daughters' participation. In the next century, their playing was often accepted as a temporary measure geared toward entertainment, not talent. Today, the issues are no less challenging. While we cannot blame softball for its very existence, we should note that the good is often the enemy of the best. It is good for women to play softball. But if playing softball perpetuates the prejudice that women cannot or should not play baseball, then softball is indeed the enemy of the best.[14]

---

[14] Thanks to Lisa Cassidy, Bill Irwin, and Holly Messitt for comments on earlier drafts of this chapter.

Ninth Inning:
Under Pressure

At some point in every ball player's career, the possibility of failure must be confronted. Fans revel in the moments when an athlete's reaction to pressure is put to the test. R. Scott Kretchmar questions the use of the intentional walk. Is it a cop-out, used to avoid competition, or is it an intelligent strategy that only shifts the balance of the contest? Heather L. Reid reminds us that Western philosophy, like baseball, is built on the premise that we know much less than we pretend.

17 | Walking Barry Bonds: The Ethics of the Intentional Walk

R. SCOTT KRETCHMAR

Imagine, if you will, a variation on the well-known final stanza of Ernest Thayer's "Casey at the Bat." This is where we learn that the Mudville hero had struck out.

> Oh, somewhere in this favored land the sun is shining bright,
> The band is playing somewhere, and somewhere hearts are light;
> And somewhere men are laughing, and somewhere children shout,
> But there is no joy in Mudville—mighty Casey was intentionally walked.

While my changes may have ruined both the story and the poem, the fact remains that since first base was open when Casey stepped to the plate, he probably would have been given a free pass. As we all know, the intentional walk has been around a long time, and it's generally regarded as a legitimate competitive strategy. It is often used to set up force outs and double plays or produce better pitching match-ups (righty-righty or lefty-lefty combinations). It might also be employed to avoid mythical sluggers like Casey, or real ones like Babe Ruth and Barry Bonds.

The employment of the intentional walk to circumvent star players appears to be increasing. In 1927, the season during which Ruth hit sixty home runs, he came to the plate on 678 occasions and received 138 bases on balls. Bonds, in his magical 2001 campaign when his 73 homers shattered Mark McGwire's long ball record, had 653 plate appearances and 177 walks—or slightly more than one free pass for every four visits to the batter's box. In 2002, Bonds was walked thirty-three percent of the time, setting an all-time, single-season record of 198 bases on balls.

Many of these free passes of course were not, strictly speaking, intentional walks. In 2002, only 68 of his 198 free passes were officially intentional. But Bonds, Ruth, and other sluggers like McGwire, Sammy Sosa, Hank Aaron, and Roger Maris have also been the recipients of what is sometimes called the "unintentional-intentional walk." In these cases, the catcher presents a normal target, but the hurler throws four consecutive pitches slightly out of the strike zone. While hitters will occasionally go after one of these bad pitches, the walk is virtually a foregone conclusion.

This is where the controversy arises. Because of the increased use of both kinds of intentional walks, hitters like Bonds have had fewer and fewer chances to display their considerable offensive skills. Some see this as a problem both for individual stars and the game of baseball. Others do not.

Where does the truth lie, and can it be uncovered? A start in answering these questions can be made by sorting out some complex issues in the philosophy of sport.

Booing the Walk

Opponents of the intentional walk claim that it is unfair to deny gifted athletes reasonable opportunities to utilize their game skills. By walking batters repeatedly, these sluggers are "taken out of the game" or at least a major part of it. They are denied a fair chance to show what they can do. This, it is argued, is unsporting.

The second argument focuses on the rights and interests of the fans. They are harmed because they are denied opportunities to see star players show their remarkable talents. People who come through the turnstiles pay good money to watch a Barry Bonds hit, not walk. They come to witness the drama between a Curt Schilling who throws ninety-five-mile-an-hour fastballs on the inside corner of the plate and a Bonds who has an incredible ability to turn on an inside pitch. Who will prevail?

When walks replace hitting, the fans never find out. They are denied heroic events, memories they can take home, and stories they can later tell to their grandchildren. Intentional walks, according to critics, are essentially non-events for the fans.

A third concern is related more to metaphysics than ethics. Some believe that baseball's inability to prevent excessive deployment of the intentional walk reveals a flaw in the game. It's a flaw because intentional walks subvert the nature of the activity—the mutual testing of pitching and fielding skills, on the one hand, against hitting and base running skills, on the other. When an intentional walk occurs, nobody's skills are tested.

All three arguments, on the surface, seem to enjoy a degree of plausibility. However, more evidence is needed to determine their merits.

Walking and Stalling

The repeated use of intentional walks in baseball, it can be argued, is like stalling in basketball. Before shot clocks were employed, a guard on one basketball team could bring the ball across the center line at the start of a contest, stand there, and let the clock run. No movement would take place—no dribbling, no rebounding, no shooting, and minimal opportunities for defending. The nature of the game was obviously violated and fans grew testy when subjected to this painfully boring strategy.

In baseball, repeated uses of the walk might be seen, by way of analogy, in the same light. The pitcher does not deploy his pitching skills, the batter has no opportunity to show his hitting skills, and the fans grow restless with yet another intentional pass.

Pitching around batters, in fact, bears many similarities to stalling. In both cases, unskilled actions are substituted for skill-based challenges. In both cases, a non-test is substituted for a real test. And in both cases, a foregone conclusion is substituted for dramatic uncertainty. Thus, it would seem reasonable to conclude that, to the extent in which a game's rules do not prevent such unwelcome substitutions, it is flawed.

Basketball, to its credit, acknowledged this problem. With virtually universal use of shot clocks and other rules, harm from the stall has now been minimized. Those who would "take the air out of the ball" either to sit on a lead or improve chances against a vastly superior opponent cannot do so for any length of time. Basketball players have to play the game, compare their skills with those of their opponents, and accept the consequences. Baseball players should be required to do likewise.

This argument by analogy may be more or less persuasive. But before one rushes out to save mistreated hitters and fans, and before one comes up with new rules to fix baseball's version of the stall, these arguments should be put to the test. Does the analogy work?

In order to answer this question, some spadework is required. All three arguments refer to things called games. An understanding of what games are and how they work is needed. Metaphysics, the study of what things are, sometimes needs to precede ethics, the study of whether actions are right and wrong. This is one of those cases.

The Nature of Games

Three general approaches to describing the nature of games might be taken. The first one starts with reflection on absolutes, on something called a Perfect Game, or Perfect Baseball.[1] Under this approach, philosophers would stipulate what a game is, identify its necessary and sufficient conditions, and (if they are good at this) end the discussion for all time.

A second option would require that individuals check their tastes and preferences. They would be asked what they would like games to be or what, in their opinion, good baseball games are.[2] Here there is no foundation for their judgments other than current wishes and feelings. In a sense these philosophers would construct an image of games that suits them.

---

[1] Sport-related works that reflect this general approach are Paul Weiss, *Sport: A Philosophic Inquiry* (Carbondale: Southern Illinois University Press, 1969) and Michael Novak, *The Joy of Sports: End Zones, Bases, Basketballs, and the Consecration of the American Spirit* (New York: Basic Books, 1976). Weiss, for example, argues that "mental vectors" can be focused on athletic perfection, even if in-the-world performances never quite reach those heights. Likewise we can reflect on ideal records and ideal games even though they cannot be found in real life.

[2] Terry Roberts, a disciple of Richard Rorty, argues that "strong poets" ought to challenge sport conventions so that players can "get more of what they want." For Roberts, nothing is sacred about baseball or, for that matter, any other sport traditions. See his "Sport and Strong Poetry," *Journal of the Philosophy of Sport*, XXII (1995), pp. 94–107.

A third option, and the one that will be pursued here, lies between a rigid realism (option 1) and an anything-goes relativism (option 2). Here philosophers would reflect on what distinctive things games are built to do and what game elements need to be in place for this function to be carried out well.

This can be called an aggressive pragmatic approach. It acknowledges that games are not like anything else in the world, and that certain constraints need to be honored when constructing and caring for these unique things. It also acknowledges that games are not fixed for all time, that evolution and culture affect person-game interactions.

John Searle used a similar approach in trying to figure out the nature of language.[3] He asked what vocabularies and sentence patterns are built to do. His answers about providing clear communication provided a foundation on which to evaluate various language conventions. Searle gave the example of "hello" as a convention for greeting people. How and when it is used follows certain rules of correct communication. When it is used appropriately, it efficiently does its job of sending a welcoming message. However, if someone were to break these conventional agreements and use "hello" out of context, say when she was leaving someone rather than greeting them, confusion might well result. The convention would no longer work. The clear communication would be lost.

The same analysis could be applied to games by asking what they are built to do. Bernard Suits and other commentators provide a number of common-sense answers. Games are built, they have said, to provide artificial tests. When something is turned into a game, it is transported from the realm of a boring activity (a tedious form of recreation where there is no test) or a real difficulty (a natural, on-the-job or work-a-day test) into the domain of gratuitous challenges (an artificial test).[4]

Artificial tests are conventions, and they need rules to inform players about goals and means—about what counts as success,

---

[3] See his *Speech Acts: An Essay in the Philosophy of Language* (Cambridge: Cambridge University Press, 1969), and *Mind, Language, and Society* (London: Weidenfeld and Nicolson, 1999).

[4] Bernard Suits, "What Is a Game?" *Philosophy of Science* 34, (June, 1967), pp. 148–156. See also William Morgan, "The Logical Incompatibility Thesis and Rules: A Reconsideration of Formalism As an Account of Games," *Journal of the Philosophy of Sport*, XIV (1987), pp. 10–20.

what counts as failure, and by what avenues players are allowed to pursue success. If someone were inventing baseball, he could say players need something to hit and some second implement that would do the hitting. But they also need an individual who would make the hitting provocatively difficult. So rules about pitchers are invented. The rulebook indicates how far away from the batter this individual must stand so that the hitting and pitching tests are not too hard and not too easy. Both challenges need to be fair and appropriately difficult. The rulebook settles on 60 feet, 6 inches.

In a similar manner, rule by rule, this convention called baseball is built—partly by insight, partly by trial and error, partly by happenstance imposed by local conditions. But this construction is always guided by criteria that outline the parameters of good artificial tests. One of these non-negotiables was already identified. A good test cannot be either too hard or too easy.

As the process moves along, other guidelines are identified. A game test should be interesting; it should have symbolic meaning for those who would play it. A game test should be for all ages. It should be something players can return to again and again and find that it remains attractive. Children should have access to it. And when one's own skills decline over the years, it would be good if the game were still able to invite these senior athletes into its domain.

It's possible that no fixed set of such criteria exist. But gamewrights and connoisseurs of games have both tacit and explicit standards on which such judgments can be made. It should be clear that the gamewrighting process is not arbitrary or otherwise haphazard. Artificial tests in every time and culture have a set of qualities that make them good or, as the case may be, not so good.

One Important Game Criterion

If games embody well-crafted problems, and if testing oneself against these problems lies at the heart of game playing, it would be reasonable to conclude that games are better to the extent to which they insure such confrontations. On the other hand, a game whose rules allowed its players to avoid its core problems would be, for that reason, defective. This conclusion would appear to provide strong ammunition for opponents of the intentional walk in baseball. This strategy, it could be said, is a form of test avoidance, a kind of stalling. If the rules of baseball do not prevent such testing defections, then the rules are flawed. And it should not be at all surprising that various harms to players and fans result from such regulatory loopholes.

In support of this conclusion it might be noted that the unbridled quest for victory has gotten so out of hand, that players paradoxically enter a game only, on occasion, to avoid it. If *not* pitching to the batter and if *not* testing one's pitching skills against a hitter's skills enhances chances for a win, so be it. The pitcher's original commitment to play the game is followed by a decision *not* to play when it becomes strategically smart to do so.

These defections make sense because external rewards and pressures to win have gotten so extreme. In response, games have had to become ever more defection-proof. Of course for true amateurs, for those who love their respective games, such rules are redundant. Amateurs have no reason to skip elements of the game just to avoid a defeat. But for those who are under extreme pressures to win, avoiding the game, under certain circumstances, makes good strategic sense. Consequently, games that are not defection- or stall-proof can be, and often are, prematurely abandoned by the very people who sought them out.

Such pressures certainly come to bear on major league baseball. The pitchers who face Barry Bonds are paid millions of dollars—not to get Bonds out, but to win games. The increased deployment of the intentional walk in recent years is certainly a response to these economic and social pressures. These forces have grown to such proportions that, remarkably enough, Bonds was once intentionally walked with the bases loaded—just so that he could not win the game with an extra base hit.[5]

Regardless of the deployment of these extreme measures, the question still remains. Is this tantamount to stalling? It is now necessary to return to the argument by analogy, put it to the test, and see if it holds up.

---

[5] On May 28th, 1998, Arizona Diamondback manager Buck Schowalter ordered the intentional walk with the bases loaded and two outs in the bottom of the ninth, with his team winning 8–6. Brent Mayne, the next Giant hitter, flied to right for the final out.

Three Counter-Arguments to the Analogy

1. Avoiding the Test

It's difficult to see how walking great hitters allows teams to avoid baseball tests. It would seem more accurate to say that this strategy changes the test. In fact, in some ways, it complicates the problems faced by the pitcher and his team.

Of course if Bonds is walked repeatedly, that part of the test is minimized. But each time he goes to first base, Bonds is one important step closer to home plate, one step closer to scoring a run for his team. And the defense now faces new challenges. Depending on the number of outs and other base runners involved, players in the field must worry about a hit and run, a sacrifice bunt, a bunt and run, a straight, delayed, or double steal, another walk, a passed ball, a wild pitch, an error, holding the runner close to the base, pitching from the stretch, testing the strength of the catcher's arm and its accuracy, the possibility of giving up a now more damaging home run, and so on.

Consequently, while walking great hitters may still be good strategy, it does not relieve the defensive team from facing baseball tests. The only change is that they are different tests—the kind that must be dealt with when extra runners are on base and the number of outs remains the same. The intentional walk is, functionally speaking, little more than a single—albeit one that cannot normally drive in a run. The defensive team, for strategic reasons, thinks that giving up a benign "single" is better than taking chances on an extra base hit. But the team also acknowledges that such a concession brings new challenges with it. The game test for the defense may have actually been enriched.

2. Harming the Sluggers

It's difficult to see how the repeated use of the intentional walk is unfair to great hitters. It would be odd in football, for instance, to say that running backs must run at least 50 percent of the time toward the all-American tackle that happens to be on the left side of the defensive line. It is common strategy to run away from such individuals to lessen the chance that they will impact negatively on the outcome of the game. So too are great scorers in basketball double teamed and great soccer players marked closely by opponents and kept from touching the ball as much as possible. In short, why would it be the case that pitchers have to pitch to Bonds any more than squads in the NBA have to play Shaquille O'Neal straight up, without any double-teams?

Because both basketball and baseball are team games, this kind of requirement makes little sense. In fact, this is why we conceptualize these activities as team tests and team contests. A team test is multi-faceted and opponents are expected, perhaps even morally required, to pick the parts of the test on which they think they can do best and avoid those parts of the problem that present the greatest difficulties. The moral axiom of always trying one's hardest, would appear to involve just such a commitment—so long as the overall game test cannot be avoided.

The baseball test, in fact, cannot be avoided because the intentional walk has no impact on the fundamental test-taking criterion in baseball—namely, the obligation to get the opposition out on twenty-seven occasions, three outs at a time. When Bonds comes to the plate with two outs in the fifth inning, the team in the field must negotiate thirteen outs before the game is over. After Bonds is given his walk, that team faces precisely the same obligation—securing the thirteen remaining outs. Bonds may be frustrated. But he and his teammates have not been treated unfairly. The challenge presented by the Giants has not been avoided; it has only been shifted to one of Bonds's teammates.

3. HARMING THE FANS

It's difficult to agree with the harm argument unless a very limited version of baseball spectating is adopted. If the game were principally about individual feats, and if the skill deserving virtually exclusive attention was the ability to hit long home runs, then the argument would have more weight. A game without such heroic, individual feats would, by definition, be a bad game.

But the game is about something else. It is about *teams* scoring more runs than their opponents, and it is about a panoply of skills and strategies that are *combined* to produce maximal positive effect. A walk combined with a successful hit and run and a sacrifice fly produces a run just as surely as a 440-foot drive to right field.

While home runs can be dramatic and are certainly one way to exhibit advanced skill, they must take their place among a host of other dramatic possibilities and a large number of other skills. In some ways, the home run is like the bright colors in a modern painting. They immediately attract attention and, for those who are not schooled in viewing modern art, they may overshadow other more subtle tones that are of equal or greater interest. But for those who appreciate the variety of baseball strategies and skills, the home run is not required. And importantly, the intentional walk is not inherently disappointing. The walk opens up new tensions, new aesthetic possibilities, new kinds of drama, new story lines.

When Bonds is walked with one out in the ninth inning and the Giants are trailing 3 to 1, baseball fans do not need to head for the exits, deeply disappointed over the fact that he did not get a chance to hit. If they are at all engaged by the game, they move to the edge of their seats. After all, in 2002, the walk brought the tying run in the person of Jeff Kent to the plate. The pitcher showed signs of tiring. Kent is a right-handed hitter, and the wind was still blowing out toward left field. How dramatic it would be if Bonds's teammate could drill one over the fence or at least keep the rally going by hitting a gapper!

The Moral and Aesthetic Superiority of Baseball

The argument by analogy does not work. The correct comparison to shortening the basketball game by stalling and "taking minutes off the clock" is not the intentional walk but rather playing fewer innings or, more precisely, "taking outs out of the game." If a baseball team wanted to sit on a lead or avoid repeated skill comparisons when facing a far superior squad, it would have to find a way to let innings go by without actually playing them. But of course, this is impossible. Baseball, in this sense, is defection-proof. This quality gives the game certain unmistakable advantages.

Baseball, golf, tennis, automobile racing, and other event-regulated games appear to enjoy a moral superiority over time-regulated contests. In baseball, as has been shown, players are required to play to the end, to honor the amount of mutual testing that was committed to at the start of the activity. Moreover, players face no temptations to shorten the game, lock in an advantage, sit on a lead, or otherwise prevent their opponents from showing superior skill in the time that remains. Ball players have to honor the nine innings. They have to play to the end.

In basketball, football, soccer, and other time-regulated contests, the moral landscape is very different. Players commit to a given amount of time for mutual testing, say 40 minutes in basketball, as required by the constitutive rules of this game. Over this duration (or something very close to it) competitors will see who can play better. It is this tacit moral obligation to play the full game that makes the stall so distasteful.

On the other hand, time-regulated games (indeed, all contests) ask that players commit to trying their hardest to prevail. But it is precisely this moral commitment that may be utilized to justify the stall. In other words, if a team is holding a comfortable lead with only four minutes left on the clock, it might well be their duty to take the air out of the ball. Using the stall, however, creates doubts about one's commitment to play the whole game. An ethical bad taste is left in one's mouth. Even though big-time sports coaches generally favor the stall, the moral unease still lingers. It is too bad that an honest battle could not have continued to the end.

Aesthetically, time-regulated games do not fare much better. These games tend to unravel at the end. The contesting becomes asymmetrical. The team that is behind tries desperately to show superior skill; the team that is ahead attempts to reduce skill-based opportunities as much as possible. The team that is behind employs high risk strategies that have little chance of succeeding; the team in the lead uses safe and generally uninteresting strategies; the team that is behind intentionally fouls, calls extra time-outs, fakes injuries—anything it can think of to stop the clock. The team that is ahead is very content not to play as long as the clock is running.

These games become drawn out. Morally questionable stalling tactics are met with morally questionable fouling tactics. Interminable free throws in basketball replace driving, defending, shooting, and the other more interesting and difficult parts of the game. Sometimes a dramatic reversal will occur, but usually the stall works and the game, after all the time-outs have been exhausted, grinds to an anti-climactic halt.

In baseball, the team that is ahead as the game enters the ninth inning usually wins. But still the side with the lead must earn its three outs. The team that is batting always has hope. Sharp breaking balls still come to the plate. If first base is open, Barry Bonds or the mythical Casey will undoubtedly be intentionally walked. And despite the unfavorable odds, Barry's and Casey's teammates will continue to take their lusty swings. Aesthetically, for the fans in San Francisco and in Mudville, this is a far more pleasing way to end the story.

18 | Socrates at the Ballpark

HEATHER L. REID

Even those familiar with both America's favorite pastime and Greece's famed philosopher must find this an odd combination. Socrates and baseball?

To many, baseball and Socratic philosophy seem to be diametrically opposed. And this is not a prejudice based on ignorance. Socrates and his student Plato are largely responsible for the beliefs that human minds and bodies are distinct sorts of things, and that the mind (or soul) and not the body, should be the focus of our attentions. As Socrates says in his *Apology*, "I go around doing nothing but persuading both young and old among you not to care for your body or your wealth in preference to or as strongly as the best possible state of your soul."[1] This emphasis on the soul seems to exclude Socrates from the ballpark. Aren't bodies and wealth precisely the two things baseball players value most? Don't philosophers disdain all physical activity, preferring to stare off into space with chin planted on fist like Rodin's statue *The Thinker*? And isn't philosophy incapable of straight answers on anything?

The answer to all three questions is a resounding, No!

Athletes of all stripes (including pinstripes) know from experience that performance in sport is as much a matter of soul as

---

[1] *The Trial and Death of Socrates*, translated by G.M.A. Grube (Indianapolis: Hackett, 1975), 30a–b.

sinew. Especially at the higher levels, physical strength and skill are only part of the equation. Where strength and skill approach parity, the difference must be made elsewhere. The drive for athletic excellence calls for spiritual qualities such as courage, creativity, self-discipline, concentration, and intelligence. Excellence in baseball is not just a matter of training the body with hours and hours of practice; it's a matter of finding the discipline and motivation within oneself to go down to the batting cages on cold rainy days, to concentrate on the ball amid life's everyday distractions, to keep believing in oneself when no one else does. The qualities that make champions in baseball's World Series are the same qualities that made champions at the Ancient Olympic Games of 776 B.C.E. The Greeks called it *aretē,* meaning excellence or virtue, and they knew that it mattered both on and off the field.

Socrates was famous for his ugly face, beautiful mind, and ironic manner. His self-designed profession was questioning Athens's wise men in the public square or *agora.* A Socratic conversation was called *elenchos,* which means 'examination', and it revealed to the men (and to the city), that they weren't as wise as everyone thought. But Socrates was not trying to show himself superior; he always claimed he knew nothing except that he didn't know. He wanted to motivate others to learn, to question authority, and to think independently. He believed that was best for them *and* for their communities.

Nevertheless he was unpopular and unappreciated. In 399 B.C.E., Socrates was tried in Athens and executed for impiety and corrupting the youth. Since then, his story has inspired thinkers and leaders as diverse as the Roman Emperor Marcus Aurelius and the American Civil Rights advocate Martin Luther King, Jr. Countless college students have studied Plato's account of Socrates's trial and execution. Authors and artists have made him a favorite subject. In some parts of the world he is a semi-religious figure, martyred for the truth. Socrates's life and ideas are routinely applied in such fields as education, politics, law, and religion.

But baseball?

Aretē is the proper and ultimate goal of baseball and philosophy. But this is not just a matter of accident or coincidence. Both Socrates's *elenchos* and athletic games like baseball are specifically constructed to cultivate and celebrate human *aretē,* and to that end they are constructed in similar ways. To illustrate this connection between Socratic philosophy and baseball, I offer four points of comparison. First, both baseball and *elenchos* are knowledge-seeking activities, grounded in uncertainty and characterized by questioning. Second, both include the risk of failure, which motivates the desire to learn, train, and succeed. Third, both require the active testing of oneself according to agreed-upon standards and rules. And finally, both include an obligation to cooperate with and challenge others.

The First Pitch: Uncertainty

The first step toward realizing the connection between baseball and Socratic philosophy is to understand athletic competition in "epistemological" terms. Epistemology is the branch of philosophy that questions how we know and understand things. Everyone knows that philosophy, which means "love of wisdom" in Greek, is an activity directed toward knowledge. What's not immediately apparent to most people is that baseball, like all athletic competition, is also directed toward knowledge and truth. But that's just because most people mistakenly associate knowledge only with books and laboratories. Knowledge is a matter of understanding ourselves, our world, anything. Think about the real reason people are fascinated with baseball. Players and spectators alike are drawn to the ballpark by the prospect of learning or proving something.

The individual player wants to learn about himself and his competitors. What kind of pitches will he throw? Will I be able to hit them? Players play the game to see what they can do, to find out things about themselves that can't be quantified by a machine. The radar gun says I can throw a ninety-mile-an-hour fastball, but only in the game will I learn if I can throw it under pressure, accurately, at the right time, without it being hit by the opposing team's cleanup batter. Likewise the spectators come to the ballpark to learn what will happen in the game. Who will win? Who will lose? Will Pedro Martinez strike out the side? Will Sammy Sosa hit a home run? Fans have their educated predictions—they know batting averages and ERAs—but they won't *know* what's to happen until they see the game played. So we all go to the ballpark eager to learn.

Everyone can appreciate the anticipation that fills the air at Busch Stadium before the start of an important St. Louis Cardinals game. What we may not realize is that pre-game jitters and excitement are symptoms of the human desire to know and learn. Often the excitement is accompanied by the nauseating dread of finding out some ugly truth, like the Cardinals relief pitchers might not be up to the challenge. Like all knowledge-seeking activities, baseball games are characterized by uncertainty; we don't *know* what will happen (despite all our efforts at statistical prognostication) so we are intrigued to find out. In fact, the allure of any particular game seems to depend on the relative uncertainty of its outcome. It's Mariano Rivera vs. Luis Gonzalez in the 2001 World Series, or Ralph Branca vs. Bobby Thompson fifty years earlier. Unlike movies or books, tape-delayed baseball games have only limited appeal. What interest we do have in them is directly proportional to what's still left to know. Perhaps we know who won, but we'll watch the tape to find out how. Maybe we just want to see for ourselves how that Gonzalez Series winning hit just cleared the infield. But once we've learned all we can, there's little interest left.

The epistemological side of baseball also explains why sports fans love upsets. Upsets take what we thought we knew (who would be the winner) and turn it on its ear by teaching us something we never expected (that Goliath had a weak spot, and that little David had something we never saw before). And when you are a player in an upset, David or Goliath, you experience something close to the very heart of sport. When the Florida Marlins win the 2003 World Series, you are reminded that Truth is never fully within our grasp, that we cannot know the future, despite even perfect records in the past. You are reminded that we as humans must admit our uncertainty in order to begin the process of learning.

And this is exactly what Socrates did. By questioning Athens's wise men in the public square, he proved that no one knows everything—even when everyone thinks that he does. Just like overconfident athletes, wisdom-loving humans shoot ourselves in the foot as soon as we *think* we have the final answer, because we lose all desire to test ourselves and improve on our opinions. We rely on our "experts," habits, or traditions to tell us the Yankees have the best team, and never think to consider that they may be wrong. We get so comfortable hearing what we want to hear, that we close ourselves off to other possibilities. When Socrates begins his trial defense in the *Apology,* the first thing he does is *warn* the audience that from him, like it or not, they will hear the truth.[2] Then he worries out loud whether this truth has any chance of standing up to the jury's beliefs and assumptions.[3] This concern surely made the jury uneasy, but that is just what Socrates needed to do. Unless he can get the Athenians to recognize the possibility that their comfortable assumptions may be wrong, the truth doesn't stand a chance. Without acknowledged uncertainty, there is no chance to learn.

But baseball, like Socrates, reveals that uncertainty in those uneasy moments before each game. The game manufactures a situation where we are made aware of the reality of our uncertainty. In the words of sportscaster Joe Garagiola, "Baseball gives you every chance to be great. Then it puts every pressure on you to prove you haven't got what it takes."[4]

No one knows what will happen, no matter how sure we feel about the worth of our prognostications; we ignore the possibility of failure at our peril. Baseball, like philosophy itself, is wisdom-loving and knowledge-seeking, an activity that aims not just for information but also for understanding. The game will answer questions about individual performances, season standings, and the effects of new grass in the outfield, but these answers are only partial and temporary resolutions of the initial uncertainty. Bigger questions loom.

In the Batter's Box: Facing up to Fallibility

A baseball game asks questions about balls and strikes that encourage both player and fan to reflect on bigger questions about life. To stand in that batter's box and stare down that corridor to the mound is to ask a question of oneself. Not just the baseball question, "Can I hit this ball?" but the character-question, "Am I up to the challenge?" Light hitting Billy Beane has admitted to facing the very real possibility that he wasn't up to the challenge. Unlike his roommate Lenny Dykstra, Beane let his

---

[2] *Ibid.,* 17c.
[3] *Ibid.,* 18a–c.
[4] http://www.americansportscasters.com/facts.html.

fear overcome him. "Lenny was so perfectly designed, emotion-
ally, to play the game of baseball. He was able to instantly forget any failure and draw strength from every success. He had no
concept of failure. I was the opposite."[5] The winning of a baseball game is meaningless in and of itself. The player really
desires to be the *kind of person* who can achieve that goal. We
want to be able to face up to the challenges presented by the
game, because the hitting of that ball with that stick demands
virtues that can be applied to life's more meaningful challenges.
It provides evidence for the player and for those looking on of
the player's growing *aretē*.

But to be able to answer baseball questions about success, a
player must stand in that batter's box and risk the possibility of
failure. Likewise philosophical questions require us to risk being
wrong. Embodied in the sincere asking of any question is the
allowance on the part of the questioner that she does not know
the answer. This admission of fallibility, so familiar to the athlete, engenders a kind of humility characteristic of Socrates, and
the object of his *elenchos*. The story goes that Apollo's divine
oracle at Delphi declared that no one was wiser than Socrates.
But rather than gratifying the philosopher, this declaration threw
him for a loop. He knew that what the oracle said must be true,
but he knew just as surely that he wasn't wise at all. "Whatever
does the god mean?" thought Socrates, "What is his riddle?"[6]
Eventually he solved the puzzle by understanding that wisdom
is the admission of ignorance. The oracle, he concluded, was
using him as an example as if to say, "This man among you,
mortals, is wisest who, like Socrates, understands that his wisdom is worthless."[7]

After this realization, Socrates took it as a divine mission to
provide the public service of revealing people's ignorance:
"Even now, I continue this investigation as the god bade me—
and I go around seeking out anyone, citizen or stranger, whom
I think is wise. Then if I do not think he is, I come to the assistance of the god and show him that he is not wise."[8] Socrates

---

[5] Michael Lewis, *Moneyball: The Art of Winning an Unfair Game* (New York: Norton,
2003), quoted in the *New York Times* (March 3rd, 2003), and cited at http://www.greater-
talent.com/lewisnyt0303.shtml.
[6] *The Trial*, 21b.
[7] *Ibid.*, 23b.
[8] *Ibid.*, 23b.

believes he's *helping* the god to make people better by reliev-
ing them of their false certainty. In this case Socrates isn't so
much *in* the ballpark as he *is* the ballpark, or his *elenchos* is a
kind of baseball game. Like sport, the *elenchos* allows no one to
rest upon his laurels. Even if everyone in town thinks you are
an expert on, say, courage, Socrates will put you to the test. And
if he shows that you don't know as much as everyone thought
you did, not only will you be responsible for finding the truth,
so will everyone else who thought that your answer required no
further thought.

Of course admitting ignorance destroys one's *reputation* for
wisdom, but the truth of your ignorance can set you free to
search for knowledge. Baseball, and sports in general, require a
similar admission of fallibility. To enter into competition is to
risk one's public reputation and even one's own self-concep-
tion. Kirk Gibson hobbled out to pinch hit with two outs in the
bottom of the ninth, with his Dodgers losing 2–1, against the
greatly feared Dennis Eckersly in the now famous opening game
of the 1988 World Series. Gibson was injured; nobody would
blame him for watching the last out from the dugout. But to
compete is to risk failure. All you can do is offer your best performance and hope it survives exposure to the competition.
Athletes with perfect records or long winning streaks know this
all too well. In 1941, Ted Williams elected to play in a double
header on the last day of season, risking his incredible .400 batting average. One bad game can seemingly erase a year-long
streak. Even on a personal level, one's self-image can be
destroyed. Athletes always risk failure, but this constant risk, this
admission of fallibility, creates the desire to learn, to train, to
improve. Williams collected six hits in the last two games, rais-
ing his average to .406. Gibson hit that home run and the
Dodgers went on to win the Series. Winning is only possible if
you are able to risk losing, just as wisdom is only possible if you
are able to admit ignorance.

Swinging for the Fences:
Engaging in Active Testing of Oneself

In time the athlete and the philosopher become accustomed to
confronting failure. Once the comfortable illusions are gone and
the reality of our imperfection is fully realized, the focus shifts

to *improvement*—to self-testing and improving oneself through competition and conversation. For the dedicated player, baseball is not so much a game as a way of living: it is a long-term commitment to training, testing, and improving. Players routinely say that they will retire as soon as they stop improving. Lou Gehrig, for example, knew it was time to hang up the cleats when he was complimented for making a routine play.[9] "If you're not getting better," the saying goes, "you're getting worse." Each season, each game, each practice session, each swing, is part of a larger process of self-improvement. They are spot-checks along the longer path towards excellence. If winning in sport really is "the only thing," as football coach Vince Lombardi allegedly claimed, then as soon as a victory was had, the desire to compete again would fizzle out. Victories are evidence of progress and improvement, but they can't quell the desire to take on the challenge again. When victory is the pinnacle of achievement, athletes will continue testing themselves, often in the public eye, even as their performance deteriorates. How else are we to understand basketball star Michael Jordan and baseball pitcher Roger Clemens still competing at age 40, though their places in history are etched in stone? The desire to know and learn doesn't wither so quickly.

Just as the baseball player must actively engage in active testing, the Socratic philosopher must never retire from conversation. When the oracle declared no one wiser than Socrates, it must have been like being crowned world champion of philosophy. But his reaction was to treat this victory as a challenge: he developed a theory about what the declaration might mean then went out and tested it by taking on whoever had a reputation for wisdom. These conversations became his own kind of athletic competitions, a means for testing himself against the great minds of his world. Socrates notes that his activities made him unpopular, eliminated the leisure time necessary for personal and public affairs, and even forced him to live in poverty, since his dedication to philosophy precluded his ability to hold a normal job. But for all this sacrifice, he reaffirmed his commitment to philosophy as beneficial both to himself and his

---

[9] Already suffering from the disease that would claim his life, Gehrig finally ended his streak at 2,130 consecutive games played.

compatriots. Socrates even claimed that his just desserts should be free meals at the Prytaneum, the honor traditionally reserved for Olympic victors, because "The Olympian victory makes you think yourself happy; I make you happy. Besides, he does not need food, but I do."[10]

Socrates's sacrifice for and commitment to philosophy may not remind us of baseball's pampered professional stars, but it may remind *them* of their early days, and it will recall for many the reality of a dedicated athlete's life. What's interesting about Socrates is that he continued the sacrifice even after being declared the champion, but that is not unlike the Cy Young Award winner regularly working on the fundamentals. Such training and testing would not be necessary were Socrates a god and therefore automatically wise. Socrates simultaneously recognizes his imperfection and his potential for near-perfection, so he actively engages in the struggle to at least approximate the ideal of wisdom. So too, even the athlete whom the masses worship like a god, must struggle daily. He enters into competition and discovers his weaknesses; he then works on those weaknesses in training and returns to competition to gauge his progress in the struggle for perfection. That philosophy should represent a similar kind of struggle is only apparent when we look closely. The agōn is a struggle not just against the competition; it's symbolic of the more general struggle against the human imperfection that pervades life itself. We strive to approach the divine ideal and the testing helps us to rise above ourselves.

A Call to the Bullpen:
The Obligation to Challenge Others

In the *Republic,* Plato offers a famous allegory of human learning as the escape from a cave.[11] We discover that the philosopher who so valiantly releases herself from the shackles of her senses, who turns from the fire, claws her way up to the mouth of the cave, whose eyes finally adjust to the bright rays of the real sun so that she may see at last the world of ideas as it is, has an obligation to descend back into the darkness and help

---

[10] *The Trial,* 36d–e.
[11] *Republic,* 514a–617a

others up the same path. And since Socrates is the closest thing to an example of this person that Plato offers, we might conclude that this obligatory service takes the form of questioning others. Socrates compares himself to a "gadfly" whose stinging questions stir up the large and lazy horse that Athens had become.[12] He makes it clear that philosophy is not just a matter of self-improvement, but that it includes an obligation to help others by testing them and facilitating their own pursuit of *aretē*.

So too, the baseball player, even after he has won multiple championships, is expected to challenge others in competition. The aging Randy Johnson must continue to struggle to improve himself and goad his fellow players to struggle to improve themselves. "Resting on your laurels" is a derogatory concept in baseball, and sport generally. (In fact the term, "laurels" refers to the crown awarded to victors at the ancient Greek Pythian games, which took place at Delphi, home of Socrates's famed oracle). Yet it would seem that if winning were everything in sport, an athlete would never descend back into the darkness of competition where the victory could be erased by a defeat. The champion would never accept the challenge of underlings, since his status is so very fragile and age is the enemy of athletic performance. Furthermore, we'd never see retired players like Dusty Baker or Alan Trammell managing from the dugout, since the objective of their struggles would have been achieved already as players.

At first glance, this aspect of baseball and philosophy are equally inexplicable. The obligation to challenge others and to continue to challenge oneself after such important goals have been met seems strange, unless the real goal is something bigger than the game, something even bigger than us. Although Hank Aaron and Roger Maris received hate mail and threats as they closed in on Babe Ruth's home run records, record breakers are generally applauded by the old record holders. "Records are meant to be broken." How can the retired champion so heartily applaud the upstart who improves on his mark? How can the aging professor coax brilliance from her struggling doctoral student? Is it because the love of wisdom and the love of athletic competition are ultimately a love for *excellence* itself—

---

[12] *The Trial*, 30e.

not just as manifest in ourselves as individuals, but excellence in general in all its manifestations? *Aretē* is the connection between sport and philosophy and every human activity that strives to celebrate what's best.

Last Pitch

As it turns out, we shouldn't be so surprised to find the ancient spirit of Socrates in our modern ballparks. Dust off the plate, and you will see that baseball and philosophy have much in common. Both activities seek knowledge, ask questions, require an admission of fallibility, encourage the constant and active testing of oneself, and include an obligation to challenge others. Furthermore, these connections are not just accidental or contrived. Baseball is an athletic competition, and like philosophy, it is directed toward the goal of *aretē,* or human excellence.

Unfortunately, this connection between baseball and philosophy is anything but automatic. Today's generation of professional players, in particular, seems to be focused on wealth, fame, and physical prowess—the three things Socrates said we should be ashamed to care for. This problem derives not from the nature of baseball, but from the people who exploit and abuse it. Philosophy is just as easily abused. You could read a Socratic dialogue, perhaps even meet Socrates in person, and learn little from the experience. Readers of *The Trial and Death of Socrates* will recall another dialogue, *Euthyphro,* in which a man hurries to prosecute his father for impiety, just at the point when Socrates proves that he has no consistent idea of what piety is. On the other hand, you can learn volumes about yourself from the same experience. Likewise, you can play baseball and learn nothing about yourself, but what an opportunity to waste! The obligation is on teachers, coaches, but especially athletes and philosophers themselves, to communicate the philosophical potential of baseball to others, while rendering their own lives and activities "examined" and therefore, in the words of Socrates, worthwhile. After all, says Socrates, "Wealth does not bring about *aretē,* but *aretē* makes wealth and everything else good for men, both individually and collectively."[13]

---

[13] *Ibid.*, 30b.

Post-Game
Press Conference

19 | Baseball and Ethics

ETHICS *is the branch of philosophy that deals with questions of right and wrong. Is it wrong to lie, cheat, and steal? Why? In formulating our moral theories, do we look at the rules, the person's character, the consequences of an action, the relationships of the people involved, the person's duty, our own conscience? Or is it a combination of factors?*

After ethicists work out the thorny issues of right and wrong, the next problem is determining what to do with people who choose to perform bad acts. This takes us to theories of punishment. Two competing philosophies today are retributive and utilitarian theories. The retributive theory states that a person who breaks the rules should be punished according to what is deserved. The bad act has disturbed the balance between individual rights and the good of society. Punishment, therefore, is needed to restore justice. The utilitarian theory states that punishment should be handed down according to the consequences it will have for all involved. Rather than look to the past and the bad act committed, the utilitarian looks to the future and whether the punishment will yield positive effects.

In 1989, Pete Rose was officially banished from baseball by Commissioner Bart Giamatti for betting on the Cincinnati Reds while he was managing the team. Because of his lifetime ban, he was not enshrined in the Hall of Fame. Since then, almost everyone interested in baseball has weighed in with an opinion. Harvard University even held a mock trial in the summer of 2003, with Johnnie Cochran defending Rose (he won, of course).

In the following argument about whether Rose should be inducted into the Hall of Fame, both authors favor the retributive theory of punishment. While acknowledging that Pete Rose may have gambled on baseball games, the authors differ about what is deserved. Mark J. Hamilton argues that Rose deserves his lifetime ban. Aeon J. Skoble argues that such a punishment is too severe, and therefore undeserved. Who will make the better argument? Wanna bet?

19a | Should Pete Rose Be in the Hall of Fame?

YES

AEON J. SKOBLE

Pete Rose finished his storied career with a lifetime batting average of over .300, with a record-setting 4,256 hits in a record-setting 3,562 games. He was named MVP of the World Series, helping the Cincinnati Reds to victory in 1975, and he was the regular-season MVP in 1973. He led the National League in batting three times, and boasted a 44-game hitting streak in 1978. His nickname, "Charlie Hustle," reflects his enthusiasm and work ethic as a player, for which he was universally acclaimed.

Rose's achievements are those of a Hall of Fame player. His inclusion in that august company should be, to use a technical term, a no-brainer. Yet he is ineligible even to be considered for inclusion, thanks to discipline meted out by then-Commissioner Bart Giamatti. Unless the ruling is rescinded, Rose will remain out of the Hall of Fame. But the question is, *should* Rose be in the Hall of Fame? The answer is an unequivocal "yes." Given his impressive record, the burden of proof ought to be on those who claim he should *not* be in the Hall of Fame. They advance precisely one argument: Rose bet on sports. He even bet on baseball. While he was a manager, he may even have bet on his own team. This, we are told, is a disgrace of such epic proportions that he should forever be banned from having his excellence recognized.

Let's grant for the sake of argument that he bet on baseball, that he bet on the Reds–exactly what is the moral wrong here?

If Rose had bet *against* the Reds, and then managed below his ability to "throw" the game, that would be a clear moral wrong: it would constitute a fraud on the spectators, a breach of trust with his employer, and a betrayal of his players. It would demonstrate a venality and lack of integrity so severe that one could make a case it would militate against his other achievements. But—there are no such allegations. The charges seem to amount to his having bet on the Reds *winning*. That, if true, would commit none of the moral wrongs just mentioned. It's as if he were saying, "I am so confident that my team and I can win, I'll even put money on it." This entails no conflict of interest, since he would thereby only incur further reason to manage to the best of his ability, which is what we would normally expect anyway.

If anything, betting on baseball might be evidence of a character flaw. For example, it might mean Rose likes gambling too much, is too "addicted" to the excitement.[1] Maybe it means he was not content with his salary and was seeking an additional revenue source. Maybe he felt "entitled" to make extra money off his spectacular abilities. Maybe he got a thrill out of skirting the rules and engaging in forbidden activity. Any of these would count as some sort of moral failing, albeit not a terrible one.

But the Hall of Fame is not the "Hall of Moral Excellence"— it is designed to honor excellence in baseball. Literally dozens of Hall of Fame members were guilty of character flaws far more severe: racism, most notably. Despising or looking down on members of other races just because they are members of other races is an ignorant and vicious sort of tribalism, surely a moral failing; specifically, failing to regard others as equally worthy of respect or dignity, failing to treat them as individuals. Some were anti-Semitic; some were homophobic. Other members of the Hall of Fame were adulterers, others were alcoholics or users of illegal drugs. At least one was an abusive spouse. Some were surely non-baseball gamblers. Some even cheated at baseball, using illegally doctored bats or balls from time to time. The Hall of Fame makes room for all these morally

---

[1] I render "addicted" in scare-quotes because I think we should be wary of the lack of free will it implies. If Rose *literally* lacked free will, surely he should not be held responsible, and thus not held ineligible.

flawed individuals on the grounds that, vices aside, they exhibited true excellence in their field. The Hall's slogan is "Preserving History. Honoring Excellence. Connecting Generations." It doesn't say anything about "Demanding Moral Perfection." If it did, Lou Gehrig would not have very much company in Cooperstown. Pete Rose's achievements are a part of baseball history, which should be connected to future generations, and his unquestioned excellence as a player deserves to be honored.

19b | Should Pete Rose Be in the Hall of Fame?

NO

MARK J. HAMILTON

On August 24th 1989 Pete Rose was banned from baseball for gambling on the game. Rose signed a document accepting the ban but not admitting any guilt. He was allowed to apply for reinstatement after a year. Since then baseball fans have been divided in their support for Rose.

I must begin by saying I love Pete Rose the ball player. Sure he was brash and cocky on the field. And most of us who are Cleveland Indians fans have never forgiven him for effectively curtailing the career of Ray Fosse by plowing him over in the All-Star game. But I was playing college baseball in S.W. Ohio in the 1970s when Pete Rose was the heart and soul of the Big Red Machine. The Reds were Rose's team and the people adored him. He was a hometown boy who became the contemporary symbol of overachievement and of how the game ought to be played: to win with every ounce of effort.

There is a strong argument, though, in support of the Major League Baseball's position that Rose should be banned. He bet on professional baseball and on the Reds while he was their manager. Is there evidence of Rose's violations? Baseball hired John Dowd, a former federal prosecutor, to conduct the investigation. Dowd calls the evidence against Rose "overwhelming." He discovered evidence Rose had run bets through his friend, Paul Janszen, to a bookie named Ron Peters.[1] Both of them tes-

---

[1] Derek Zumsteg, "Evaluating the Dowd Report," www.baseballprospectus.com/news/20021031/zumsteg.html.

tified against Rose as did Janszen's girlfriend Danita Marcum. Another bookie, "Val," took bets directly from Rose and through Steven Chevashore. Besides the testimony of these characters, there are phone records of calls from the Reds clubhouse to bookies, financial and bank records that show continued betting during the baseball season, and betting slips with Rose's signature and prints on them. The evidence is compelling. The testimony of the witnesses was corroborated by handwriting experts and a wealth of phone records. Rose also admitted to illegal betting on basketball and football, and the gambling records provided by the witnesses indicate that the gambling payments to bookies continued through the baseball season, long after football and basketball had ended.[2]

Rule 21(d) is visible in every major league locker room: "BETTING ON BALL GAMES. Any player, umpire, or club official or employee, who shall bet any sum whatsoever upon any baseball game in connection with which the bettor has a duty to perform shall be declared permanently ineligible." This rule recognizes the need to keep the game fair though its conventions, so that any player or manager who gambles on the games violates an essential rule of the game.

What is wrong with managers having enough confidence to bet on their own team? The wager could make him short-sighted. He may be so interested in winning today's game to get out of the debt, he might not act on the best interests of the team he is managing. He might sacrifice winning the season for the sake of winning today for personal benefit. What if he has a large gambling debt and he is trying to make it all up in tonight's game? For example, such a manager could sacrifice future chances at victory in order to win tonight by overextending his top relief pitcher. He could become more interested in personal advantage than in the long-term success of the team. Or if a manager gets in debt to bookies he could attempt to clear his account by providing inside information about his team.

Rose is a tragic figure of contemporary sport. He continues to deny he bet on baseball despite all the evidence to the contrary. By admitting Rose back into baseball and thus into the Hall of Fame without making him admit his actions, showing

---

[2] Sean Lahman, "Answers to Frequently Asked Questions about Pete Rose," http://www. baseball.com/data/rose-faq/html.

great remorse, and renouncing his behavior, baseball would be saying that Pete Rose is above the rules of the game and above respecting the game. The game would lose integrity and Major League Baseball would be saying that their rules have no weight and authority; they do not really matter.

Commissioner Giamatti may have stated it best on the day of Rose's ban:

> The banishment for life of Pete Rose from baseball is a sad end of a sorry episode. One of the game's greatest players has engaged in a variety of acts which have stained the game, and he must now live with the consequences of those acts. By choosing not to come to a hearing before me and by choosing not to proffer any testimony or evidence contrary to the evidence and information contained in the report by the Special Council to the Commissioner, Mr. Rose has accepted baseball's ultimate sanction, lifetime ineligibility."[3]

---

[3] http://www.dowdreport.com.

20 | Baseball and Political Philosophy

POLITICAL PHILOSOPHY *is the branch of philosophy concerned with how to run a State. What is the role of government? What is justice? How can we create a more just society?*

Discussions about justice, freedom, and power inevitably turn to questions of money. Political philosophers like Adam Smith and Karl Marx have written thousands of pages on the best ways to distribute wealth. Smith argued that an individual must be free to join the economic market without governmental restraints. Marx believed that only a more egalitarian distribution of money would prevent the inevitable injustices between the rich and the poor.

Without money, we become disempowered and without power, we lose our freedom and self-worth. On the other hand, too much money can also serve to limit freedoms. Think of the destructive lives and deaths of pop music stars: Elvis Presley, Kurt Cobain, Tupac Shakur. Problems inevitably follow from having too much and too little money.

In 2001, Alex Rodriguez (A-Rod) signed a ten-year contract with the Texas Rangers totaling $252 million. While many Americans struggle to pay their rent, and nearly half the world's population lives on less than two dollars a day, American sports heroes live large. Is this just? In the ensuing debate, Albert Duncan argues that A-Rod has earned his millions honestly and justly. Joel Shuman claims baseball is larger than any one individual and people like the fans need to be considered as well. The *authors may wax philosophical about whether ballpark beer is "less filling" or "tastes great," but both agree that $6.00 a cup is an expensive way to quench your thirst.*

20a | Does A-Rod Deserve So Much Money?

YES

ALBERT DUNCAN

The high salaries of professional athletes continue to be a controversial issue. The seemingly outrageous annual amounts paid to baseball players such as Texas's Alex Rodriguez ($22 million), Toronto's Carlos Delgado ($18.7 million) and Boston's Manny Ramirez ($17.2 million), have further fueled the controversy. Compared to decades ago, players' salaries have increased dramatically. For example, Babe Ruth, perhaps baseball's greatest player, received a salary of $70,000 in 1927. This amount, when corrected for the effects of inflation, would be worth just over $714,000 today. Yet the average annual salary paid to baseball players in 2003 is $2.5 million.

Even after inflation, baseball players make much more now than ever before, but the fact is, players like A-Rod are not overpaid. They are not paid according to the mental and physical effort used in performing an activity, nor are they paid according to the amount of resources they employed developing those skills. They are paid according to the influence they have on others, their economic impact, and for the uniqueness of their talent. Therefore, the high salary received by professional athletes is a just and natural outcome of a capitalist society. They have earned it.

Our economic system is a market system, governed by the interaction of supply and demand. Wages, production, and prices are all intertwined and determined in this dynamic process; goods and services are usually allocated to those who value them most. According to basic economic reasoning, consumers aim to maximize their satisfaction of the goods and services they consume.[1] It is that desire (maximization of satisfaction) of fans that helps nourish the strong demand for sporting activities. The significant impact that outstanding professional athletes such as Rodriguez, Sammy Sosa, Roger Clemens, Mark McGwire, Derek Jeter, and Barry Bonds have on others stems from the fact that these athletes make significant contributions to the maximization of fans' satisfaction.

That impact can also be seen by the difference in television ratings and game attendance when those stars are involved. In 2001, when Bonds was on course to break the record for most home runs for a season, fans packed the stadiums everywhere he played. He was maximizing consumers' satisfaction where entertainment was concerned. The same can be said of the home run derby of Sosa and McGwire in 1998. With the acquisition of McGwire, the St. Louis Cardinals sold about 600,000 more tickets in 1998 than 1997. During that period, ticket prices increased by 15 percent and there was a $5.5 million increase in revenue. According to economist Roger Abrams, "Studies have shown that an elite player might add ten to fifteen wins to a ball club's season total. The revenue increase that results from higher attendance may more than cover the player's salary."[2]

The economic impact of sporting activities in the United States is enormous. Sporting activities are not just for entertainment; they are business entities as well, with a multiplicity of spillover effects. The manner in which ball clubs generate revenue through broadcasting rights, merchandising and sponsorship, as well as the way popular sports figures are used to promote products, demonstrates the flourishing business aspect of professional sports. Every Major League team plays eighty-one regular season home games per season, which can result in tremendous economic benefits for local economies. According to *CRE Real Estate*, the economic impact on local economies of such a team together with its stadium lies between $175 million

---

[1] William E. McEachern, *Macroeconomics: A Contemporary Introduction,* sixth edition (Cincinnati: South-Western Publishers), p. 71.

[2] Roger Abrams, *The Money Pitch: Baseball Free Agency and Salary Arbitration* (Philadelphia: Temple University Press, 2000), p. 33.

and $225 million. Beneficiaries are not limited to those associated with the teams. They also include restaurants and bar workers, vendors, hotel workers and those involved in both public and private transportation.

Outstanding baseball players are celebrities who are idolized by many. Their unique skills and their exciting styles of play have tremendous impact on others. That impact has given us an insatiable desire to be entertained by them. Our demand is influencing their salary. Are they overpaid? No, they are worth their salary. It is the market forces at work.

---

[3] *CRE Real Estate Issues*, vol. 21, no. 3 (December, 1996) at http://www.melaniphy.com/Article.htm.

20b | Does A-Rod Deserve So Much Money?

NO

JOEL SHUMAN

For the love of money is the root of all evil.

—St. Paul

Yes, Alex Rodriguez makes too much money. Then again, so do most major league baseball players; obscenely inflated salaries are but one thread in the fabric of problematic economic practices that have corrupted and may well soon destroy Major League Baseball. I make this claim with a bit of equivocation; equally vivid among my childhood memories are my father's being glued to the radio or television rooting on (and often cursing) the 1960s Pittsburgh Pirates and his frequently regaling me with stories about the Wobblies, Mother Jones, and Eugene Debs. My dad's ways of seeing the world evidently stuck with me, as to this day I remain—in spite of what many would say is the implausibility of both positions—a Pirates fan and something of a socialist. Just so, a part of me will always believe that if a player from a middle or working-class background—especially one as good as Rodriguez—can get twenty-five million a year from a group of rich owners who probably got their money on the backs of workers, so much the better.

But the present situation in Major League Baseball, where the *average* annual player salary is approximately $2.5 million— more than fifty times the average household income in the United States—is hardly a compelling example of class struggle.

I suspect most fans, hearing such numbers, think about the economics of baseball the same way they think about Microsoft or Enron or Martha Stewart: very rich people fighting with *really* rich people over sums of money that are beyond the average person's imagination. As with so many aspects of contemporary American life, baseball has been captured by the latest version of the ideology of the market, and that captivity threatens to destroy the game at its highest level of play. Such a claim, of course, begs the question of what is the meaning of baseball. And because baseball is such a profoundly *human* activity, anything we say about what baseball is for presupposes some account (to borrow from the title of a wonderful book by Wendell Berry) of what *people* are, and of what they are for.

According to classical and neoclassical economic theory, women and men are most essentially rational, self-interested, acquisitive individuals, driven always and everywhere to act in our economic self-interest. If this is indeed the case, then all of our activity is fundamentally economic. Business, metaphorically if not literally, describes everything we do, baseball included. And if baseball is finally a business, then it is perfectly appropriate that A-Rod get a $252 million contract, for that, like $40 seats, $5 hot dogs, and $6 beers, is what the market currently will bear. In the long run, some teams will flourish and others will fall by the wayside, and this should not concern us, for that is the way the market works.

But we are more than self-interested individuals, and baseball is much more than an instantiation of market economics. We are creatures, made for friendship with one another. Such friendships must be cultivated; we achieve them not through the pursuit of our own self-interests, but through our mutual participation in common projects—projects like playing or watching baseball. Baseball is a kind of activity that the philosopher Alasdair MacIntyre calls a *practice*, a complex, inherently social activity directed first of all toward goods *intrinsic* to that activity. The intrinsic goods achieved by participating in a practice, MacIntyre explains, are never solely the possession of those individuals who achieve them; in some sense they remain the possession of the practice and all of its participants. We participate in practices because our participation is good in itself; our pursuit of such common goods binds us together as members of communities and makes us better than we would otherwise have been. Such participation offers us ways to resist the corrosive impersonal forces of the market, which have no place for tradition or community.

This means that A-Rod's achievements–like his 57 home runs in 2002—never belong solely to Alex Rodriguez. For as a baseball player, A-Rod is part of a traditioned community formed by the practices of playing, coaching, umpiring, and yes, of watching and appreciating baseball. That doesn't mean that A-Rod does not deserve to be well paid for the remarkable skills he has developed over the years. The exchange of money from fans to owners to players is part of the tradition that is baseball, and players good enough to play in the major leagues, especially those of A-Rod's caliber, ought to be well-compensated. But the exchange of money is only one part of the tradition, a part ultimately in service to the tradition. When it threatens the integrity of the game, whether by alienating fans or creating a competitive imbalance or by pricing small-market teams out of the league, it has become something other than part of the tradition that is baseball.

21 | Baseball and Metaphysics

METAPHYSICS *is the branch of philosophy that deals with questions about the real world. Everyone, it seems, has an opinion on what defines "real." Hip-hop stars tell us to "keep it real." MTV has their* Real World. *Other TV networks have their "reality" shows. Now that the "real" has invaded pop culture, you'd think we'd be closer to understanding what is real and what isn't. For a more comprehensive understanding of reality, though, we need to turn to the metaphysicians.*

What is real? Is there reality beyond our senses? In the East, Taoists and Buddhists believe the real world is invisible. Jewish, Christian, and Muslim philosophers argue that the real world is with God, an all-knowing, invisible power. In the eighteenth century, empiricists like David Hume argued that our senses discover what is real. Later, phenomenologists like Edmund Husserl advised us to return to the things themselves in order to determine what is real.

Baseball players have long had their own opinions about invisible forces and the real world. Remember the 1989 movie Major League, *and Dennis Haysbert's performance as the voodoo-worshipping Pedro Cerano on the crackpot Indians? Superstitions are now a part of the game. But are these unseen forces real? That's a question only a metaphysician can answer, and thankfully, we have two. Steven Streeter argues that the mysterious baseball forces are real and can be scientifically measured. Neil Feit claims that it is irrational to believe in any-thing that can't be clearly explained. Read on. A little argument never hurt anyone (knock on wood).*

21a | Does Superstition Help Performance?

YES

STEVEN STREETER

If Roger Clemens kisses Babe Ruth's monument before a game, does that help him pitch better at Yankee Stadium? Or if John Franco wears his father's firefighter's t-shirt for good luck, does that improve his on-field performance? Some may dismiss these rituals as ridiculous superstitions, but in baseball the subtle effect of superstitious belief has a positive and measurable effect on performance. The difficulty is in proving this positive influence. Many of us are convinced only by concrete, black and white visible results, measurable in quantifiable numbers and statistics.[1]

Of course it's very difficult to measure the subtle energy created by superstition because this energy is invisible to the human eye. But science has been able to measure invisible energy fields such as the efficacy of prayer, the reality of the dreamworld, and even subatomic particles. These invisible forces are measured by sophisticated instruments and through inference, noting their influence on surrounding entities that can be quantified. For example, no one has ever seen a black hole, but we know they exist because we can measure the effect of their gravitational force on surrounding celestial bodies.

Thus it is with superstition. We measure its effectiveness in baseball by its effect on the performances of players and on the

---

[1] See Chapter 15 in this volume.

game itself. Players understand the power of superstition, and they follow the rules: no talking about a no-hitter while it is in progress, no changing your routine while on a hitting streak, no wearing the unlucky number 13, no lending your bat to another player.

Other baseball superstitions are more personal. Babe Ruth, Joe DiMaggio, and Willie Mays stepped on second base when they ran in from the outfield, Vida Blue wore the same baseball cap for years, manager Gene Mauch wouldn't clean his uniform if his team won, and Nomar Garciaparra has a standard ritual at the plate where he pulls on each batting glove and taps his toes. Dave Concepción, the great Reds shortstop of the 1970s and 1980s, defied conventional baseball superstition by wearing the number 13, but he would shower in his uniform during a slump to wash away the bad energy.

Superstition thrives where mysterious twists and variables are abundant. In baseball, there are variables from game to game, and even from pitch to pitch. Pitchers are notoriously superstitious because they know there is no easy explanation as to why their curve ball is breaking one day and is flat the next outing. And hitters understand that the precise combination of timing, sight, rhythm, and muscle reaction must be perfect in order to successfully hit a baseball past diving fielders. Intuitive players know there are forces and rules that are beyond their rational understanding, so they do what they can to align themselves with these forces to produce successful results.

This phenomenon, though, goes beyond mysterious forces. Attention to baseball superstition brings awareness and precise concentration, and these qualities produce quantifiable results. When Sparky Anderson who, as a manager, won championships in both the American and National leagues, came out of the dugout to relieve a pitcher he would walk slowly, carefully avoiding stepping on the foul lines. This careful adherence to superstition sent a message to his team that attention to detail mattered, and that the players needed to be aware that the lines were there to set the boundaries of fair and foul. Like the rules of superstition the lines must be respected, and not crossed or stepped on haphazardly.

So attention to the guidelines of superstition helps one's concentration and awareness, which translate into proper preparation and an intensity of focus. All this helps the player succeed;

if he is prepared he may know how to pitch a tough hitter with men on base, and an intensity of focus may help the hitter determine which kind of pitch is coming his way, how many outs there are, or when to take the extra base. These are specific instances of how awareness can improve performance. And there are more subtle, though still measurable successes which can be inferred from the respect given to the forces of superstition: that if one believes, *à la* American philosopher William James, that adherence to superstitious forces improves one's performance, then that belief becomes reality.

Superstition, which is shared throughout the baseball community and is manifested through ritual and tradition, has become ingrained within the laws governing the sport, and has become an integral part of the mystique of big league success.

21b | Does Superstition Help Performance?

NO

NEIL FEIT

A baseball player is superstitious when he irrationally believes that a certain phenomenon influences his performance, or perhaps his team's performance. In typical cases, the relevant phenomenon is a pattern of behavior on the part of the player himself: wearing a peculiar item of clothing, following a certain route to the ballpark, eating chicken before every game (as Wade Boggs did), or even wearing a particular uniform number (Rickey Henderson once paid a teammate $25,000 for the right to have number 24; for Larry Walker, the number is 33). Of course, one can eat chicken before the game purely for dietary reasons, in which case the behavior is not superstitious—it does not result from superstitious beliefs.

A superstitious belief is unjustified because it is not supported by adequate evidence. Moreover, a superstitious belief probably entails that there is some magical or unexplainable connection between the phenomenon and one's performance, or at least that the phenomenon affects one's luck (rather than one's skill or physical and psychological capacities). In any event, we recognize clear cases of superstition when we see them. We also talk of players' routines and rituals (I will ignore any differences there might be between them). A routine or ritual is superstitious only if it results from superstitious beliefs. Examples of non-superstitious routines include stretching and batting practice.

It does seem possible that a player here and there is helped by his superstition. However, as I see it, this is generally not the case. Let's take a closer look. A person is helped by a thing–whatever exactly the thing is–if the person would have been worse off without the thing. Given any dimension of baseball performance (such as batting average or ERA), we may say that a superstition has helped one's performance in that dimension provided that, if it had not been practiced, the performance would have been worse than it actually is. We can call this the *counterfactual account* of helping.

If the counterfactual account is right, there is little reason to think that superstition generally helps one's performance. This is because there is little reason to think that a given superstitious player would perform worse than he actually performs, if he were not superstitious. In fact, there is fairly good reason to think that if a given superstitious player were cured of his superstition but not otherwise changed, his performance would not differ significantly: after all, his athletic ability would remain unaffected. It would be difficult to test directly whether superstitious players hit or pitch better than they would if they were not superstitious; but the matter seems amenable to empirical testing that bears indirectly on it. Perhaps it can be determined who has a batting superstition and who doesn't (to take one example). Perhaps a sufficiently large and unbiased sample can be chosen from each group. My suspicion is that the batting averages of the superstitious players would not be significantly better than their more rational peers with similar abilities. In any case, there is little empirical evidence for the claim that superstition helps performance, and the burden is on those who wish to see it. We might like to think that Sparky Anderson's refusal to step on the base lines (as reported by Steven Streeter) helped his players' performances; but this has not been shown. Moreover, any effect on performance needs to be shown to result from the fact that his behavior was superstitious. We would have to be convinced that if Anderson was really not superstitious, and just wanted to keep the chalk off his shoes, his behavior would not have had similar benefits.

Streeter is right to focus on things like awareness and concentration. However, I would bet that when ball players think about their superstitions, they think in terms of good luck rather than increased concentration. I am not denying that a player's routine can enhance his performance; but as we have seen, a routine need not be superstitious. We may not have an adequate conceptual analysis of superstition; but it is clear that many routines are not associated with superstitious beliefs. For example, stretching, batting practice, and warm-up routines, if they are associated with beliefs about performance at all, are likely associated with reasonable and justified beliefs that they enhance performance. Other routines, including various routines performed just before or after stepping into the batter's box, might reasonably be believed to increase one's concentration or to clear one's mind of distracting thoughts (much like a golfer's pre-shot routine is said to do). Finally, even if a belief of this kind turns out to be unjustified, it might not entail the existence of any magical or inexplicable connections between one's routine and one's performance, so the mere lack of adequate justification for the belief is not sufficient for it to be superstitious.[1]

---

[1] I would like to thank Raymond Belliotti, Stephen Kershnar, Dale Tuggy, and Julia Wilson for helpful discussions and comments on earlier drafts of this chapter.

22 | Baseball and Legal Philosophy

LEGAL PHILOSOPHY *is the branch of philosophy that deals with the nature of laws. While Social and Political Philosophy addresses larger questions of the State, philosophers of law look specifically at the laws that help make up the State.*

When, in the now famous Brown v. Board of Education case of 1954, Thurgood Marshall argued that American separate but equal policies promoted inequality, his arguments were based on both law and philosophy. Today, legal philosophers like Ronald Dworkin focus on how judges can, and should, shape American law.

Because of the special status baseball enjoys in American culture, legal eagles of the judiciary have never been far from the ballpark. In 1919, for example, Judge Landis led the investigation into the Black Sox scandal, involving White Sox players accepting cash payments from gamblers in exchange for throwing the World Series. When Landis served Shoeless Joe Jackson with a lifelong banishment from the game, he began a precedent of linking baseball rules with American law.

The issue of steroids has brought senators and baseball scholars to the plate. Now it's time for the philosophers to take a swing at it. Why are drugs like aspirin considered legal, but not some steroids? In the following debate, Michael J. McGrath claims steroids use taints the game, while Simon Eassom believes it all comes down to a matter of taste. Which argument will pump you up?

22a | Should Steroids Be Banned?

YES

MICHAEL J. McGRATH

The May 2002 edition of *Sports Illustrated* revealed one of sports' most poorly kept secrets: baseball players use performance enhancing drugs. The cover of *SI* prominently featured a quote from former MVP Ken Caminiti, who confessed that regular doses of steroids were as much a part of his training regimen as batting practice: "At first I felt like a cheater. But I looked around, and everybody was doing it." Of course, it is no secret that baseball players utilize whatever means, both legal and illegal, they can to improve their chances of success. The impact of steroids, however, is much more profound than a Gaylord Perry Vaseline ball or even a Sammy Sosa corked bat.

Baseball is America's pastime, and as such, many Americans scrutinize any issue that questions the integrity of Major League Baseball. For this reason, the issue of ethics in the major leagues is in many ways a microcosm of the moral principles of the United States. When Caminiti and former players Mark McGwire and José Canseco admitted that they had used steroids, their confessions not only were an embarrassment to baseball, but also an affront to the nation. In June of 2003, Major League representatives addressed Congress on the issue of performance enhancing drugs. The concern of the politicians was evident. North Dakota Senator Byron Dorgan (D) commented on the topic of steroids: "We've got an issue to face as a country . . ."[1]

---

[1] http://sportsillustrated.cnn.com/baseball/news/2002/06/10/congress_steroids_ap.

Arizona Senator John McCain (R), called attention to perhaps the most serious consequence when he noted that the sale of Androstenedione soared in 1998, the year Mark McGwire hit 70 home runs, breaking Roger Maris's single-season home run record. McGwire admitted that he regularly used the drug. McCain noted, "Like it or not, professional athletes serve as role models."[2] Whether baseball players choose to be or not, they are role models. Do we want the very public figures of our nation's pastime espousing the practice of succeeding at all costs? What does this philosophy say about America's morals? Both senators agree that the consequences of performance enhancing drugs are far reaching. Fortunately, there are players who also recognize the serious consequences of this issue. According to Craig Counsell of the Arizona Diamondbacks, the allure of more money drives players to "get an advantage somewhere, even if it involve[s] crossing an ethical line."[3] The New York Mets' Tom Glavine, one of MLB's most respected veterans, addressed the use of drugs from the Kantian point of view that there should be universal principles according to which we all live: "Those of us who don't do it, we feel like we aren't on an even playing field and that's something that shouldn't happen."[4]

There is no doubt that steroids and other performance enhancing drugs cause irreparable damage to the users' bodies. A *Saturday Night Live* skit pokes fun at these dangerous consequences. Guest host Patrick Swayze and Chris Farley are panelists on a show about the benefits of bodybuilding. All of the "bodybuilders," however, appear with deformed facial features, oversized shoulders and arms, and puny legs. Of course, the skit is an exaggeration, but the numerous injuries and side effects directly linked to steroids are not. While the player who considers steroids his breakfast of champions may not appear as freakish as Chris Farley and Patrick Swayze do in their skit, some performance enhancing drugs are responsible for changes in the body's physical appearance, one of which is shrinkage of the testicles due to the body's inability to produce testosterone; other serious side effects include high blood pressure, heart disease, liver damage, stroke, blood clots, urinary and bowel problems, and impotence.

---

[2] *Ibid.*
[3] http://sportsillustrated.cnn.com/si_online/special_report/news/2002/05/29/steroids_reax.
[4] *Ibid.*

Immanuel Kant's ethical theory argues that a principle is morally correct if it is good for all people at all times and under all circumstances.[5] We cannot make individual exceptions. The use of performance enhancing drugs can in no way represent this philosophy. Sure, Caminiti won the MVP award, and McGwire and Canseco hit a lot of home runs, but the ends do not justify the means. They never do, according to Kant. The presence of steroids, Andro, and the many other supplements in major league locker rooms compromises the integrity of the game. If MLB condones the use of steroids, America's pastime will become like professional wrestling, a "sport" devoid of any professional code of morals. Just ask World Wrestling Federation wrestler Davey Boy Smith. Wait, that's not possible. At the age of 39, Smith died of a heart attack, the direct result, according to the medical examiner, of prolonged steroid abuse.

---

[5] For a good description of Kant's ethics, see Chapter 7 in this volume.

22b | Should Steroids Be Banned?

NO

SIMON EASSOM

I'm not going to talk about drugs. Instead, I am going to refer to Performance Enhancing Technologies (PETs) for three reasons. First, the word "drug" has so many connotations–including associations with addiction, illegality, and crime—that the issue of drug-use in sport is obfuscated by an immediate negative attitude towards drug culture. Second, I want to ask whether the use of drug-use in baseball *in principle* is wrong. Third, pets are nice!

Let's assume for the sake of argument that the chemical substances (stimulants such as ephedrine and steroids such as nandralone) and biological procedures (such as blood doping or gene therapy) used to enhance performance are legal, safe, and freely available (many of the banned substances on the International Olympic Committee's list are all three). Are there any good reasons why they shouldn't be used in a sport such as baseball? In other words, before we get side-tracked by such considerations as to whether or not the acceptance of drug-use in baseball coerces children into harmful or illegal practices, let's consider whether or not there's anything wrong in essence with certain PETs.

In any sport, the rules limit the means by which a participant can achieve the goal of the game. These rules tend to *define* the sport by establishing its constituent components and setting its procedural standards. Baseball is baseball because it is a game played with a ball, pitched to a player with a bat who, after hitting the ball, tries to run around the bases without being tagged. In theory, the number of bases could be greater or fewer than at present, the number of players on the team could be increased or decreased, the size of the ball could be different, the number of strikes before you're out altered, and so on. The specifics are really a matter of culture and tradition and they could be altered to a certain degree without changing the essence of the game of baseball. In fact, there are a very large (but probably finite) number of potential formats of the game that could all meaningfully be called baseball. We just happened to have settled on a particular version we like and this is the standard. Why change it?

Within these parameters it is perfectly reasonable to try to achieve the goals of baseball as efficiently as possible with as much success as possible: to hit the ball more often, harder, further, to pitch the ball faster, etc. These things can be achieved by new technologies, theoretically, in two kinds of ways: by changing the means by which they are achieved or by improving the efficiency with which the means are applied. Let's call these two kinds of technology *aids* and *enhancers*. In the former case (technological aids), the size and shape and fabric of the bat could be changed to make hitting and hitting further easier to achieve. The pitcher could use a sling or even some sort of firing device like a canon. Catchers could wear gloves with large nets attached, and so on. But, you might protest, these technologies applied to aid performance might not be desirable because they tend to *de-skill* the activity—they change it for the worse because they make it harder to distinguish between the better and worse players and teams.

In the latter case, technologies can be applied to improve the way things are already done. Technology can be used that helps the hitter see pitches better, new techniques of pitching can be developed using biomechanical modelling, new materials can be used in the manufacture of gloves, the swing weight and balance of the bat can be altered to enable the hitter to swing faster. In each case, these technologies *enhance* the performance but do not necessarily de-skill the game. The pitcher still has to pitch, the hitter still needs to anticipate the pitch and demonstrate tremendous hand-eye coordination to hit the ball. It is a perfectly reasonable ethic of competitive professional sport to try to improve performance. Not only do these technologies enhance the performance, they enhance the game. We all like to watch big hitters going yard and pitchers striking out sluggers.

Substances such as steroids, used by players to bulk up muscle mass, increase strength, and thereby increase swing speed are performance-enhancing technologies just like relaxation techniques, mental rehearsals, diets, batting cages, video-replays, and weight-training sessions. They don't de-skill or re-skill the activity. They don't make the bat bigger, the pitch slower, or the outfield smaller. They are not like Popeye's spinach. But, they make for more excitement. It made no difference to my enjoyment watching Mark McGwire break Roger Maris's thirty-seven-year-old home-run record in 1998 knowing that McGwire trained using androstenedione.

What we allow or disallow in the satisfaction of our thirst for more exciting and spectacular baseball games is a matter of taste, not morality (of aesthetics, not ethics). There's nothing wrong (in principle) with the use of steroids to enhance performance. Their use is no more "unnatural" than many other practices we freely condone. They do not alter the game or destroy its integrity. Ban them because you don't *like* them, but you won't find reasons inherent in what baseball actually is that make their use inherently wrong.

23 | Baseball and Aesthetics

AESTHETICS *is the branch of philosophy that is concerned with aesthetic qualities, such as beauty, sublimity, ugliness, elegance, coolness, coherence, or dramatic impact—but most of all, beauty. What is beauty? How can we learn to recognize it? Is beauty in the eye of the beholder or is it out there in the world?*

According to Plato, beauty is an immortal force in the world that one's soul can experience only in small doses, and only when in love. Contemporary philosopher Arthur Danto describes beauty as "a necessary condition for life." Because beauty is so difficult to behold, and so important to our lives, philosophers help show us how to find it in our day-to-day world.

Any search for beauty will naturally lead us to nature, and then to art. It is in paintings, music, sculpture, literature, and film that we can experience beauty most clearly. But most of us need help. We take music appreciation classes, join book clubs, and watch Ebert and Roeper *to help us appreciate true beauty.*

Baseball, of course, is beautiful. The stadiums and uniforms are visual treats, the sounds of the ball hitting the bat or popping into the catcher's mitt takes us back to a more innocent time, as does the smell of peanuts on a hot summer day. In the following debate, Vincent L. Toscano and Larry Raful make competing aesthetic arguments for the best baseball movie. Both argue that beauty should involve form and content. It should be beautiful

319

to look at like a Roy Hobbs home run into the lights, and it should also take us to a time that we immediately associate with goodness and warmth. Both authors got their ideas by listening to the voice in the cornfield, "If you write it, they will read."

23a | What's the Best Baseball Movie?

The Natural (1984)

VINCENT L. TOSCANO

There are so many reasons to select *The Natural* as the best baseball movie. First are the fine performances from a top notch cast. Robert Redford has the blond boyish good looks and athletic ability to play Roy Hobbs, and he brings to that character not only a dash of the All-American boy but also hints of some deeper, darker aspects of character. Barbara Hershey is quite alluring as Harriet Bird, the mysterious and deadly "lady in black" who claims Hobbs as her final victim. Wilford Brimley's craggy features and long-suffering demeanor give Pop Fisher, the manager of the NY Knights, a kind of nobility as he chases his dream of a pennant. Robert Duvall plays the reporter Max Mercy with the aura of sleazy sanctimony one might expect from the media that makes athletes heroes one day and goats the next. Kim Basinger portrays Memo Paris, Pop Fisher's niece and willing accomplice in the scheme to have the Knights lose; then the judge can take the team from Pop. Her performance as the seductress who woos Hobbs to distract him from his game hints at a character torn between love of money and just love. Finally, as Iris, the girl from Hobbs's past and the mother of the son he didn't know he had, Glen Close exudes a purity and dignity that rescues Hobbs from the clutches of Memo.

Then there is the story line adapted somewhat faithfully from Bernard Malamud's novel, until the dramatic changes needed to produce the Hollywood ending (in the book, Hobbs strikes out). As a young baseball phenom, Hobbs's magical baseball talents are squandered by his pride (The Fall), leaving him out of baseball for fourteen years. He returns as a mid-30-year-old "rookie" sensation and once again is led astray until he is saved (Redemption) by the love of a good woman. In the final scenes Hobbs's integrity is challenged by the corruption of the Judge but he resists the bribe and delivers the climactic home run that gives the Knights their pennant and saves the team for Pop Fisher.

Finally there is the look of the movie created by Director Barry Levinson and Cinematographer Caleb Deschanel. The use of an amber lens provides a visual lushness. For important scenes, such as young Roy's late afternoon confrontation and strikeout of The Whammer, and Iris rising from her seat to help Roy break out of his slump, the halo lighting evokes the mythic and mystical character of the film. The final moments when Hobbs hits the game winning home run and sets off a cascade of lights and sparks are akin to the finale of any good Fourth of July fireworks display.

The movie is also a marvelous cultural artifact of the Reagan era. It seems to me that the sources of Ronald Reagan's appeal had much in common with the qualities that made *The Natural* a popular success. Most adult Americans living in the 1980s could fully appreciate Roy's simple answer when Iris asks "What happened to you?" His reply, "My life didn't turn out the way I planned." Since the mid-1960s American society had endured continued turmoil produced by assassinations, increasingly violent protests for peace and equality, and revelations of "dirty tricks" at the highest levels of government, followed by Presidential disgrace and resignation. Each year seemed to bring another blow to our most cherished ideals and visions of America as an "exceptional" country. America's once dominant economic position was being challenged by foreign competition, OPEC, and a globalized economy that left in its wake a rust belt of plants and businesses that could no longer compete. The country was in a deep funk, a "crisis of confidence" a "malaise" of spirit.

Enter President Reagan. He insisted that the American dream was still alive, that we could still work our will in the world, that capitalism and the unfettered free market would restore our prosperity. Simple nostrums were spoken with simplicity, sincerity, and conviction. The world was still one of infinite possibilities; forget about Vietnam, about Iran or Lebanon. "Reagan is not only a comfort but a necessity" argued Gary Wills. "He is the kindly fanatic . . . a rabble soother at a time when people . . . need to be assuaged, to have anxieties dispelled, complexities resolved."[1] Are not these the essential qualities and functions of cultural mythology? One might add, are not these the ingredients of *The Natural* which corrects the moral failures of Hobbs's behavior presented in Malamaud's novel?

Set in prewar America, the film extols the values of a simpler, more rural country. For an America that seemed lost but hoped for better, Reagan was a gift. As Roy says to Iris when it is time for her son to meet his father, "Yes, a father makes all the difference." And, at the right moment, so does a father figure in the White House.

---

[1] Gary Wills, *Reagan's America: Innocents at Home* (Doubleday, 1987), p. iv.

23b | What's the Best
Baseball Movie?

*It Happens Every
Spring* (1949)

LARRY RAFUL

There are two kinds of baseball films. One is the "you guys sit in the theater and we'll put on a movie so you can root for the hero" kind of film. The two Kevin Costner movies (*Field of Dreams* and *Bull Durham*) are in this league, as is *The Natural*. All three are tremendously entertaining and pure fantasy. Why "fantasy?" Because we can't relate to any of the three characters. We can only view them from afar, root for them, and admire them. We want Roy Hobbs to hit the homer, but no one I know identifies with Robert Redford's character. We have never heard voices in cornfields and then driven off across the country seeking The Voice. And maybe you have, but I know I've never met a baseball fan like Annie Savoy in *Bull Durham*.

And the other kind of baseball film? That's the kind made to entertain by allowing us to place ourselves into the movie, to allow us to seriously identify with the protagonist. "Gee, if it were only *me* up there instead of *him*." These baseball movies allow common shlubs to place themselves in The Show, to somehow release our earthly bonds for a few minutes and soar, to somehow, by hook or crook, wind up on the diamond. These, too, have an element of fantasy, but the fantasy happens to the common man. It allows that person, simply, to play baseball at the major league level, or at least at a level of excellence that helps his team win. And, I submit, playing baseball at that level is a dream millions of people have at some point in their lives, because almost all of us have once held a baseball or softball, or a glove on our hand, or swung a baseball bat.

The best baseball movie of all time comes from this type of film plot. In one of the earliest of the baseball movies, Ray Milland goes from baseball fan extraordinaire and befuddled chemistry teacher to the greatest pitcher of his time, in the 1949 classic, *It Happens Every Spring*. You know it's going to be a great movie with a title like that and an opening quote from Albert Einstein.

A quick synopsis (in case you have never seen this movie, and if you haven't, what kind of a baseball fan are you?): mild mannered Vernon Simpson (Milland) is a die-hard Cardinals fan (you have to love him turning on the radio under the podium during class, while expounding on a chemical formula, so he can keep up with the game), who is trying to finish his experiments with chemically treated wood. Into Vernon's lab flies a wayward baseball, breaking test tubes and ruining the experiment. Lo and behold, the ball, soaked with the resulting mixture of chemicals, will avoid any contact with wood. Get it? Well, Vernon gets it, partly because the Cardinals desperately need a pitcher. Vernon takes two lunkheads on the college baseball team out to the diamond and proceeds to look like Walter Johnson, easily striking one of them out with the mystery juice rubbed on the ball. (The lunkhead catching is none other than Alan Hale, who later left college baseball and became the Skipper of the S.S. Minnow on *Gilligan's Island*.)

Vernon takes a hasty and mysterious leave of absence, shows up at the Cardinals batting practice, wows them all, and then joins the team. He names himself King Kelly, starts winning games with no hitters and shutouts, and becomes friends with a crusty catcher, who, when told by the manager "Kelly is not indispensable" replies, Yogi-Berra-like, "Yeah, but we can't get along without him." At one point, Monk the catcher hurts his finger, puts a wood splint on his hand, and hilarity ensues when he tries to handle the juiced ball. He's even got a little Damon Runyon in him: "Leave us have no secrets between us."

Well, I could tell you about the exciting conclusion, but let's just say that the Cards win the Series, Kelly can't ever play again, and he goes home to head a new research lab and to marry his sweetheart Debbie.

The movie is just lovely in so many ways, at so many levels. It's in black and white, and is from a time long ago when all was well with the world. We could laugh at ourselves, and we could laugh at so many oddities that are no longer politically correct to parody. And, like so many films that were to follow, a person could watch this movie and think how wonderful it would be to be in the big leagues for one season, for a few games, for one World Series, to help his team win it all once, just once.

But there is a catch, of course. As much as we are entertained by Vernon, there is no mention in the movie of morality. Well, Vernon, I hate to break it to you, but you were cheating. That's right—cheating! And what is odd is that we don't mind this particular dishonesty at all. We are entertained and amused by heavenly helpers in *Angels in the Outfield*, by the antics of the Devil and Lola in *Damn Yankees*, and by the wondrous curves of King Kelly's breaking pitches. Yet when we actually walk through the turnstiles at the ballpark, we scream the loudest at the very thought of any cheating, because baseball is a pure game, and needs to be played at the purest level. We will not tolerate anything else.

And that's why this type of movie—the common man finds some magic and helps his team–is more of a real baseball movie than the fantasy type movies. Anyone who has held a bat has thought about hitting a home run in a major league park, and anyone who has ever held a baseball thinks about striking out a fearsome slugger. Because it will never happen, because there is no mystery juice and there are no angels or devils in the outfield, it is entirely understandable and even unremarkable that we are amused and entertained by baseball movies that come directly from our dreams, while we continue to live normal, and honest, lives.

24 | Baseball and Education

THE PHILOSOPHY OF EDUCATION *deals with questions concerning teaching and learning. After ethicists help us determine what goodness and happiness are, we then must decide how best to help others attain them.*

Educational issues naturally lead us to schools and schooling. How should we teach children the skills necessary to be happy? Aristotle believed that other people have an enormous impact on our character training. American philosopher John Dewey published Democracy and Education *in 1916, extolling the importance of preparing children to participate in society. Both philosophers agree that social environment directly affects our personalities.*

Team sports like baseball can help teach children the values of teamwork, sportsmanship, and friendly competition. But sports can also reaffirm negative values like violence, selfishness, and gender bias. This dual nature of sports highlights the importance of having good role models today.

Baseball has its share of good and bad role models. When Pittsburgh Pirate Randall Simon swung his bat at a fan running the beloved sausage race in 2003, questions about today's role models were rightly raised. In the following debate, Edward A. Sullivan and Graham Harman take on the argument. While Sullivan believes children who had the good fortune to watch Ted Williams and Jackie Robinson had better role models,

Harman points out the tremendous advancements today's ball players have made on and off the field. Both philosophers agree that good role models are essential to child development, but only one of them has a sausage suit in his closet.

24a | Were Baseball Players Better Role Models Then or Now?

THEN

EDWARD A. SULLIVAN

Thucydides once said that "the bravest are surely those who have the clearest vision of what is before them, glory and danger alike, and yet not withstanding go out to meet it."[1] Ted Williams and Jackie Robinson exhibited bravery unknown to today's ball players.

I remember seeing Ted Williams play the first time I went to see a Red Sox game. It was the summer of 1946, and my older brother and his friends took me to Fenway Park. We rode the bus to Lechmere Station and then took the trolley car to Kenmore Station. When we got to the ballpark, the Red Sox were taking batting practice and the Chicago White Sox players were playing catch in front of their dugout. When Williams stepped in for batting practice, a quiet came over the ballpark and the White Sox players stopped playing catch. I watched in awe as Williams hit two majestic towering fly balls, one landing in the bullpen, the other in the seats well beyond the bullpen. What a joy baseball was and the game hadn't even started!

Williams missed most of the 1952 and 1953 seasons, serving the country in the Korean War. During one of his missions, Williams literally displayed "courage under fire." When his jet

---

[1] Thucydides, *The Peloponnesian War*, vol. 2, Daniel Grene, ed., translated by Thomas Hobbes (Ann Arbor: University of Michigan Press, 1959), p. 111.

was hit by enemy fire, he managed to crash-land while it burned. Later, when he was inducted into the Baseball Hall of Fame in 1966, Williams again called on his courage, speaking out against the injustice of Negro League players not getting into the Hall of Fame. He said, "I hope some day Satchel Paige and Josh Gibson will be voted into the Hall of Fame as symbols of the great Negro players who are not here only because they weren't given the chance." As a result of Williams's speech, Negro League players began to be inducted into the Hall. Satchel Paige and Bob Gibson were voted into the Hall in 1971 and 1972 respectively. Williams saw an injustice, was brave enough to protest it, and made a difference.

Jackie Robinson displayed his bravery in another way, facing the burden of second-class citizenship. Even before arriving in Florida for spring training in 1946, Robinson and his wife were unable to fly from New Orleans to Pensacola because white people had been assigned their seats. They could not eat in the "white only" coffee shops at the airport. They found that once they arrived at the Dodger training camp, white baseball players stayed at a hotel that did not admit blacks. When his wife attended spring training workouts, she was forced to sit in the section reserved for blacks, the Jim Crow section. During spring training, the Montreal Royals (Brooklyn's minor league club) had to cancel exhibition games in Sanford, Deland and Jacksonville, Florida, Savannah, Georgia, and Richmond, Virginia because the cities had regulations forbidding Negroes and whites from competing with each other.

I remember stopping at the Natural Bridge in Virginia, while traveling from Boston to Oak Ridge, Tennessee in the summer of 1959. Having grown up in the north I was not prepared for what I saw at this national historic landmark, within three hours travel time of Washington, D.C.: water fountains marked "White only" and "Colored only," restrooms marked "White men only," "White women only," "Colored men only," "Colored women only." This was my first experience of the discrimination that blacks living in the south experienced every day. This was part of the experience that Robinson had each year as part of spring training in the south.

It took courage for Robinson to confront this insidious form of racial hatred. As part of the deal that Robinson worked out with Brooklyn's general manager, Branch Rickey, Robinson would have to face the taunts and racial slurs without speaking out or fighting back. When this was made clear, Robinson asked Rickey, "Do you want a coward, a ball player who's afraid to fight back?" To which Rickey replied, "I want a ball player with guts enough not to fight back."[2]

Ted Williams and Jackie Robinson courageously overcame difficulties far greater than any of the wealthier players today confront. If you're looking for role models, you can do no better than them.

---

[2] Quoted in Harvey Frommer, *Rickey and Robinson* (Lanham: Taylor Trade Publishing, 1982), p. 11.

24b | Were Baseball Players Better Role Models Then or Now?

NOW

GRAHAM HARMAN

Baseball players are better role models today than in past decades, no matter how counterintuitive this may seem. The tendency to believe the opposite is based largely on the universal illusions generated by the passage of time.

In the *Apology*, Socrates begins his defense by complaining that his most dangerous accusers are those now dead. Having slandered Socrates and passed into the grave, his deceased enemies have left us one-sided warnings about the Socratic vices, while escaping any scrutiny or cross-examination themselves—like those insufferable people who insult us even while leaving the room to avoid reprisal. A similar phenomenon occurs with retired and departed baseball players, who leave the field of play amidst Cooperstown plaques and dreamy anecdotes from aged broadcasters, basking in a glow that no active player can possibly match.

The first deed of time is to erase all moments of mediocrity and turn any past period into a caricature filled with peaks and valleys. Think back to your college years, and you will remember life-changing books, drunken escapades, and poignant romances, not the tedious drudgery of the laundry room and flash-card learning. But when comparing two eras of your own life, or even of Major League Baseball, it is important to consider the overall tenor of their daily rhythms, not just the exceptionally high and low points of each period.

If we consider the low points, there can be no question that the olden days sank to more abhorrent depths. The great morality play of baseball in our time has been the Pete Rose scandal. But even the worst accusations against Rose belong nowhere near the swamp of the 1919 Black Sox or the sordid maneuverings of the vile Hal Chase. For every sensationalized smear about drug use among today's players, there are a half-dozen stories from the past about drunken brawls and seedy off-season adventuring. You were offended by John Rocker's remarks to *Sports Illustrated*? But Rocker is a flat-out Berkeley multiculturalist compared to Ty Cobb and Cap Anson. The corked bat of Sammy Sosa would have been all in a day's work during your father's childhood. Today's reporters remember well the rudeness of Barry Bonds and Steve Carlton, but this will someday be lost beneath their numbers, just as the personal crudity of Rogers Hornsby and Ted Williams is now forgotten by all but historians.

We might also compare some of the high points of the sport in the two eras. Here as well, the modern players are equal to or better than their elders. Who could make a better case for the greatness of yesteryear than Lou Gehrig, with his legendary iron man streak and his dignity amidst mortal decay and death? Only one era has a Gehrig. But Cal Ripken's durability proved superior to Gehrig's, and was no more dependent on artificial means for extending the streak. It may be true that none of our players have faced the specter of death quite as directly as Gehrig. But recall cancer patient Brett Butler roaming center field without saliva glands, or the heart-rending Dave Dravecky of 1989, pushing his diseased throwing arm to the point of injury and eventual amputation. No old-time player exceeded the courage and grit of the wounded Kirk Gibson in the 1988 World Series, his screams of pain echoing from the clubhouse batting cage before his historic home run.

But let's not make the case based on peaks and valleys alone; let's consider the overall level of the sport in the two eras. Baseball today provides better role models just as society today provides a better model. The racist climate of "golden age" baseball has given way to about as racially tolerant a space as exists anywhere in American society. My beloved Chicago Cubs acquired a number of valuable players in their 2003 playoff run (Karros, Grudzielanek, Lofton, Estes, Ramirez, Glanville, Simon).

Would it ever occur to any but the crassest of baseball fans to consider the racial proportions of all of these trades? Hardly. Indeed, in our time it would take a good deal of mental effort even to *think* about this irrelevant issue, which means as little to any general manager or fan these days as the astrological signs involved in a trade—a far cry from what would have happened before World War II. And as for foreign players, no Chicagoan thinks of Sammy Sosa or Magglio Ordoñez as unwelcome strangers. We welcome Dominicans, Mexicans, Venezuelans, and now Japanese into our national game without anything more than the tiniest incidents. Players today remain in top physical condition throughout the year, while enduring levels of round-the-clock television and internet scrutiny unknown in the past.

Finally, let's not avoid the issue of organized labor. One could debate whether the Player's Union has now overreached in its demands or harmed the financial health of the game. What seems *beyond* debate is that the Union has been in the right for at least the majority of its existence. The pre-Curt Flood baseball player was little more than chattel, property of his team for life, vastly underpaid in comparison with the profits generated by his sport. Whatever the painful effects of the 1981 and 1994 strikes, today's players have taught us far more than yesterday's about solidarity, fairness, and the dignity of human labor.

The illusions of time have given baseball players of the past a nobility even greater than what they actually possessed while in action. The same will happen with today's game. We in our elderly years will brag about stars like Sosa, Clemens, Henderson, and Bonds. But perhaps even more importantly, we will have every right to boast about our era of cosmopolitan baseball, gentlemanly baseball, educated and family-friendly baseball. Would anyone really rather have Chase, Cobb, the Black Sox, and the Reserve Clause?

The Team

GREGORY "Smash 'em" BASSHAM is Director of the Center for Ethics and Public Life and Chair of the Philosophy Department at King's College, Pennsylvania. He is the co-editor of *The Lord of the Rings and Philosophy: One Book to Rule Them All* (Open Court, 2003), the author of *Original Intent and the Constitution: A Philosophical Study* (Rowman and Littlefield, 1992), and the co-author of *Critical Thinking: A Student's Introduction* (McGraw-Hill, 2002). Greg's lifetime wiffle ball statistics are posted on his website.

JAY "Whiz Kid" BENNETT is a Principal Scientist with Telcordia Technologies. He is the editor of *Statistics in Sport* (Arnold, 1998) and co-author of *Curve Ball* (Copernicus, 2001). Jay is a Fellow of the American Statistical Association and a past Chair of its Section on Statistics in Sports. Born in Philadelphia the day after the Phillies won their first pennant in thirty-five years, he endured thirty years more before being rewarded with another; it was worth the wait.

MICHAEL "OH Ichiro" BRANNIGAN is Professor of Philosophy and Chair of the Philosophy Department at La Roche College in Pittsburgh. He is also Executive Director of the college's Institute for Cross-Cultural Ethics. In between innings, he has written his politically correct share of articles and books on Asian philosophy and medical ethics and has been awarded international fellowships. He is now working on a book on ethics across cultures and another on global biotechnologies. With Japanese and Irish roots, he remains loyal to the Red Sox. This somewhat explains his interest in Custeriana as well as his nickname, a near-homonym for the Japanese *mo ichido* ("one more time").

ERIC "Shoeless" BRONSON heads the Philosophy and History Department at Berkeley College in New York City. He edited *The Lord of the Rings and Philosophy: One Book to Rule Them All* (Open Court, 2003) with Gregory Bassham, and has been a regular contributor to the Philosophy and Popular Culture series. He also produced the award winning documentary *My Lazy White Friends*, and wrote the short film *Ruckus!* with Dean Ishida (Farouche Films, 2004). Eric was the commissioner of Rabstick Park (1986–1989), and was the first person in recorded history to break his nose in a wiffle ball game.

TED "The Panther" COHEN is a professor at the University of Chicago, where he is a former chairman of the Department of Philosophy. He is a former president of the American Society for Aesthetics. Among his recent publications is *Jokes: Philosophical Thoughts on Joking Matters*. During the latter part of his ball-playing career, he occasionally played catcher, priding himself on his quick work around the plate, and denominating himself "The Panther," a name children in the game generously awarded him on a day when he was forced to leave the field with a dislocated finger.

ALBERT "Wicket" DUNCAN is an Adjunct Professor of Economics at Berkeley College, New York City, and at The Borough of Manhattan Community College, New York. He believes that baseball is America's religion and star players should get much more than Sunday School offerings. So should economics professors.

SIMON "The Lip" EASSOM is Principal Lecturer in Sports Ethics and honoured Teacher Fellow of De Montfort University, England, in the Department of Sport Sciences. His recent publications include a short volume *Explaining Ethics*, an edited volume *Sport Technology: History, Philosophy, and Policy,* and a forthcoming book entitled *Cyborg Sport: Primate Play*. He spent a season in the U.S.A. rooting for the Indians, but now avoids Cleveland. His philosophical pitch tends to be more spit than curve.

RANDOLPH "Hack" FEEZELL is Professor of Philosophy at Creighton University in Omaha, Nebraska. He is the author of *Faith, Freedom, and Value: Introductory Philosophical Dialogues* (Westview, 1989), and co-author of *How Should I Live? Philosophical Conversations About Moral Life* (Paragon House, 1991), and *Coaching for Character: Reclaiming the Principles of Sportsmanship* (Human Kinetics, 1997). His most recent book is *Sport, Play, and Ethical Reflection* (University of Illinois Press, forthcoming). His most important ethical work is undoubtedly the unpublished *Sophomore Sensation*, a shameless rip-off modeled on Clair Bee's wonderful antiquarian Chip Hilton books. Although his baseball skills have faded, he still handles a fungo pretty well and throws excellent BP.

NEIL "Diesel" FEIT is an Assistant Professor of Philosophy at the State University of New York at Fredonia. His main area of research is in the philosophy of mind and language, but he has published articles in a variety of other sub-fields, including the philosophy of sport. Born and bred in the Bronx, Neil is a devoted Yankees fan, despite having been dragged out to Shea Stadium too often in his youth.

MARK "Hammy" HAMILTON is an Associate Professor of Philosophy and Faculty Representative to the NCAA at Ashland University, where he teaches courses in Philosophy of Religion, Ancient and Medieval Philosophy, Sports Ethics, and C.S. Lewis. He coached eight years of College baseball in the 1980s. As a high school, college, and semi-pro player he was known as a contact hitter, which is a nice way of saying he did not have any power. Some called him "Kuyp," after former Indians second baseman "Punch and Judy" hitter Duane Kuyper, even though in his twenty years of baseball, "Hammy" hit twice as many homers as Kuyper did in his big league career—two compared to Kuyper's one.

GRAHAM "Oil Can" HARMAN is Assistant Professor of Philosophy at the American University in Cairo, Egypt. He is the author of *Tool-Being: Heidegger and the Metaphysics of Objects* (2002) and *The Carpentry of Things: Reviving Phenomenology* (forthcoming), both published by Open Court. From 1996 to 1998 he served as the Chicago staff writer for sportsextra.com. His first experience with philosophy was the accidental discovery of *The Bill James Baseball Abstract* at age fourteen.

LESLIE "Smiley" HEAPHY is an Assistant Professor of History at Kent State, Stark Campus. She wrote, *The Negro Leagues, 1869–1960* (McFarland, 2003). She is also the Women in Baseball Committee chair for SABR (Society of American Baseball Research). Leslie encourages her students to step up to the plate and get involved in their history projects.

"Hammerin'" PAUL HORAN is a lawyer in New York and a former law clerk for the Hon. William H. Walls, U.S.D.J., District of New Jersey. Once each spring, he watches a video of Game Six of the 1986 World Series; he cheers every time.

JOE "-fer five" KRAUS is Assistant Professor of English at King's College. He is the co-author of *An Accidental Anarchist* (Academy Chicago, 2001), and his work in American literature, particularly on ethnicity and the figure of the gangster, and on plagiarism has appeared in *The American Scholar, Centennial Review, Issues in Writing, MELUS*, and elsewhere. He has been misreading signs since his inglorious little league career of the mid-1970s.

R. SCOTT "The Curse of Rocky Colavito" KRETCHMAR is a professor of Exercise and Sport Science at Penn State University. A long-time Cleveland Indian fan, he was raised in northern Ohio and played baseball for Oberlin College, gaining all-conference status all four years. A torn rotator cuff forced a shift in attention from practice to theory. He is author of *Practical Philosophy of Sport*, has been President of the International Association for the Philosophy of Sport, was elected Fellow in the American Academy of Kinesiology and Physical Education, has served as Chair of the Penn State Faculty Senate, and is the current Faculty Representative to the NCAA for Penn State. Having published numerous articles on the philosophy of sport in highly respected academic journals, he has come to following insightful conclusion about his Indians. "They will be back . . . but probably not during the lifetime of anyone currently reading this book!"

ARYN "Sweet Spot" MARTIN studies and teaches at Cornell University in the Department of Science and Technology Studies. Her scholarly work is in the history and sociology of genetics, and she has a special interest in counting, be it chromosomes or runs batted in. As a Canadian, she is an ardent fan of the Toronto Maple . . . er . . . Blue Jays.

PELLOM "Woody" McDANIELS III sits on the Board of Directors at the Negro League Museum in Kansas City. He was a defensive lineman for the Kansas City Chiefs and the Atlanta Falcons in the National Football League from 1992 until 2000. He has published a book of poetry, *My Own Harlem* (Addax, 1998), and founded *Arts for Smarts* in 1993 to expose children to the fine and applied arts. Pellom is currently in the American Studies program at Emory University, where he intends to incorporate some old pigskin moves in his dissertation defense.

MICHAEL J. "Señor Smoke" McGRATH is Assistant Professor of Spanish at Georgia Southern University. He is the author of *Religious Celebrations in Segovia, 1577-1697* (Mellen Press, 2002) and the editor of Calderón de la Barca's *El mágico prodigioso* (*The Prodigious Magician*; Juan de la Cuesta Hispanic Monographs, 2003). In addition, his articles on sixteenth- and seventeenth-century Spanish literature have appeared in journals both in the United States and Spain. "Señor Smoke" played baseball in Madrid for two years and holds his team's record for most wins by a pitcher from Indialantic, Florida.

WILLIAM J. "Bump" MORGAN is a professor in the Cultural Studies Section, Ohio State University. He is interested in the ethics of popular culture, and especially in the ethics of sports. He has published widely on the latter topic including a book entitled, *Leftist Theories of Sport: A Critique and Reconstruction*. He is currently at work on another book tentatively titled, *Why Sports Still Morally Matter*. He traces his interest in baseball back to his boyhood hometown, Williamsport, Pennsylvania, better known as the home of little league baseball, where he first learned to play the game. Though a reasonably adept fielder, he was better known for his hapless hitting.

"Wahoo" LAWRENCE RAFUL teaches legal ethics at Creighton Law School in Omaha, Nebraska (just down the road from the birthplace of Wahoo Sam Crawford). His main occupation is his lifelong commitment to the San Francisco Giants, and only married his Dodger-fan wife when she promised to raise the children as Giants fans.

HEATHER L. "Wheels" REID is Associate Professor of Philosophy at Morningside College in Sioux City, Iowa. A specialist on Plato, she is also author of *The Philosophical Athlete* (Carolina Academic Press, 2003) and part of the editorial board of *The Journal of the Philosophy of Sport*. She prefers to bike around the basepaths.

ALEX "Chico Escuela" RUCK is studying philosophy and history at the University of Vermont. An infielder on the 1995 14th Ward (Pittsburgh) championship team, he helped his father, Rob Ruck, make *Kings on the Hill: Baseball's Forgotten Men*. Alex is hoping to bring winter ball to Vermont.

ROB "Escuela Viejo" RUCK teaches history at the University of Pittsburgh. He is the author of *Sandlot Seasons: Sport in Black Pittsburgh* and *The Tropic of Baseball: Baseball in the Dominican Republic*, and was the project director and writer for *Kings on the Hill*, an Emmy-winning documentary on the Negro Leagues. Rob's son likes to remind him who is the real king of the hill.

J.S. "The Natural" RUSSELL teaches philosophy at the University of British Columbia and at Langara College. He has published articles in moral and political philosophy, philosophy of law, and philosophy of sport. In his spare time, he coaches youth baseball, where he has been on the receiving end of a few bad calls.

THOMAS D. "Lefty" SENOR is Associate Professor of Philosophy and Chair of the Philosophy Department at the University of Arkansas. He has published papers on the philosophy of religion, epistemology, and political philosophy, and has served on the Executive Committee of the Society of Christian Philosophers. Despite his universalist tendencies, Senor believes that an especially hot corner of hell is reserved for baseball writers who did not vote for Ryne Sandberg as a first-ballot Hall of Famer.

JOEL "The Goat" SHUMAN is a native West Virginian who teaches moral theology at King's College in Wilkes-Barre, Pennsylvania. A frequent public speaker and the author of numerous popular and scholarly articles about theology and medicine, he has written *The Body of Compassion: Ethics, Medicine and the Church* and *Heal Thyself: Spirituality, Medicine, and the Distortion of Christianity* (with Dr. Keith Meador). A father of three, he lives with his family in Mountain Top, Pennsylvania, from whence he continues to insist that Roberto Clemente was the greatest right fielder. Ever. Joel's sons call him "goat."

AEON J. "One-Man Gang" SKOBLE is Assistant Professor of Philosophy at Bridgewater State College. He is the co-editor of the anthology *Political Philosophy: Essential Selections* (Prentice-Hall, 1999), as well as co-editor of *The Simpsons and Philosophy* (Open Court, 2001) and the forthcoming *Woody Allen and Philosophy* (Open Court, 2005). He writes on moral, political, and social theory for both scholarly and lay journals, and is editor of the annual journal *Reason Papers*. His next project is a comparative study of motivation and virtue in Marcus Aurelius and Don Mattingly.

JASON "Mailman" SOLOMON is a lawyer who currently serves as Chief of Staff to the President of Harvard University. His biggest accomplishment came in junior high school, when he founded one of the first rotisserie leagues in the Northeast—the Parallel Baseball League (PBL)—with his co-author. And no, he didn't cheat.

STEVEN "Streetball" STEETER is an English Professor at Berkeley College in New York City. He says he doesn't really believe in superstition, but just in case, he has his fingers crossed.

EDWARD "The Kid" SULLIVAN is Director of Secondary Education at Providence College. He is the author of *The Future: Human Ecology and Education* (ETC Publications). He has published numerous articles and has given presentations on the causes and solutions to some of the problems facing education. As a charter member of the Red Sox Nation (he went to his first Red Sox game in 1946), he suffers from frustration each year from April to October. This frustration is compounded because he is also a fan of the San Diego Padres.

VINCENT L. "Foghorn" TOSCANO retired as an Associate Professor of History at Marist College where he also served as Assistant Academic Vice President as well as Dean of the Division of Humanities. He is the author of *Since Dallas: John F. Kennedy in the American Imagination*. His baseball credits include a visit to the Yankee clubhouse during Joe DiMaggio Appreciation day when his uncle gave him a ball signed by the 1951 Yankees. Two days later he lost the ball and had to go to work for forty years to recoup the money it is now worth.

WILLIE "Mad Dog" YOUNG is an assistant professor of Theology at King's College. He is the co-editor of the *Journal of Scriptural Reasoning*, and has published several articles on postmodern religious thought. In his spare time, he conducts bunting clinics for t-ball players. "Today's players just don't know how to bunt, so I think it's important that we reach them early, and really just focus on the fundamentals," he says.

Index